HTML5

HTML5

DESIGNING RICH INTERNET APPLICATIONS

MATTHEW DAVID

AMSTERDAM • BOSTON • HEIDELBERG • LONDON • NEW YORK • OXFORD
PARIS • SAN DIEGO • SAN FRANCISCO • SINGAPORE • SYDNEY • TOKYO
Focal Press is an imprint of Elsevier

Focal Press is an imprint of Elsevier
30 Corporate Drive, Suite 400, Burlington, MA 01803, USA
The Boulevard, Langford Lane, Kidlington, Oxford, OX5 1GB, UK

Notices
Knowledge and best practice in this field are constantly changing. As new research and experience broaden our understanding, changes in research methods, professional practices, or medical treatment may become necessary.

Practitioners and researchers must always rely on their own experience and knowledge in evaluating and using any information, methods, compounds, or experiments described herein. In using such information or methods they should be mindful of their own safety and the safety of others, including parties for whom they have a professional responsibility.

To the fullest extent of the law, neither the Publisher nor the authors, contributors, or editors, assume any liability for any injury and/or damage to persons or property as a matter of products liability, negligence or otherwise, or from any use or operation of any methods, products, instructions, or ideas contained in the material herein.

Library of Congress Cataloging-in-Publication Data
David, Matthew, 1971-
  HTML5 : designing rich Internet applications / Matthew David.
    p. cm.
  Includes index.
  ISBN 978-0-240-81328-8
 1. HTML (Document markup language) 2. Multimedia communications. 3. Web site development. I. Title. II. Title: Visualizing the Web.
  QA76.76.H94D4184 2010
  006.7'4–dc22   2010018716

British Library Cataloguing-in-Publication Data
A catalogue record for this book is available from the British Library.

ISBN: 978-0-240-81328-8

For information on all Focal Press publications
visit our website at www.elsevierdirect.com

11   12   13   14   5   4   3

Printed in the United States of America

Working together to grow
libraries in developing countries

www.elsevier.com | www.bookaid.org | www.sabre.org

ELSEVIER   BOOK AID
             International   Sabre Foundation

Praise for the Book

HTML5 isn't one thing, but many different improvements rolled under one name. Knowing where to start can be tricky. Fortunately, this book presents the major concepts in a logical sequence. Topics flow easily from explanations to bite-sized projects, flavored with the author's practical advice. It's a handy introduction to HTML5, and I'm looking forward to the paper copy!

—Sam Wan, UI engineer

With the arrival of HTML5 and CSS3, those working with the web face a host of new challenges. HTML5: Designing Rich Internet Applications puts solutions at your fingertips; the content is concise and easily referenced, and the accompanying projects help convert learning to real-world action.

—Toby Pestridge, Toby James Creative

Matthew David proves that developing in HTML5 right now can be exceptionally rewarding with this the first major update to the language in over ten years. Matthew has provided us a great frame of reference of what's to come and what we can start using now!

—Conrad Fuhrman, partner/lead developer, ThreeSphere LLC

HTML5 is quickly gaining technological influence as more devices and browsers support it every day. Matthew David introduces you to key concept, and dives in for a comprehensive look to prepare you for tomorrow's internet.

—Joel Martinez, Codecub.net

Matthew David has continued his mastery of presenting new and seemingly complex topics in a practical, easy-to-understand manner. This book will not only bring programmers and designers into the next generation of web development, but also redefine their concept of what can be done in a browser—presenting limitless opportunities for years to come.

—Ryan Moore, author of Foundation ASP.NET for Flash

Dedication

No one person writes a book. For this book to be published I need to thank a lot of people. First, I have to thank Focal Press and, in particular, Paul Temme who took a risk on developing one of the first HTML5 books and working with me to develop the Visualizing series. I also have to thank Anais Wheeler for always ensuring I hit my deadlines and checking that I had sent her all the files needed.

I also want to thank my friends and colleagues at Jewelers Mutual who listened to me talk about CSS3, HTML5, and which browser supported what technology. I will take the glassy-eye looks they gave me as deep, attentive interest.

Finally, I need to thank my beloved family who put up with me disappearing for hours at a time to write my next great book. I love you guys. I could not have completed this project without you.

CONTENTS

Section 2

PREFACE

Incredibly, it has been more than 20 years since the first release of HTML, the HyperText Markup Language. In the early days of web development, HTML underwent a series of rapid evolutions from simple text to including images and adding CSS to format text.

Then in 1997 the introduction of HTML4 hit the market and everything came to a stop. Sure, we saw the release of XHTML, but there was very little advancement in HTML as a language. Why the hold up? The reason is based on three major factors: computers were limited in what they could process, the connection to the Web was limited to the speed of a user's dial-up modem, and the Web was busily being molded into a new medium.

However, the Web has evolved. Today, computers are blinding fast with many of us running SmartPhones faster than desktop behemoths of just 6 years ago. Connection to the Web is now measured in megabytes per second, and the Web is now a standard we all rely on. It has become increasingly apparent that HTML4 just does not cut it for modern Web users. Bottom line: We need a new standard.

A group called the Web Standards Project began developing HTML5 in 2007. The goal of the project is ambitious: Develop an HTML standard that is capable of running full applications in a web browser. HTML5 introduces a broad set of new technologies, including:

- New HTML elements
- Geolocation APIs
- Drag-and-drop APIs
- Local data APIs
- Forms 2.0
- Video and audio support
- SVG and CANVAS graphics
- CSS3
- Two- and three-dimensional animation
- JavaScript 2.0

It seemed, for a while, that the new HTML5 standard would not come to pass. Nay-sayers scoffed that the standard was good in print, but would never make it to the Web. Then a funny thing happened: FireFox began adopting elements of HTML and was quickly followed by Apple's Safari web browser. Three final actions drove home the importance of HTML5:

- Google released the web browser Chrome with HTML5 as a key feature.
- The World Wide Web Consortium Group (W3C) halted work on XHTML 2.0 and adopted HTML5 as the new Web standard.
- The Web went mobile.

It can be argued that the implementation of feature-rich web browsers on iPhones, Android phones, and WebOS phones has clinched the deal for HTML5. Today, mobile web developers can build web sites that surpass desktop equivalents.

The missing part in all of this technology was Microsoft. Uncharacteristically, Microsoft was silent about their support for HTML5. Many saw Internet Explorer dying slowly, to be surpassed by newer, more nimble browser technologies. This changed in spring 2010 when Microsoft released a developer copy of Internet Explorer 9 and formerly joined the HTML5 working group. All major web browsers are now adopting HTML5.

The focus of this book is to introduce you to HTML5. You will be taken behind the scenes of this new technology and shown how you can integrate HTML5 into your web sites today. The five sections in the book include an article and a project, which build on to each other to deliver a final, 100% HTML5-compliant web site.

HTML5 is not a flash-in-the-pan technology. It is a firmly supported standard that will be used to build web applications for the next 10 years. Now is the time to start learning how you can use this new standard to wow your clients.

HTML5 TAG STRUCTURE

The core to all Web design is HTML, the code that sits behind every web page and allows users to create stunning web sites. Today's web sites can do amazing things. Can you imagine not being able to use solutions such as Google's Gmail, Microsoft's Bing, or view content on YouTube? Web sites have moved from static pages to complex applications. The core HTML language requires more and more functionality to meet our needs. To this end, a new standard has been introduced—HMTL5.

Where HTML Code Can Be Found

Not sure how to find HTML? It can be located on any web page by right-clicking your mouse and selecting View Page Source, as shown in Figure 1.1.

It will depend on your web browser how the HTML code is presented. No matter what you are doing on the Web—developing a PHP shopping cart, implementing an ASP.NET application, updating your latest blog entry, or playing an online game—every solution on the Web must use HTML at some point. If not, then your web browser will not be able to view the page correctly.

HTML5. doi: 10.1016/B978-0-240-81328-8.00006-9

3

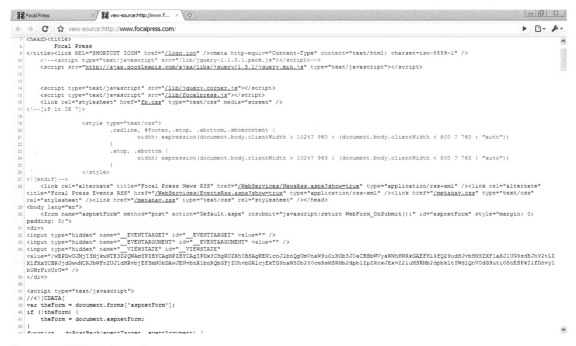

Figure 1.1 HTML code can be viewed in any web browser. Here, Google's Chrome is color coding the HTML code.

The Evolution of the Web

Back in the days of 1995 when the Web was just gaining mainstream attention, it was assumed that you needed a computer (preferably Windows 95) running Microsoft's Internet Explorer to view the Web. Yes, you could also use Netscape's Navigator, but Microsoft took care of that problem by 1999. There was not much of a change to this model for about ten years.

The change to the desktop PC Internet browsing model began with the easy installation and adoption of wireless networks. A bulky computer or even a laptop to connect online was no longer needed; rather, users only needed a device that had enough power to go online and get what they needed wherever they were.

The first few Internet-powered devices were crude at best, but it did not take long for mobile devices to catch up with PCs. The change came with Apple's release of the iPhone and iPod Touch, which both support one of the most advanced web browsers. Apple's mobile devices shipped running a mobile version of their web browser called Safari. Does "mobile version" mean that features were cut from the full Mac OS X version? In a word: No. Mobile Safari is built using an open-source web browser called WebKit. Apple makes the bold claim that their iPhone web browser displays web pages exactly the same way as a full browser running on a Windows PC. Indeed, to add insult to injury, Apple took the boast even further: The iPhone web browser supports much of the latest core Web technologies that Microsoft's Internet Explorer does not support. Namely, the iPhone, back in 2007, was already supporting HTML5 and Microsoft was a long way from this support (Figure 1.2).

Today, we assume that most devices will connect to the Internet. It is not just the realm of the PC—game systems, Blu-Ray DVDs, MP3 players, cameras, storage SD flash cards, and more devices connect to the Internet every day. HTML, this core language that runs how we view the Web, is changing to support a post-PC world that connects to the Internet.

Figure 1.2 The iPhone's mobile Safari already boasts strong support for HTML5 technologies.

The Rocky Road from HTML4 to HTML5

Tim Berners-Lee developed the Hypertext Markup Language (HTML) in 1989. The Internet has been around since the 1950s, but it had a fundamental flaw—connecting from one disconnected source to another was very difficult. Tim Berners-Lee addressed this issue by creating two technologies:

- HTTP, the Hypertext Transfer Protocol, a service protocol to enable web servers to run.
- HTML, the Hypertext Markup Language, a scripting language to allow the presentation of text with embedded links to documents on the same server or a different server.

The revolutionary spin on Berners-Lee's HTML language is that the link embedded in the page did not need to know if the web page it was linking to existed. If the page did not exist, then you received an error. If the page did exist, then you jumped from one web site to another.

A second reason for the success of HTML is that the language is very easy to learn and use. HTML uses a simple concept of tags that start and end a section. For instance, the following will show as a block of text when viewed through a web browser.

```
<p>
Lorem ipsum dolor sit amet, consectetur adipiscing
elit. Nam ac tortor elit, ac posuere erat. Nullam non
lectus libero, in vestibulum ligula. Lorem ipsum dolor sit
amet, consectetur adipiscing elit. Nam venenatis faucibus
arcu, consectetur blandit magna pellentesque et.
</p>
```

The tag concept for writing web pages is easy to learn and use. Needless to say, the World Wide Web really caught on. By the early 1990s it was becoming clear that the Web, in particular HTML, was going to be a very big thing. At that time a fortunate event happened: Tim Berners-Lee decided not to cash in on the success of the Web and instead formed a coalition to standardize popular Web technologies. This group, called the World Wide Web Consortium (W3C; *www.w3c.org*) is an open standards body made up of representatives from many different companies such as Apple, Microsoft, Adobe, Sun, Google, Real Networks, Oracle, IBM, and many more. A goal of the W3C is to prevent any one company from forcing a technology onto users. This is important, as Microsoft was effectively trying to do this as they dominated the Web from 1997 to 2007.

The W3C has produced many popular technologies used by software companies each and every day. These include HTML, XML, Web Services Protocol (SOAP), and the PNG graphics format, among many others. Each of these standards are proposed, defined, ratified, and published with group approval. One of the first set of standards to go through this process was HTML.

Berners-Lee's first version of HTML is very different from the version we use today. For instance, Berners-Lee did not care for design and did not include any way to format text in the first release of HTML. Images were also an afterthought. Between 1989 and 1997 HTML went through four major standard ratifications.

The last major release of the HTML standard was in 1997 with HTML4. The standard proposed the inclusion of Cascading Style Sheets Level 1, or CSS1, as a method of controlling the design of pages; the use of PNG graphics as an open bitmap graphics standard; the adoption of a standard Document Object Model to allow JavaScript applications to run consistently across web browsers; and introduced the first release of XML to control data structure. As HTML matures as a language, the demands for what it can accomplish increase.

Web 2.0 Applications and Solutions

The challenge with today's Web is that it is not the same place created in the 1990s. The W3C tried addressing the evolution of the HTML standard with a new, updated standard called XHTML 2.0. The contributing vendors did not warmly accept the technology standard and a subsequent standard, HTML5, developed by the Web Hypertext Application Technology Working Group (WHATWG), is now in active development. The result is XHTML 2.0 has died on the vine, and all of the major technology companies, including Microsoft, are pledging to support HTML5.

Overall, all web browsers have adopted the HTML4 standard. Web site development can now be easily accomplished using tools such as Adobe's Dreamweaver and Microsoft's Expression Web. But, it has taken a decade to get here. Arguably, Microsoft is the company that has been the weakest in supporting Web HTML standards with their Internet Explorer. It is only with the release of Internet Explorer 8 that Microsoft was compliant with HTML4—a full 12 years after the standard was published.

New web browsers (Apple's Safari, Opera Web Browser, Google's Chrome, and Mozilla's FireFox) and new Web-enabled devices (Apple's iPhone, Google's Android, Palm's Pre, and RIM's BlackBerry) are pushing what can be done on the Web. Each of these competitive companies agrees on one thing: HTML5 is the next standard, and they are already supporting it.

What Is Included in HTML5

Unlike earlier improvements to HTML, the new HTML5 specifications are taking a much broader look at what is needed to support web site development and programming for the next decade and beyond. HTML5 can effectively be broken down into the following segments:

- Core page structure
- Visual presentation
- Graphical tools
- Rich media support
- Enhancements to JavaScript

The structure of this book follows these five distinct categories for HTML5.

Enhancements to Core Tag Language

Raise your hand if you have ever written any HTML code? Okay, everyone's hand is now in the air. The reality is that most of us have grown up building and using HTML4/XHTML code syntax structure. Now along comes HTML5: Do we have to relearn everything? No, and that is good news. HTML5 gracefully supports older code practices. This allows you to migrate code from one standard to another.

For instance, the following XHTML code is supported in HTML5.

```
<BR/>Lorem ipsum dolor sit amet, nec a ultricies.
<BR/>Egestas ipsum in, praesent ut et, vulputate vel.
<BR/>Dapibus magna a.
<BR/>Felis sit, vestibulum pede.
```

You can also write this example in HTML5 and older web browsers will view the content. Let's take the previous example and write it using new HTML5 element syntax.

```
<br>Lorem ipsum dolor sit amet, nec a ultricies.
<br>Egestas ipsum in, praesent ut et, vulputate vel.
<br>Dapibus magna a.
<br>Felis sit, vestibulum pede.
```

The break line element, `<br>`, in HTML5 has dropped the XHTML support for the closing /. The code, however, will work in XHTML browsers.

Of course, this does not mean that HTML5 is all backwards compatible. Many of the new HTML5 elements are not supported in older web browsers. Browsers supporting HTML5 are:

- FireFox 3.0+ (all operating systems)
- Safari 3.0+ (Windows OS X and iPhone OS 1.0+ operating systems)

- Google Chrome (all operating systems)
- Opera 9.5+ (all operating systems)

New Elements Are Introduced to HTML5

HTML5 introduces new elements to allow you to control your code. Broadly, the new elements cover these main functions:
- Blocking of content on the page
- Media management
- Form structure

The blocking of content in HTML is traditionally accomplished using either complex tables or the infamous DIV element. HTML5 introduces several new elements that allow you to easily insert blocks of content into the page. Conveniently, these new elements have names that identify what the block of content accomplishes:
- HEADER
- SECTION
- ARTICLE
- ASIDE
- FOOTER
- NAV

The role of the new page layout elements is to better describe specific parts of a document. Think of the new tags as behaving in a similar way to how you approach writing a document in Microsoft Word. A typical Word document is built up of sections of content that can be separated in paragraphs, sidebars, and header and footer sections. The new blocking elements in HTML5 approach HTML code in logical sections, or blocks.

The FORM element, in HTML5, has also received its first major upgrade since HTML2, back in 1994. Forms 2.0, as it is sometimes referred to, enables you to add the following visual effects to form fields:
- Format the form for adding only telephone numbers.
- Allow a form field that is picking a web address to validate it against the client browser history.
- Format a field to only accept valid email addresses.
- Enable a field to pick from a calendar to choose a date.
- Force a field to be the first default field in the form.
- Highlight fields that are required.

With Forms 2.0, the rich functionality you need in a form is built directly into HTML—there is no need for Ajax, Flash, or any other technology.

Blocking Content on the Page

The updated HTML5 structure is looking to more accurately describe areas of content on the screen. This is called *blocking* in HTML5. We use blocking every day as we develop web pages. An example of this is a typical blog posting. The structure of a blog is something like this:

- Title the blog post.
- Add a date for the post.
- Add links to related content.
- Add the content the blog is about.
- Include figures to support your content.
- Possibly add a side note about the content.
- Allow users to post comments on your post.
- Include a central navigation to the site.
- Add a header and footer to the page.

Using conventional HTML4 markup techniques you can list all of this information in either complex tables, paragraph elements (<p>), or use the DIV element to block content on the page. The following example is an extract from Wikipedia describing HTML5 using HTML4 techniques (see also Figure 1.3). The HTML elements are in ***italics***.

```
<p><b>HTML5</b> is the next major revision of <a
href="/wiki/HTML" title="HTML">HTML</a> (Hypertext Markup
Language), the core <a href="/wiki/Markup_language"
title="Markup language">markup language</a> of the <a
href="/wiki/World_Wide_Web" title="World Wide Web">World
Wide Web</a>. The <a href="/wiki/Web_Hypertext_
Application_Technology_Working_Group" title="Web Hypertext
Application Technology Working Group">Web Hypertext
Application Technology Working Group</a> (WHATWG) started
work on the specification in June 2004 under the name Web
Applications 1.0<sup id="cite_ref-0" class="reference"><a
```

Figure 1.3 HTML4 code displayed in Google's Chrome.

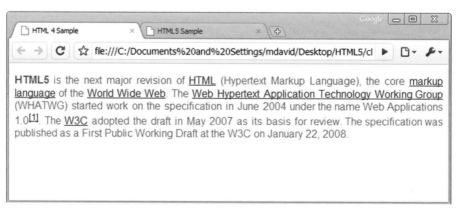

```
href="#cite_note-0"><span>[</span>1<span>]</span></a><
/sup>. The <a href="/wiki/W3C" title="W3C" class="mw-
redirect">W3C</a> adopted the draft in May 2007 as its
basis for review. The specification was published as a
First Public Working Draft at the W3C on January 22,
2008.</p>
```

Unfortunately, the HTML4 approach does not tell much about what the data mean. A role of HTML5 is to make syntax more meaningful. Using HTML5 you can leverage the new ARTICLE element to block out the section of the page for your main article. Additional emphasis to specific content can be applied using the MARK element. Finally, date/time information within your HTML can be highlighted using the TIME element.

Here is the same content from *www.wikipedia.org*, but in HTML5 (see also Figure 1.4).

```
<article>
<m>HTML5</m> is the next major revision of <a href="/
wiki/HTML" title="HTML">HTML</a> (Hypertext Markup
Language), the core <a href="/wiki/Markup_language"
title="Markup language">markup language</a> of the
<a href="/wiki/World_Wide_Web" title="World Wide Web">
World Wide Web</a>. The <a href="/wiki/Web_Hypertext_
Application_Technology_Working_Group" title="Web Hypertext
Application Technology Working Group">Web Hypertext
Application Technology Working Group</a> (WHATWG) started
work on the specification in <time>June 2004</time>
under the name Web Applications 1.0<m><a href="#cite_
note-0"></m></a>. The <a href="/wiki/W3C" title="W3C"
class="mw-redirect">W3C</a> adopted the draft in <time>May
2007</time> as its basis for review. The specification was
published as a First Public Working Draft at the W3C on
<time>January 22, 2008</time>.
</article>
```

Figure 1.4 The content is displayed using HTML5 in Google's Chrome. The display looks the same visually, but the code is structured more logically.

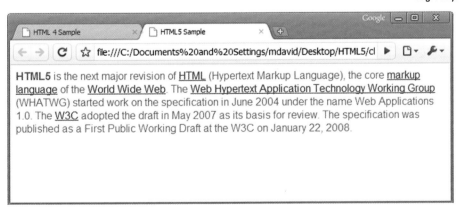

The structure, emphasis, and description of different types of content are wrapped using the new ARTICLE, MARK, and TIME elements. The code is much easier to read and the content has more meaning.

The new move to describing more accurately the web page content has several benefits. The first is for search engines, such as Google.com or Microsoft's Bing.com, which can use the blocked content to identify regions on the page. The second is with organization. It is simply easier to organize content when you know what the content is. Finally, more effectively organizing content allows for the future development of the Semantic Web, a device where content is found, shared, and created across web site domains more easily.

In this chapter you will see how to content block your HTML code using the following:

- The new DOC type to identify the web page as containing HTML5 content.
- The SECTION element to separate content more easily.
- The ARTICLE element to identify the main content on a page.
- The NAV element to identify navigation on a screen.
- Use HTML Forms 2.0 to have even more control over your web forms.
- Apply new HTML element attributes.
- Understand why specific elements are not included in HTML5.

Modifications to Content Sections

The vast majority of content on the Web is text based. You can look at sites such as Wikipedia, Twitter, and Facebook for validation. Millions and millions of pages of content are created every day. In mid-2008 Google hit a significant milestone where their search engine indexed its trillionth web site (that is, 1,000,000,000,000—yes, 12 zeros!).

A goal of HTML5 is to make finding, organizing, and sharing billions and billions of pages more easy. With HTML5, you are looking to place meaning to the content that you are adding to the page.

There are several different categories of content type in HTML5. Broadly speaking, HTML5 now allows you to do the following:

- Block the overall content of a page
- Text-level content structure

These two levels of content structure will add meaning to your web page.

Making DOC Type Easier to Work With

The first line of HTML in any web page identifies the version of HTML the page contains. This is called the DOCTYPE. The DOCTYPE has its roots tied to SGML. SGML requires a DTD (document type definition) reference to accurately render the web page. With XHTML three different DOCTYPEs were introduced. Ultimately, this was complex to manage.

With HTML5 you have one, simple DOCTYPE, which is `<!DOCTYPE html>`. The new DOCTYPE will automatically inform the web browser that the page content is in HTML5. The DOCTYPE is not case sensitive.

Organizing Code Using Blocking Elements

There are few ways in HTML4 to define content. The most common is to use the P element to identify the start and end of a paragraph, or the DIV element to identify the start and end of a section of content. Both do not adequately describe the content. You can see blocking applied to most web pages. Figure 1.5 illustrates how you may block out a web page such as *www. focalpress.com*.

With HTML5 a new element, the SECTION element, clearly identifies a block of content. This method is called *block level semantics*. With HTML5 there are several elements that block content:

- SECTION
- ARTICLE
- HEADER
- FOOTER
- ASIDE
- FIGURE
- NAV

The new names for each of these elements identify the type of content they block on a page.

Figure 1.5 The Focal Press web site is split into logical blocks of content.

Using the SECTION Element

The SECTION element is part of a new set of elements that describe the content on a page. You can think of the SECTION element as enclosing a significant part of a page, in the same way that a chapter in a book is a significant section of the book. An example of the SECTION element follows.

```
<SECTION>
<ARTICLE>
<P>Nulla facilisis egestas nulla id rhoncus. Duis
eget diam nisi, quis sagittis nulla. Fusce lacinia
pharetra dui, a rhoncus sapien egestas ut. Ut lacus
ante, semper sed interdum a, posuere egestas ante. Nullam
luctus arcu sed sapien dignissim quis posuere ipsum
placerat.</P>
</ARTICLE>
<ARTICLE>
<P>Lorem ipsum dolor sit amet, consectetur
adipiscing elit. Nunc vehicula ipsum sit amet eros
adipiscing volutpat. Sed gravida urna vel sapien commodo
pretium.</P>
</ARTICLE>
<UL>
<LI>Praesent ut sapien quam. </LI>
<LI>Aliquam erat volutpat. </LI>
</UL>
</SECTION>
```

You can clearly see in Figure 1.6 that the two paragraphs, wrapped in the P element, and the two bullet points are part of the same content wrapped in the SECTION element.

The SECTION element is an efficient way to organize content in your code.

Figure 1.6 The role of the SECTION element is to organize content into logical sections.

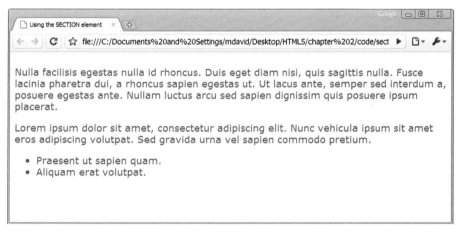

Using the ARTICLE Element

The ARTICLE element is used to clearly identify content in a web page. Blogs are a good example where content is clearly identified. The main section of a page is the content that you can wrap using the ARTICLE element. You can have additional HTML elements included within an ARTICLE. The following blog from *http://blog.whatwg.org/* is an example that shows how you can use the ARTICLE element in HTML.

```
<ARTICLE>
<H1>Spelling HTML5</H1>
<P> <TIME>September 10th, 2009</TIME> by Henri Sivonen</P>
<P> What's the right way to spell "HTML5"? The short
answer is: "HTML5" (without a space).</P>
</ARTICLE>
```

In Figure 1.7 you can see how the ARTICLE content is displayed in a web browser.

More than one ARTICLE can be added to a page. You should think of the ARTICLE element as a tool that logically breaks up content. Similar content separated by the ARTICLE element can be contained within a SECTION element.

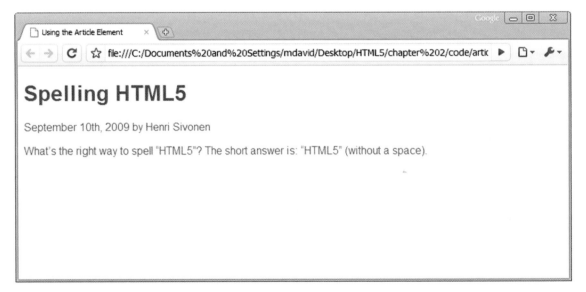

Figure 1.7 Use the ARTICLE element to block the main content on your page.

Using the HEADER and FOOTER Elements

The top and bottom of a page created with Microsoft Word or any other word processing software is a place reserved for the header and footer information page. This includes page number, copyright notice, and other details. Web pages are no different. Header and footer information is found on most web pages. You

Figure 1.8 The Focal Press header section.

can see in Figure 1.8 on Focal Press' web site that header information is used.

You can see the use of the header on the page. It contains the Focal Press logo, the element line, high-level links, and a search box. HTML5 allows this area of content to be clearly identified as either a header or a footer using the new HEADER and FOOTER elements.

For instance, a HEADER for Focal Press would look like the following.

```
<HEADER>
<SECTION><a href="/"><img src="/images/fplogo.png"
border="none" alt="Focal Press logo" title="Focal Press
Home"/></a> learn | master | create</b>SECTION>
<NAV>
<ul><li><a title="Digital Imaging and Photography"
class="first"
href="/photography.aspx">Photography</a></li><li><a
title="Production, Postproduction, and Motion Graphics"
href="/film_video.aspx">Film &amp; Video</a></li><li><a
title="Animation, 3D, and Games"
href="/animation_3d.aspx">Animation &amp; 3D</a></li><li><a
title="Audio Engineering and Music Technology"
href="/audio.aspx">Audio</a></li><li><a
title="Broadcast and Digital Media"
href="/broadcast.aspx">Broadcast</a></li><li><a
title="Theatre and Live Performance"
href="/theatre.aspx">Theatre</a></li><li><a class="offsite
last"
```

```
href="http://www.elsevierdirect.com/imprint.jsp?iid=100001"
>Bookstore </a></li> </ul>                </NAV>
    </HEADER>
```

The FOOTER section to a page is also viewed on most web pages. An example FOOTER in HTML5 will look as follows:

```
<FOOTER>
<P>Copyright © 2009 Focal Press, Inc.</P>
</FOOTER>
```

Unlike normal page layout, the HEADER and FOOTER are not exclusive to just the head and foot of a web page. You can have a header and footer placed around the ARTICLE or SECTION element if those pieces require specific header and footer content.

Using the ASIDE Element

The role of the ASIDE element is to describe content that is related to but is not part of the main content on the web page. You can think of the ASIDE element as fitting the role of a sidebar reference or an aside found in books and articles. The following example shows how the ASIDE element can be used with the ARTICLE element.

```
<ARTICLE>
<P>Lorem ipsum dolor sit amet, consectetur adipiscing
elit. Vivamus sed eros at metus pulvinar convallis id quis
purus. Sed lacinia condimentum viverra.</P>
    <P>Lorem ipsum dolor sit amet, consectetur adipiscing
elit. Vivamus sed eros at metus pulvinar convallis id quis
purus. Sed lacinia condimentum viverra.</P>
    <ASIDE>
<H1>What is Lorem Ipsum?</H1>
<P>Lorem Ipsum is simply dummy text of the printing and
typesetting industry.</P>
    </ASIDE>
    </ARTICLE>
```

The main content of the page and a support aside can be clearly separated using the ASIDE element, as shown in Figure 1.9.

Apply formatting, using CSS, to visually show where the ASIDE is on the screen.

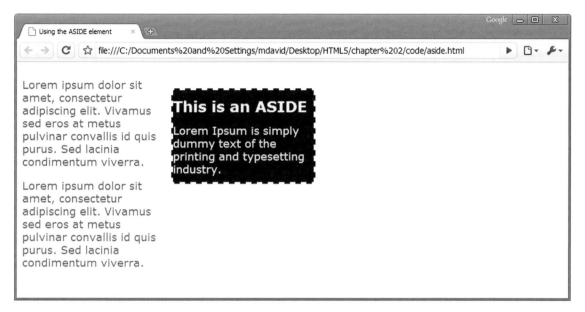

Using the DIALOG Element

Conversation and comments are common place on the Web. The DIALOG element allows you to identify conversation on a screen. There are three main parts to the DIALOG element:

- The wrapping DIALOG element that identifies a conversation.
- A DT element that identifies the speaker.
- A DD element that identifies the conversation.

Using the DIALOG element to block conversation can look as follows.

```
<DIALOG>
<DT>Josie Smith </DT>
<DD>HTML5 is a great way to block semantic elements on
a page. </DD>
<DT>Ian Jones </DT>
<DD>Yes, you are absolutely right. </DD>
<DT>Josie Smith </DT>
<DD>Conversation can now be easily identified. </DT>
<DT>Ian Jones </DT>
<DD><P>Blocking allows you to accomplish several things
such as:</P>
<UL>
<LI>Clearly identifying blocks of content on a page</LI>
<LI>Making it easier to construct page designs</LI>
</UL>
</DD>
</DIALOG>
```

Figure 1.10 illustrates how this may be presented on the screen.

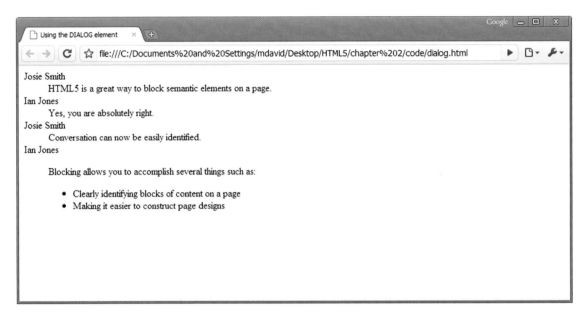

Figure 1.10 You can control comments and conversation with the DIALOG element.

Opening and closing the conversation is the main DIALOG element. Each new conversation starts with a DT element that identifies the speaker. For instance, Ian Jones is identified using the following DT element:

```
<DT>Ian Jones </DT>
```

Ian's conversation is then wrapped between a DD element. Here is a close-up example.

```
<DD><P>Blocking allows you to accomplish several things
such as:</P>
<UL>
<LI>Clearly identifying blocks of content on a page</LI>
<LI>Making it easier to construct page designs</LI>
</UL>
</DD>
```

You can see that additional HTML elements can be placed within the DD DIALOG element such as list, paragraph, or even an article.

Using the FIGURE Element

Inserting images into a web page is common practice. Identifying the image and supporting text as a figure is much more difficult. The FIGURE element clearly identifies an image and supporting description as being part of a set. This set is called a *figure group*. As with many of the previous new HTML5 elements, the FIGURE element is a method of blocking related content with itself.

```
<FIGURE>
<LEGEND>Figure 12. Using the FIGURE element </LEGEND>
<IMG alt="The FIGURE element is another example
of block semantics in HTML5" src="figure_element.jpg"
border="0" height="140" width="240"/>
</FIGURE>
```

As with the DIALOG element, the FIGURE element also has an additional element you can use within it. The LEGEND element identifies the text that is to be associated with the image. The FIGURE element can be used multiple times on a page.

Using the NAV Element

The final HTML5 blocking element is NAV. Navigation is important to any web site. The role of the NAV element is to clearly identify groups of links that when grouped together form navigation.

Navigation can take many different roles on a single web page. The different types of content that can be grouped together as navigation include, but are not limited to, the following:

1. Top-level links typically found in the top right corner of a web page.
2. Links that move you through data such as "Next" and "Previous."
3. Links found in the footer of a web page.

The following is an example of navigation grouped using the NAV element.

```
<NAV>
<a href="/home.html">Home</a> | <a
href="aboutUs.html">About Us</a> | <a
href="contactUs.html">Contact Us</a>
</NAV>
```

Of all the blocking elements in HTML5, the NAV element is one of the easiest to use.

Text-Level Semantic Additions and Changes

HTML5 is expanding text-level semantic changes. The goal of these additional elements is to clearly identify fundamental qualities such as time, numbers, progress, and emphasis. These elements augment existing HTML4 elements that include VAR, CODE, KBD, TT, and SAMP.

Using the MARK Element

Do you want to highlight or place emphasis on a section of text without necessarily having the text formatted? The MARK element looks to do exactly that. The following example from Wikipedia shows that the word "HTML5" should have extra emphasis.

```
<P><M>HTML5</M> is the proposed next standard for HTML
4.01, XHTML 1.0, and DOM Level 2 HTML. <M>HTML5</M> has
been said to become a game-changer in Web application
development, making obsolete such plug-in-based rich
Internet application (RIA) technologies as Adobe Flash,
Microsoft Silverlight, and Sun JavaFX.</P>
```

It is important to note that unless you apply CSS to the MARK element, you will not see the emphasis change on the HTML on the screen.

Using the TIME Element for Measurement

In addition to drawing emphasis to a section of text using the MARK element, you can also identify text as being a measurement of time. The TIME element identifies a specific time and can be added as follows:

```
<TIME>April 23, 2010</TIME>
```

This format is acceptable. A more complete use of the TIME element is to add a datetime attribute. The following example is more easily understood by machines.

```
<TIME datetime="2009-12-24T23:00:00">11:00 O'Clock on
Christmas Eve</TIME>
```

The goal of the TIME element is to describe the date/time text on the page.

Using the METER Element

The METER element identifies a numeric value over a specific range. For instance, you can use it to identify the distance of a runner in a race, the price for groceries, or any numeric value. In the following example you can see that the price for a can of tuna is a value with the METER element wrapped around it.

```
<P>Tuna is going on sale today for the amazing price of
just <METER>$2.00<METER>!</P>
```

Additional specific attributes can be added to the METER element to show a range in the value. The attributes you can use are:
- value
- min

- max
- low
- high
- optimum

The following example demonstrates using the additional METER attributes.

```
<P>The distance you swam in the contest was<METER
value="120" min="0" max="200" low="80" high="200"
optimum="200">120 yards</meter></P>
```

The value is the number of yards actually swam. The minimum is the minimum number of yards you can swim, with the maximum number of yards being 200. The low value is the lowest number of yards actually swam, and the high value represents the most yards swam with the optimum value representing the optimum number of yards.

Using the PROGRESS Element

The PROGRESS element represents the progress for an ongoing process. For instance, you can use this element if you are downloading an image on a web page, a file, or loading up some new data.

There are two attributes for the PROGRESS element for `value` and `max`. The `value` is the current value for a download at this specific point in time. The maximum value is the total value. For instance, you can identify a downloaded file in the following example:

```
<PROGRESS value="245998" max="100000">25%</PROGRESS>
```

The PROGRESS element is, by itself, static. You will need to tie the element to a JavaScript program to track the progress of what you are tracking.

Applying HTML5 to Make HTML Code Easier to Read

Let's take the example of the blog identified at the start of this chapter and show how a typical web page is now changing with HTML5 markup. Following is a typical blog entry with HTML4 markup. The code is split into several main sections:

- Header content
- Link to the main blog
- Blog article
- Comments on the blog
- Navigation
- Footer and header information

Are Elements Case Sensitive?

 You can write your HTML elements in lowercase and uppercase. Heck, you can even mix it around. For example, the following three are all acceptable.

```
<SECTION>FIRST
SECTION</SECTION>
```

```
<section>second
section</section>
```

```
<Section>Third
Section</Section>
```

For consistency, pick and use a standard that makes the most sense to you.

The following section is the header content, or the hidden content in a web page that describes the document.

```
<?xml version="1.0" encoding="UTF-8"?>
<html xmlns="http://www.w3.org/1999/xhtml">
  <head>
    <title>Example Blog in HTML4</title>
  </head>
<body>
```

The following section is the top header content of the HTML4 page. You will see that the code is forced to use the DIV tag along with additional ID information to describe the content.

```
<div id="page">
  <div id="header">
    <h1><a href="www.someblogpost.com">HTML
Element Language is Awesome</a></h1>
  </div>
```

The following content is the main article for the blog post. Again, notice the use of the DIV element. In this instance you will see that the code requires DIV elements to be nested within each other.

```
<div id="container">
  <div id="center" class="column">
    <div class="post" id="html_element_language">
      <h2><a href=
    "/blog/html/html_element">
    HTML Elements are Awesome</a></h2>
      <div class="entry">
        <p>Yesterday I started to write in Word and
realized that everything uses markup to separate content,
we simply don't always see it. For instance, in Word you
define the start and end of content; if you want to create
a table of contents you define specific content to be for
a TOC; you define specific content for figures and page
structure. This is the same as HTML5!</p>
      </div>
    </div>
  </div>
```

Here you can see comments made on the blog. Holy nested DIV elements, Batman!

```
<div id="comments">
<div id="speaker">
<p id="comment">You bring up a great point. </p>
<p id="comment">It is great that you take time to make
these comments. </p>
  <p id="comment">You hit the nail on the head. </p>
  </div>
  </div>
  </div>
```

Here is the navigation to move you back and forth between blog entries.

```
<div class="navigation">
  <div class="alignleft">
    <a href="/blog/page/2/">&laquo; Previous
Entries</a>
      </div>
    <div class="alignright"></div>
  </div>
</div>
```

Here is the navigation to place a sidebar for the blog.

```
<div id="right" class="column">
  <ul id="sidebar">
    <li><h2>Info</h2>
    <ul>
      <li><a href="/blog/comment-policy/">Comment
Policy</a></li>
        <li><a href="/blog/keywords/">Keyword List
List</a></li>
      </ul> </li>
    </ul>
  </div>
```

The final part of the page is the footer section.

```
<div id="footer">
  <p>Copyright 2009 Matthew David</p>
  </div>
</div></body></html>
```

As you can see from the example the DIV element is used extensively to structure content. The content, however, does not have any semantic organization. What does all this content mean?

Now, let's look at the same content structured for HTML5. The opening meta-information, including DOCTYPE, opens the code.

```
<!doctype html>
  <head>
    <title>Example Blog in HTML4 </title>
  </head>
<body>
```

The first action is to define the content that will appear at the top of the web page using the HEADER element, as follows.

```
<header>
    <h1><a href="www.someblogpost.com">HTML
Element Language is Awesome</a></h1>
  </header>
```

The main blog and comments are wrapped together with a SECTION element. As you look at the HTML code you can see that the content is associated.

```
<section><h2><a href=
  "/blog/html/html_element">
  HTML Elements are Awesome</a></h2>
```

The main content on the page is wrapped in an ARTICLE element, as follows.

```
<article>
    <p>Yesterday I started to write in Word and
realized that everything uses markup to separate content,
we simply don't always see it. For instance, in Word you
define the start and end of content; if you want to create
a table of contents you define specific content to be for
a TOC; you define specific content for figures and page
structure. This is the same as HTML5!</p>
    </article>
```

The associated comments at the bottom of the page are blocked together using the DIALOG element.

```
<dialog>
  <dt>John Smith</dt>
  <dd> It is great that you take time to make
these comments.</dd>
  </dialog>
```

It is typical to find navigation at the end of a blog posting that lets you move to the next or previous article. You can use the NAV element to block the links.

```
<nav>
<a href="/blog/page/2/">&laquo; Previous Entries</a>
</nav>
```

The closing SECTION element clearly shows the end of the content:

```
</section>
```

The bottom of the page is a footer section with additional navigation.

```
<footer>
<nav>
  <ul>
    <li><h2>Info</h2>
    <ul>
    <li><a href="/blog/comment-policy/">Comment
Policy</a></li>
    <li><a href="/blog/Keywords/">Keyword List</a>
</li>
  </nav>
  <p>Copyright 2009 Matthew David</p>
</footer>
</body>
</html>
```

It is clear where the main article for the page starts as it is wrapped in the ARTICLE element; it is clear where comments are added as they are placed within the DIALOG element. The same can be said for navigation, headers, and footers on the page. There are no clustered DIV tags in this example.

Additional HTML5 Elements You May Or May Not Use

The HTML5 elements covered are the most common elements you will use. There are additional elements, including:

- The EVENT-SOURCE element catches server-sent messages.
- The OUTPUT element sends messages you may get from a JavaScript program.
- The RUBY, RT, and RB elements allow you to add Ruby annotations.

Working with HTML5 Forms

If you have ever shopped online and purchased a book, CD, or gift, then you have used a form during the checkout process to enter your name, address, and credit card information. The FORM elements you are using are the same elements added to HTML2 in 1994 and they have not changed since. In contrast, your use of the Web has changed dramatically.

With HTML5 comes a well-needed update to web forms and data management. The W3C had already begun modernizing the FORM element, called Forms 2.0, before HTML5. However, it has now been rolled into HTML5. The new implementation of FORMS now includes support for features that previously had to be accomplished with clever JavaScript and Ajax tricks.

Browsers Supporting Forms 2.0

The updated FORM element is very new and is only now starting to be included in the latest web browsers. At the time of writing, only the Opera 10 web browser supports Forms 2.0. However, it is widely expected that FireFox, Chrome, and Safari will soon too support Forms 2.0.

What Has Changed in HTML Forms 2.0

The biggest change with HTML5 Forms is the extension of the core INPUT element with new attribute types. The following is a list of the new types you can use in HTML5:

- `<input type="search">`: This attribute allows you to specify the element for searching.
- `<input type="number">`: This attribute allows you to convert the input type into a visual spin box.
- `<input type="range">`: This attribute allows you to convert the input type into a visual scrub bar.

- `<input type="color">`: This attribute allows you to convert the input type into a visual color picker.
- `<input type="tel">`: This attribute allows you to format the input for a telephone line.
- `<input type="url">`: This attribute allows you to specify a web address.
- `<input type="email">`: This attribute allows you to specify an email address.
- `<input type="date">`: This attribute converts automatically into a date picker.
- `<input type="month">`: This attribute automatically converts into a month picker.
- `<input type="week">`: This attribute automatically converts into a picker that allows you to select a week.
- `<input type="time">`: This attribute allows you to add a timestamp.
- `<input type="datetime">`. This attribute is for precise, absolute date and timestamps.
- `<input type="datetime-local">`: This attribute is for local dates and times.

As you might expect, the new attributes still support the existing `text`, `password`, and `submit` attributes. Using the new INPUT elements will look as follows for a form.

```
<FORM>
<label >First Name </label>
<input name="FirstName" type="text">
<label >Last Name </label>
<input name="LastName" type="text">
<label >Date Of Birth </label>
<input name="DOB" type="date">
<label >Email Address </label>
<input name="email" type="email">
<label >Your Personal Web Site</label>
<input name="WebSite" type="URL">
<label >How Many Hours Do You Surf The Web Each Week?
</label>
    <input name="SurfWeb" type="range" min="1" max="20"
value="0"><output name="result" onforminput="value=a.
value">0</output>
    </FORM>
```

As you can see from Figure 1.11, applying the different INPUT attributes is very easy in HTML5. The only exception is the sliding RANGE type. The RANGE is a visual tool that allows you to choose a value by sliding a scrub bar. The scrub bar allows you to select a value between the minimum (min) and maximum (max) values. The value is then captured and sent back to the form using the OUTPUT element.

First Name

Last Name

Date Of Birth

Email Address

Your Personal Web Site

How Many Hours Do You Surf The Web Each Week? 0

Figure 1.11 The new FORM types allow you to easily create complex forms.

Inserting the Cursor Automatically into a Specified Field

A second, and useful, addition is the ability to set a form element to be the default starting element in the form. The `autofocus` attribute can only be used one time in a form. The attribute does not have a value. If you elect to add it to an INPUT value then the cursor will automatically focus on that element. The following shows how to set the focus for an INPUT element:

```
<input name="FirstName" type="text" autofocus>
```

You can only use the `autofocus` attribute once per form.

Making an INPUT Field Required

You can also set an INPUT element using the `required` attribute. As with the `autofocus` attribute, the `required` attribute has no values. If you add the attribute then the form field is required. Here is an example using the `required` attribute.

```
<input name="FirstName" type="text" required>
<input name="MiddleName" type="text">
<input name="LastName" type="text" required>
```

In this example you can see that the first and third INPUT elements are required and the second is not. If the field does not have any data entered into it then a message will pop up asking for a value (Figure 1.12).

Figure 1.12 An error message pops up if you do not enter a value when the `required` attribute is set.

Adding the Placeholder Text

As you can see, HTML5 added many additional tweaks that allow you to control data captured in your forms. A further addition is an attribute called `placeholder`. You have probably seen placeholder text in many forms online. FireFox has a placeholder in the browser's search box. The light-gray box specifies

Figure 1.13 Using the placeholder attribute to add text that prompts user input.

the default search engine. When you click on the field the text disappears. See Figure 1.13.

Following is how you add placeholder text to an input field.

```
<FORM>
<input name="search" type="text" placeholder="Google
Search">
<input type="submit" value="Search">
</FORM>
```

You can put all of these different techniques together to create compelling HTML5 Forms. The following example can be accomplished with JavaScript in current web browsers without the use of HTML5. The difference is that HTML5 accomplishes the same results in far less code.

```
<FORM>
<label >First Name </label>
<input name="FirstName" type="text" autofocus required>
<label >Last Name </label>
<input name="LastName" type="text" required >
<label >Date Of Birth </label> required>
<input name="DOB" type="date">
<label >Email Address </label>
```

```
<input name="email" type="email">
<label >Your Personal Web Site</label>
<input name="WebSite" type="URL" placeholder="Enter
your own Web site address">
<label >How Many Hours Do You Surf The Web Each Week?
</label>
<input name="SurfWeb" type="range" min="1" max="20"
value="0"><output name="result" onforminput="value=a.
value">0</output>
</FORM>
```

The new attributes for HTML5 have been highlighted so you can see how they are used.

Controlling Data with HTML5

Forms are used to add, modify, and delete data. HTML5 is the first version of the HTML standards to directly address the need for managing data both on the server and locally on your computer. There are three key ways in which data can be more effectively managed in HTML5:
- Extending the functionality of HTML5 Forms
- Displaying data
- Storing data
The following sections explore these three different methods.

Extending the Functionality of HTML5

A dropdown list in a web form is typically accomplished using the SELECT element. With HTML5 you can replace the values in a SELECT element by extending the default INPUT element with dropdown options. This is accomplished using the new DATALIST element. The DATALIST element allows you to create an array that can be associated with an INPUT element (Figure 1.14). The following example demonstrates the DATALIST element used to list different colors.

```
<label>Select a color</label>
<input list="mylist" type="text">
<datalist id="mylist">
<option label="Red" value="Red">
<option label="Blue" value="Blue">
<option label="Green" value="Green">
</datalist>
```

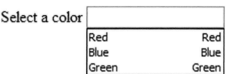

Figure 1.14 The DATALIST element gives you more control over how to organize an array of data in HTML.

The attribute value of "mylist" binds the DATALIST with the INPUT element. The values of the DATALIST can be shared with other elements on the screen.

Displaying Data in HTML5

The DETAILS and DATAGRID elements are two ways in which to add interactivity to your data. The DETAILS element allows for additional information to be highlighted on the content. For instance, the following example will show additional information.

```
<p>Click for Additional Information.
<details open="open">
<p>The details for this content will be shown when you
select it with the mouse.</p></details>
</p>
```

Additional interactivity is accomplished with the inclusion of the DATAGRID element. DATAGRID gives you interactivity that you would expect to see with a grid control in a tool such as Microsoft's Access. It is simply a way to structure data. The resulting data can be displayed in tree, list, or tabular format (Figure 1.15).

```
<datagrid>
<p>HTML5</p>
<p>Ajax</p>
```

Figure 1.15 The DATAGRID element is used to organize content in a default list format.

```
<p>XHTML</p>
<p>HTML 4</p>
</datagrid>
```

The data can be formatted with CSS.

Storing Data Locally Using Web Storage

Cookies are the typical way you save and store data locally for a web site. With HTML5 the amount of data you can store locally has been dramatically increased. The new Web Storage standard that is included with HTML5 allows for massive amounts of data to be stored. Instead of using text-based cookies, Web Storage is a local database that sits within the web browser.

The significant benefit of having a database in the web browser is that you can now program your web applications to store data locally and continue running when they are not connected to the Internet. You can see this already being used with Google's Gmail, Calendar, and Docs services. The web applications run whether you are connected to the Web or not.

The advantage of offline web application management does not make much sense for traditional PCs, but it becomes very important when your web application is running through a mobile device such as Apple's iPhone. Google's Gmail service for the iPhone is designed to allow you to work even when you are not connected to the Internet. For instance, you are waiting to take your commuter train and you are checking your Gmail account. You get on the phone as you're reading an email and decide to reply to the message. As you are typing your message the train starts to move and you are taken out of a 3G or EDGE network and loose Internet connectivity. The HTML5 Web Storage feature allows your application to keep running. You can reply to your email message and even write new messages without ever knowing that you are not connected to the Internet. The local database stores your contacts and a specific number of emails and responses. The next time your phone is connected to a network, your email messages are sent and new messages are received. It is all done without you even knowing.

How Are Data Stored Locally?

The database being used by Google, Opera, Apple, and FireFox to enable HTML5 Web Storage and offline browsing support is the open-source database called SQLite. You can get more information at *www.sqlite.org*.

Web Storage is achieved using JavaScript. The following example is of a form that allows you to enter a value. When you click the mouse out of the area of the INPUT element, the data will be stored locally in your web browser using the Web Storage database.

```
<section>
  <header> <h1>Using Web Storage</h1> </header>
  <article>
    <section>
      <p>Enter a value and then click out of the INPUT
field for the value to be stored</p>
        <label for="local">Enter a Value </label>
        <input type="text" name="local" value=""
id="local" required autofocus>
    </section>
  </article>
</section>
```

The main guts of the code are managed through JavaScript. Below your HTML elements add the following SCRIPT elements. You are going to add JavaScript in the SCRIPT elements.

```
<script>
</script>
```

Add the following JavaScript function.

```
function getStorage(type) {
  var storage = window[type + "Storage"],
    delta = 0,
    li = document.createElement("li");
  if (storage.getItem("value")) {
    delta = ((new Date()).getTime() - (new Date()).
setTime(storage.getItem('timestamp'))) / 1000;
      li.innerHTML = type + "Storage: " + storage.
getItem("value") + "(last updated: " + delta + "s ago)";
    } else {
      li.innerHTML = type + "Storage is empty";
    }
  document.querySelector("#previous").appendChild(li);
  }
```

The JavaScript is completing three tasks:
1. It is creating a new local database called Storage.
2. A field called `value` is being added to the Storage database.
3. A timestamp field is also added to the Storage database.

The following JavaScript will save any value you enter into the INPUT element.

```
getStorage("local");
  addEvent(document.querySelector("#local"), "keyup",
function () {
```

```
      localStorage.setItem("value", this.value);
      localStorage.setItem("timestamp", (new Date()).
getTime());
    });
```

You can now enter a value into the INPUT field. The value is captured and stored in a database. If you close the web page and then reopen it, the value you entered will be saved.

New HTML5 Attributes

An attribute is a setting that allows you to apply additional functionality to your element. Elements often have specialized attributes such as the INPUT element's use of the `required` attribute to specify the field as being required. There are, however, some new global attributes you can use in HTML5.

The new `draggable` attribute has a value of true or false. This attribute is tied to the new drag-and-drop application programming interface (API) included with HTML5 that allows you to drag any element on the page.

The `contenteditable` attribute allows you to specify if content can be edited in the web page. The following example allows you to edit all of the content within the SECTION element.

```
<section contenteditable="true">
  <h1>Edit this content</h1>
  <p>You can select, edit, and create your own content
in this space</p>
</section>
```

Adding Style to Your Elements

All of the elements covered in the chapter define blocks of content on a web page. They do not, however, add any visual style to the content. This is done using Cascading Style Sheets (CSS). The `class` attribute from HTML4, used to reference specific styles in a CSS document, still applies in exactly the same way with HTML5. The only difference is the CSS3 gives you many more options for creating visually pleasing designs.

Most of the attributes from XHTML and HTML4, such as `id`, `class`, and `style`, are still available in HTML5.

What Is Not Being Supported in HTML5

HTML5 is dropping support for several older and less used HTML elements from earlier versions of the HTML language. You will see a trend that many of the elements that are being dropped were previously used to apply formatting or design to an object on the screen. For instance, the MARQUEE element, which allowed you to create a scrolling text in your web page, is now dropped. You can now duplicate the same scrolling bar using JavaScript, standard HTML, and CSS. There is no need to keep the older element.

The following is list of the elements that are not supported by HTML5:

- BASEFONT—can be duplicated with CSS
- BIG—can be duplicated with CSS
- CENTER—can be duplicated with CSS
- FONT—can be duplicated with CSS
- S—can be duplicated with CSS
- STRIKE—can be duplicated with CSS
- TT—can be duplicated with CSS
- U—can be duplicated with CSS
- FRAME—can be duplicated with iFrame or CSS
- FRAMESET—can be duplicated with iFrame or CSS
- NOFRAMES—can be duplicated with iFrame or CSS
- ACRONYM—can use the ABBR element
- APPLET—can use the OBJECT element
- ISINDEX—use FORM controls instead
- DIR—has been widely replaced by the UL list element

Depreciated Element Support in Web Browsers

HTML5 does not support a bunch of older elements. This does not mean that your favorite web browser will drop support for these elements. You will need to check on a browser-by-browser basis for which elements are being supported in an effort to allow web pages to render correctly.

In addition to elements that have been removed, there are some elements that have modified functions, including:

- The A anchor element without an HREF attribute now represents a "placeholder link."
- The ADDRESS element is now scoped by the new concept of sectioning.
- The B element now represents a span of text to be stylistically offset from the normal prose without conveying any extra importance.
- The HR element now represents a paragraph-level thematic break.
- For the LABEL element the browser should no longer move focus from the label to the control unless such behavior is standard for the underlying platform user interface.
- The MENU element is redefined to be useful for actual menus.

- The SMALL element now represents small print (for side comments and legal print).
- The STRONG element now represents importance rather than strong emphasis.
- Quotation marks for the Q element are now to be provided by the author rather than the user agent.

In addition to HTML elements not being supported in HTML5, there are also several attributes being dropped. You will see that the attributes are being dropped as they replicate stylistic presentations already handled by CSS.

- The `align` attribute on CAPTION, IFRAME, IMG, INPUT, OBJECT, LEGEND, TABLE, HR, DIV, H1, H2, H3, H4, H5, H6, P, COL, COLGROUP, TBODY, TD, TFOOT, TH, THEAD, and TR.
- The `alink`, `link`, `text`, and `vlink` attributes on BODY.
- The `background` attribute on BODY.
- The `bgcolor` attribute on TABLE, TR, TD, TH, and BODY.
- The `border` attribute on TABLE, IMG, and OBJECT.
- The `cellpadding` and `cellspacing` attributes on TABLE.
- The `char` and `charoff` attributes on COL, COLGROUP, TBODY, TD, TFOOT, TH, THEAD, and TR.
- The `clear` attribute on BR.
- The `compact` attribute on DL, MENU, OL, and UL.
- The `frame` attribute on TABLE.
- The `frameborder` attribute on IFRAME.
- The `height` attribute on TD and TH.
- The `hspace` and `vspace` attributes on IMG and OBJECT.
- The `marginheight` and `marginwidth` attributes on IFRAME.
- The `noshade` attribute on HR.
- The `nowrap` attribute on TD and TH.
- The `rules` attribute on TABLE.
- The `scrolling` attribute on IFRAME.
- The `size` attribute on HR, INPUT, and SELECT.
- The `type` attribute on LI, OL, and UL.
- The `valign` attribute on COL, COLGROUP, TBODY, TD, TFOOT, TH, THEAD, and TR.
- The `width` attribute on HR, TABLE, TD, TH, COL, COLGROUP, and PRE.

How to Gracefully Migrate Sites to Work with the New HTML5 Standard

HTML5 introduces a lot of new features. This can be daunting for web developers who have to support current browsers such as Microsoft Internet Explorer 6–8. There needs to be a way to gracefully migrate web sites to the new technologies in HTML5.

Fortunately, Modernizr is a great open-source solution that allows you to detect the use of HTML5-specific technologies and provide options for HTML5 browsers to use older HTML4 technologies to still correctly display the page. You can download the JavaScript files for Modernizr at *www.modernizr.com*. The compressed files are only 7 Kb and will not take up much space on your web site.

Add the Modernizr files to the root of your web site. You can reference them from your web page as follows.

```
<!DOCTYPE html>
<html>
<head>
  <title>Detecting HTML5 content with Modernizr</title>
  <script src="modernizr.min.js"></script>
</head>
<body>
```

With the JavaScript added to the page you can now write script that allows you to swap in HTML5 when the web browser can support it or insert an older format for older browsers. For instance, you can have the following HTML5 INPUT element on your page:

```
<input type="date" name="DOB" id="DOB">
```

Add the following JavaScript to reference Modernizr, and older web browsers will swap out the HTML5 attribute with an Ajax alternative.

```
if (!Modernizr.inputtypes.date){
  createDatepicker(document.getElementById(DOB));
}
```

Using tools such as Modernizr ensures that all users coming to your web site can view the content and that new HTML5 content is targeted to the right audience.

What You Have Learned

In this chapter you have been introduced to key new elements found in HTML5. The purpose of the HTML5 elements is to identify blocks of text specified using the SECTION, ARTICLE, NAV, DIALOG, ASIDE, FIGURE, HEADER, and FOOTER elements.

Within a block of text are additional elements that place specific emphasis on content. Using the MARK element you can add emphasis to a specific section. Time and measurement can also be emphasized with the TIME and METER tags.

Finally, applications are becoming first-class citizens on the Web with the introduction of enhanced FORM elements and the new data management tools in HTML5.

PROJECT 1: BUILDING A WEB SITE USING HTML5 BLOCKING ELEMENTS

In the article chapter of this section you were introduced to the new SECTION, ARTICLE, NAVIGATION, ASIDE, HEADER, and FOOTER elements in HTML5 that allow you to apply a more easily readable structure to your web site design. In this project chapter you will be building an entire web site that uses the new HTML5 blocking elements to illustrate how you can more effectively structure your code.

The site will consist of four pages, as follows:

- Home page
- Product page
- News page
- Contact us page

Each of these pages demonstrates how you can use HTML5 in your web site design. By the time you have completed this project you will able to apply blocking to your new site design.

Creating a Template for Your Web Site

Each of the pages in the site will highlight specific elements used in HTML5. To make things easy for you, let's set up one page that you can reuse as a template for the other pages in the project site. It is easier to manage your site when the HTML code is consistent on each page. Finding and replacing sections becomes a matter of cut and paste. For this project, the default home page contains all of the elements and structure you will need for the entire site. The home page will be used as the template.

Before you start coding your HTML let's take some time to explore how the default home page is structured. You will want to use a tool that allows you to easily draw blocks on the page to visually show where you will place the content. Figure 1.1Proj uses PowerPoint to block out the page.

Styling Your Site with CSS

The project in this chapter is no exception. A Cascading Style Sheets (CSS) style document is included with the project files. Look for the file called "style.css" that is used to apply all of the visual design elements used in this project.

Professional Tools You Can Use to Manage Your Site

Tools such as Adobe's Dreamweaver and Microsoft's Expression Web support Dynamic Web Templates (DWT) files that you can use to create a template to reuse in your site. This will save you a lot of time as you manage your web site.

HTML5. doi: 10.1016/B978-0-240-81328-8.00001-X

39

Default Page Structure

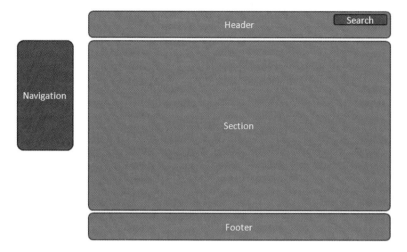

Figure 1.1Proj Rectangles drawn into a PowerPoint slide visually illustrate the different areas of content in the home page.

Figure 1.1Proj shows that there are four basic sections to each web page. HTML5 allows you to block out the following sections:

- Header
- Section
- Navigation
- Footer

The basic structure for the page looks like the following in HTML5.

```
<!DOCTYPE html>
<head>
<meta content="en-us" http-equiv="Content-Language"/>
<meta content="text/html; charset=utf-8" http-equiv=
"Content-Type"/>
<link href="style.css" rel="stylesheet" type="text/
css"/>
<title>Company Home Page</title>
</head>
<body>
<header>      </header>
<navigation>  </navigation>
<section>     </section>
<footer>      </footer>
</body>
</html>
```

The default page opens with the HTML5 DOCTYPE element that declares that the page supports HTML5. The rest of the HTML code within the HEAD element has not changed in HTML5. It is not until you start creating the content for the home page that you will see the new HTML5 elements.

The new blocking elements in HTML5 accurately describe where the content goes. In HTML4 and XHTML you can only achieve this same type of layout using DIV elements that are difficult to manage. It is easier to understand what each section is attempting to achieve when you name the elements as HEADER, FOOTER, SECTION, and NAVIGATION.

Now that you have a basic structure for the page, you can start filling in each section with content.

Customizing the HEADER Element

The HEADER element in the project example contains only one key part: a search engine. To add a Google Search engine, insert the following code.

```
<header id="header" class="headerStyle">
        <form method="get" action="http://www.google.
com/search">
        <input type="text" name="q" size="15"
maxlength="255" value="" placeholder="Search"/>
        <input type="submit" value="GO"/>
        <input type="hidden" name="sitesearch" value=
"www.focalpress.com"/>
        </form>
    </header>
```

The HEADER element has two additional attributes: `id` and `class`. The `id` is a value that, if you insert JavaScript into the page, you can use to identify the HEADER element on the page. The `class` attribute `headerStyle` links to a style defined in the CSS file. The `headerStyle` describes the placement and visual presentation of the HEADER element on the screen.

Inside the HEADER element is the FORM element. The FORM element takes any content entered in the INPUT element and sends it to Google. The first INPUT element is using a new HTML5 Forms attribute. The `placeholder` attribute allows you to add ghosted text into the input form that disappears when you start typing your own content, as shown in Figure 1.2Proj. A final hidden INPUT element forces the search engine results to only search *www.focalpress.com*.

| Search | GO |

Welcome to our Site

Cras ut justo eu arcu varius viverra in a enim. Nulla varius pharetra luctus. Ut scelerisque consequat velit at accumsan.

Sed euismod eros ut massa commodo egestas. Ut fringilla tincidunt ligula quis blandit. In et vestibulum orci.

Donec et metus sed purus ultrices interdum vel non purus. Nulla nisi velit, vulputate nec sodales vitae, dignissim quis odio. Praesent malesuada pulvinar leo, vel ultricies metus eleifend at.

Figure 1.2Proj The form on the page uses the `placeholder` attribute to add content.

Customizing the NAVIGATION Element

The NAVIGATION block contains the links that will be used in the site. The following HTML describes the links on the screen.

```
<navigation id="NavigationLink"
class="navigationStyle">
        <a href="default.html">Home</a>|<a
href="products.html">Products</a>|<a href="news.
html">News</a>|<a href="contactUs.html">Contact Us</a>
    </navigation>
```

The NAVIGATION element, as with the HEADER element, has two attributes: id and class. The class attribute links to the CSS style navigationStyle. You will see in Figure 1.3Proj that there is additional content around the NAVIGATION element.

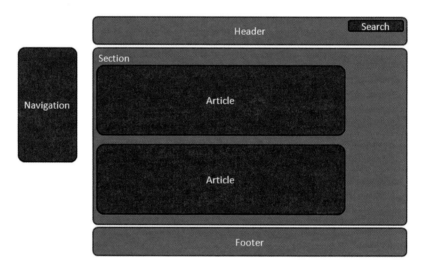

Figure 1.3Proj The NAVIGATION element is placed on the left side of the page.

A SECTION element is used to define where the company name and NAVIGATION are placed on the screen.

```
<section id="navigation" class="leftSection">
<p id="CompanyName" class="companyNameStyle">COMPANY
NAME</p>
    <navigation id="NavigationLink" style="" class=
"navigationStyle">
        <a href="default.html">Home</a>|
<ahref="products.html">Products</a>|<a href="news.
html">News</a>|<a href="contactUs.html">Contact Us</a>
    </navigation>
    </section>
```

You can see from this code example that the SECTION element contains both P and NAVIGATION elements. Each element now accurately describes the different types of content on the screen.

Customizing the Main SECTION Element

The center area of the web page is reserved for the main content. The HTML for this section can be described as easily as follows:

```
<section> </section>
```

Typically, you will find that the main section of any web page will contain more content. The template page is going to be set up with two areas for additional content within the SECTION element, as shown in Figure 1.4Proj and the following code.

How to Format Vertical Text

A CSS3 feature called Transform is used to change the angle of the text from horizontal to vertical.

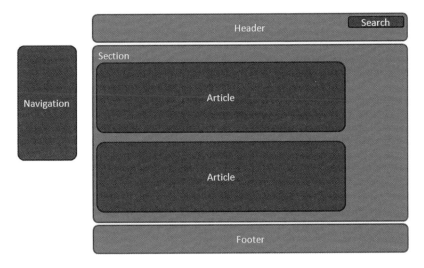

Figure 1.4Proj The SECTION element contains two ARTICLE elements.

```
<section>
<div id="section_articleOneIdentifier" style="position:
absolute; left: 355px; top: 105px; width: 1px; height:
60px; z-index: 3">
        <hr class="style2" style="height: 60px; width:
1px"/></div>
   <article id="article_one" style="position: absolute;
left: 420px; top: 100px; width: 315px; height: 195px;
z-index: 2">
        <h1>Header 1</h1>
        <p>Add Content here</p></article>
   <div id="section_articleOneIdentifier" style="position:
absolute; left: 355px; top: 355px; width: 1px; height:
60px; z-index: 3">
```

```
            <hr class="style2" style="height: 60px; width:
1px"/></div>
      <article id="article_two" style="position: absolute;
left: 420px; top: 350px; width: 315px; height: 195px;
z-index: 2">
            <h1>Header 2</h1>
            <p>Add Content here</p>
      </article>
      <hr class="HRstyle" style="position: absolute; left:
420px; top: 320px; width: 315px; height: 2px; z-index: 3"/>
      </section>
```

Two ARTICLE elements are placed within the SECTION element. The `id` attribute for both ARTICLE elements is unique to allow you to easily identify which element is which. Instead of linking to an external CSS class, a `style` attribute is used for both ARTICLE elements. The `style` attribute is using CSS, but it is localized to that single element and is not shared with other elements.

Each ARTICLE element also contains H1 and P elements. The H1 element is a header that will be used to lead in each article title. The P element is a paragraph element for content. Placeholder text is added to the H1 and P tags so you can see where the content is when you view the page in an HTML5-compliant web browser.

The final HR element is a visual separator between the two ARTICLE elements.

Customizing the FOOTER Element

The final element to modify is the FOOTER element. The following code describes the FOOTER element.

```
<footer id="footer" class="footerStyle">
      <hr class="HRstyle"/>
      <p class="Copyright">Copyright © 2010 Focal
Press</p>
</footer>
```

Typically, the FOOTER element does not contain much information. An HR (horizontal rule) element is used to visually separate the FOOTER element from the content on the page. Below the HR element is a P (paragraph) element that contains copyright information. Again, CSS is used to style and position the elements on the screen.

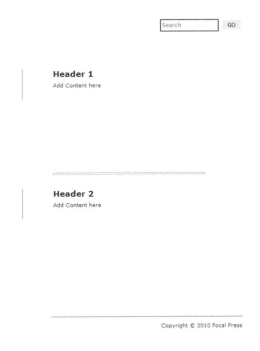

Figure 1.5Proj A template web page created using HTML5 blocking elements.

At this point you can save your HTML. Name your file "template.html." Your page should look the same as Figure 1.5Proj.

Creating the Site's Home Page

In many ways, the home page for your site is the easiest to create. You have already done all the heavy lifting in creating the template for the site. For the home page, all you have to do is switch out the content you entered as placeholder text with the text you want to have displayed on your home page.

Open the "template.html" file and save the file as "default.html." This will be your new home page file.

Each of the ARTICLE elements in the main SECTION element will be modified to reflect new content. Using a unique ID for each ARTICLE makes it easier to work with each section. Find the ARTICLE with the ID article_one and replace the HTML code with the following.

```
<article id="article_one" style="position: absolute;
left: 420px; top: 100px; width: 315px; height: 195px;
z-index: 2">
```

Using *Lorem Ipsum*
Lorem Ipsum is a fake language you can use to fill up space on a screen to illustrate where text should be placed. This prevents your customers from reading the text and commenting on typos instead of looking at the overall visual presentation.

```
    <p id="section_articleOneIdentifier" style="position:
absolute; left: 355px; top: 105px; width: 1px; height:
60px; z-index: 3">
    <hr class="style2" style="height: 60px; width: 1px"/>
</p>
    <h1>Welcome to our Site</h1>
    <strong>Cras ut justo eu arcu</strong> varius viverra
in a enim. Nulla varius pharetra luctus. Ut scelerisque
consequat velit at accumsan.<br/><br/>
    <strong>Sed euismod eros</strong> ut massa commodo
egestas. Ut fringilla tincidunt ligula quis blandit. In et
vestibulum orci.<br/><br/>
    <strong>Donec et metus sed</strong> purus ultrices
interdum vel non purus. Nulla nisi velit, vulputate nec
sodales vitae, dignissim quis odio. Praesent malesuada
pulvinar leo, vel ultricies metus eleifend at.
</article>
```

This code keeps the content within the ARTICLE element. A search engine, such as *www.Google.com* or *www.Bing.com,* can now accurately identify this content as informational and pertinent to the page. Identifying pertinent information is the goal of a search engine and will help in allowing a page to appear higher in the list of Google or Bing's search results page.

The second ARTICLE element contains the following HTML code.

```
    <article id="article_two" style="position: absolute;
left: 420px; top: 350px; width: 315px; height: 195px;
z-index: 2">
    <p id="section_articleOneIdentifier" style="position:
absolute; left: 355px; top: 355px; width: 1px; height:
60px; z-index: 3">
    <hr class="style2" style="height: 60px; width: 1px"/>
</p>
    <h1>What we do</h1>
    <p>Nullam tincidunt pulvinar ornare.</p>
    <p><strong>Our Products</strong></p>
    <p>Phasellus dictum elementum erat, rutrum pellentesque
tellus imperdiet ac. Sed quis porttitor eros.</p>
    <p><strong>Our Services</strong></p>
    <p>Etiam gravida dui a purus sollicitudin tempus
blandit sem pulvinar.</p>
    </article>
```

The second ARTICLE uses different HTML to format the text. The new HTML elements do not restrict you from using additional elements within them, giving you maximum creative freedom to code a page the way you want it coded.

This is it. Save the page and view it through your favorite HTML5-compliant web browser. It should look like Figure 1.6Proj.

Figure 1.6Proj The home page.

Adding a Product Page That Uses the MARK Element

The product page, when viewed through your web browser, will look very similar to the home page. Figure 1.7Proj shows the product page.

Figure 1.7Proj The product page.

The difference with the product page is that, behind the scenes, the MARK element is being used to specify content in each ARTICLE element. The MARK element is another way in which you can specify content on a page for a search engine to pick up and use.

The following HTML is from the ARTICLE with the ID `article_one`.

```
<h1><m>The Gizmo Product</m></h1>
<m>The Gizmo Product</m>varius viverra in a enim. Nulla
varius pharetra luctus. Ut scelerisque consequat velit at
accumsan.<br/><br/>
    <strong>Sed euismod eros</strong><m>The Gizmo
Product</m> egestas. Ut fringilla tincidunt ligula quis
blandit. In et vestibulum orci.<br/><br/>
    <strong>Donec et metus sed</strong> purus ultrices
interdum vel non purus. Nulla nisi velit, vulputate nec
sodales <m>The Gizmo Product</m> quis odio. Praesent malesuada
pulvinar leo, vel ultricies metus eleifend at.</article>
```

The goal of the product page is to emphasize the placement of specific words on a page.

Adding a News Page That Uses the TIME and ASIDE Elements

The third page you are going to create is the news page. The news page uses two elements that help provide additional information about content and provide structure content on the screen. Figure 1.8Proj shows what the news page looks like.

Figure 1.8Proj The news page uses the ASIDE element to define a sidebar on the page.

Let's start by adding the sidebar shown on the screen in the figure. Open the "template.html" file and save it as "news.html." The sidebar is created using the ASIDE element. As with other blocking elements, the goal of the ASIDE element is to help you structure your content. In this example, you are going to go one step further and format the position and presentation of the ASIDE element using CSS.

The following HTML code creates the ASIDE.

```
<aside id="aside" style="position: absolute; left:
740px; top: 200px; width: 150px; height: 190px; z-index: 6;
background-color: #808080; color: #FFFFFF;-moz-border-radius:
10px;-webkit-border-radius: 10px;padding: 5px;">
  </aside>
```

The `style` attribute defines the position, background color, and border radius so you can see the ASIDE element on the page. Place the ASIDE element within the SECTION element. The following HTML can be added within the ASIDE element tags. This is the content for the ASIDE.

```
    For additional information on press releases please
contact:<br/><br/>
    Production Information<br/>
    John Marshall<br/>
    <a href="mailto:jmarshall@email.com">jmarshall@email.com
</a><br/><br/>
    Corporate Information<br/>
    Jenny Smythe<br/>
    <a href="mailto:jsmythe@email.com">jsmythe@email.com
</a><br/><br/>
    Phone Calls:<br/>
    (920) 555-1212<br/>
```

Both of the ARTICLE elements contain information that is newsworthy. A date for each news article specifies the publication date. Using the TIME element you can highlight the time content for each article on the page.

Following is the title and date for the first article.

```
    <h1>The news is hot!</h1>
    <p><time>April 1, 2010</time></p>
```

In this instance, the TIME element captures the information between the two tags and identifies it as a date. The second news headline uses the `datetime` attribute to be more specific with the date.

```
    <h1>What we do</h1>
    <p><time datetime="2010-03-15T10:32:17">March 15, 2010
</time></p>
```

Here, the text between the TIME elements states March 15, 2010. The `datetime` attribute allows additional information to be

Web Browser Support for HTML5 Forms
Currently, Opera 9.5+ has the strongest support for HTML5 Forms. Google's Chrome, Apple's Safari, and Mozilla's FireFox are incrementally building support for HTML5 Forms into each successful release of their browsers. Google, in particular, is anxious to build stronger support for HTML5 Forms to help support the evermore complex web services, such as Gmail and Docs.

added. In this case, the `datetime` attribute adds a timestamp to the date explaining that the article was published at 10:32 AM and 17 seconds.

Creating a Contact Us Page That Uses the New Form INPUT Attributes

Earlier in this chapter you built a search engine form that sends requests to Google. The Contact Us form builds on the fundamentals introduced with the Google Search form and introduces you to more complex ways in which you can display data.

Figure 1.9Proj shows the Contact Us form as it is presented in Opera 10. As you use the form you will see the following interactions have been included:

Figure 1.9Proj HTML5 Forms support many new tools that enable you to capture data.

- The form automatically places the focus of the cursor into the *First Name* field and the field is required.
- The *Middle Name* field is disabled, preventing a user from entering data into it.
- The *Age* field is a numeric scroll that allows you to pick from an age range of 18–100.
- The *Email* field has a visual cue to tell you that you must enter a valid email address.
- The *How did you hear about us* field is a dropdown menu that allows you to choose from several options.
- The *When would you like us to contact you* field is a selectable date tool.
- The final field, *How many of our products do you own*, is a slider allowing you to choose from 0–10.

The new attributes for the INPUT element enable you to accomplish complex design without having to develop complex scripting solutions or leverage nonstandard technologies such as Adobe Flash or Microsoft SilverLight.

What has not changed in HTML5 Forms is the way you send data using computer graphic interface (CGI) or server-side-technologies such as PHP, ASP.NET, ColdFusion, or JSP. You can use any CGI solution to transmit data captured in a web form. HTML5 only gives you more options to capture the data. Once you have the data, they are still data.

To create the Contact Us form you will need to take a copy of the "template.html" file and save it as "contactus.html." Open the "contactus.html" file in your favorite text editor. The form will be added to the main SECTION block of the page.

The first elements to add are the opening and closing FORM elements, as follows.

```
<h1>Contact Us</h1>
<p>For more information, contact us:</p>
<form method="POST" action="http://fp1.formmail.com/
cgi-bin/fm192">
</form>
```

In this code you have a title and brief sentence introducing the form. The FORM element uses the `POST` method to submit the contents of the form. In this example I am using the free FormMail service to submit the contents of the form. You can use this for your forms, too; the `action="http://fp1.formmail.com/cgi-bin/fm192"` submits the data from the form to a free CGI/Perl script.

INPUT form elements are placed in-between the opening and closing FORM elements. The following three INPUT elements are hidden. The role of these elements is to pass data to CGI/Perl script letting it know that the form is valid and where to send the results when someone has completed the form.

```
<input type="hidden" name="_pid" value="119137">
<input type="hidden" name="_fid" value="FNNZXGED">
<input type="hidden" name="recipient" value=
"matthewadavid@gmail.com">
```

Here you can swap out the recipient email with your own.

The visual elements of the form use the LABEL and INPUT elements to present themselves on the page. The LABEL element identifies the text as a label and is typically used with forms. As with the TIME, MARK, and METER elements, the LABEL element is a new HTML5 blocking feature. Each form INPUT element has a preceding LABEL describing the element. The LABEL element does not have any additional attributes. The following is the LABEL for the first field in the form:

```
<label>First Name:</label><br/>
```

A BR element is used to force a single line break after the LABEL element.

The following HTML code allows you to force the cursor to start in this field by adding the autofocus attribute. The required attribute also prevents the form from being submitted until a value has been entered into the First Name field.

```
<label>First Name:</label><br/><input name= "FirstName"
type="text" autofocus required><br/><br/>
```

The Middle Name INPUT field has been visually disabled. You can use the disable feature to lock and unlock fields dynamically using JavaScript.

```
<label>Middle Name:</label><br/><input
name="MiddleName" type="text" disabled>
```

The Last Name field is also a required field using the required attribute.

```
<label>Last Name:</label><br/><input name="LastName"
type="text" maxlength="25" required><br/><br/>
```

The Age field is a numeric stepper tool that allows you to scroll through a specific range of numbers. In this case, you can choose a number from 18–100. Figure 1.10Proj shows age 27 selected.

Contact Us

For more information, contact us:

First Name:

Middle Name:

<- disabled

Last Name:

Age:

27

Email:

How Did you hear about us:

When would you like us to contact you:

How many of our products do you own

10

Submit

Figure 1.10Proj The numeric stepper tool allows you to choose a number from a range.

The visual effect of the numeric stepper is created through setting the attribute settings of `type`, `min`, and `max`. Following is the HTML code for the Age field.

```
<label>Age:</label><br/><input name="age" type="number"
min="18" max="100"><br/><br/>
```

The `type` attribute identifies the INPUT element as a numeric stepper. Placing a minimum and maximum value forces the element to be restricted between those two numbers.

The Email field uses the INPUT type attribute `Email` to force the visual email icon to appear at the beginning of the field. Figure 1.11Proj shows the use of the `Email` type and `required` attribute.

Figure 1.11Proj The Email field uses the `Email` attribute to add a visual icon indicating that the field requires a valid email.

The code to add these `Email` and `required` visual cues is as follows.

```
<label>Email:</label><br/><input name="email"
type="email" required><br/><br/>
```

As you can see, all you need to do is identify the INPUT as `type="email"` and insert the `required` attribute.

The most complex INPUT element allows you to choose from three items in a dropdown menu, as shown in Figure 1.12Proj.

Contact Us

For more information, contact us:

First Name:

Middle Name:

<- disabled

Last Name:

Age:

Email:

How Did you hear about us:

http://google.com	google
http://yahoo.com	yahoo
http://bing.com	Bing

to contact you:

How many of our products do you own:

0

Submit

Figure 1.12Proj Using the new DATALIST feature, you can add more complex data to dropdown menu selections.

The dropdown menu is accomplished by creating a datalist and linking it to an INPUT element. The following code creates the list. The key attribute is the id attribute in the first line; the ID in the datalist can be linked to other elements on the page.

```
<datalist id="mylist">
<option label="google" value="http://google.com">
<option label="yahoo" value="http://yahoo.com">
<option label="Bing" value="http://bing.com">
</datalist>
```

An INPUT element can now be linked to the datalist using the following code.

```
<label>How Did you hear about us:</label><br/><input
name="HowDidYouHear" type="uri" list="mylist"><br/><br/>
```

The INPUT element uses the `list` attribute to link the ID of the datalist. The datalist values are now injected into the INPUT element.

Frequently, you will see a tool used in web pages that enables you to select a date. With HTML5 you can add a date picker simply by identifying the INPUT element as the DATE type. The following code is all you need to add.

```
<label>When would you like us to contact you:</label>
<br/><input name="ContactDate" type="date"><br/><br/>
```

You can see from Figure 1.13Proj that changing the `type` attribute to `date` adds a sophisticated date picker.

Figure 1.13Proj Selecting a date in HTML5 is easy with the new DATE type.

Before selecting the Submit button, you can answer the last question in the form by using the slider and choosing a number from 0–10. The value you select appears as a number to the right of the slider.

Using the slider and displaying the value you select uses both a new `type` attribute in the INPUT field and the new OUTPUT field. The slider uses the new `range` attribute. As with the `number` attribute, the `range` attribute also supports minimum and maximum values. You can also force the slider to start at a specific number using the `value` attribute. The following code defines the INPUT as a `range` with the `min` set at 0, the `max` set at 10, and the `value` set at 5, positioning the slider in the center.

```
<label>How many of our products do you own:</label>
<br/><input id="slider" name="sliderValue" type="range"
min="1" max="10" value="5"></input>
```

You will also see in this code that the ID of the INPUT element is `sliderValue`. The OUTPUT element can link to the ID and post the value into the web page. The following code shows you how to do this.

```
<output name="NumberOfProducts" value="5" onforminput=
"value=sliderValue.value">5</output><br/><br/>
```

The final element to add to the FORM is the BUTTON element, as follows:

```
<button type=submit>Submit</button>
```

As you can see, nothing special is applied to the BUTTON element. Sorry, just plain old-fashioned HTML here, folks.

Summary

The project covered in this chapter illustrates how you can successfully use the HTML5 blocking elements to more effectively manage your HTML code. Without having to resort to complex and confusing HTML TABLES or DIV elements, the new HEADER, SECTION, ARTICLE, ASIDE, NAVIGATION, and FOOTER elements logically place content on the screen.

Additional elements M, TIME, METER, and LABEL allow you to highlight specific elements on the page. This is useful for search engines to find specific content you want to emphasize.

The new FORM attributes allow you to add a slew of new visual tools to capture data. The new INPUT types are both sophisticated and simple to insert. You no longer need to work with complex Ajax libraries to add a date picker. All you need to do is modify an INPUT type.

The role of these new elements is to enable you to more easily control the content as it is presented in HTML. How that data are presented is controlled using CSS. This chapter introduced you to CSS, but it is covered in much more detail over the next section of the book, Picture CSS3.

PICTURE CSS3

Tags are used in HTML5 to place and organize content at a level that is descriptive. This does not mean that the page will look good. Presentation of content on the page is controlled using Cascading Style Sheets Level 3, or CSS3, in HTML5.

Using CSS3 to describe how your page should look, however, is not new. The technology was first introduced in 1997 and is now, in HTML5, in its third major release, named CSS3. The good news is that all CSS1 and CSS2 standards are fully supported by popular web browsers.

For this book you will use CSS to format web pages. There are good reasons why you want to do this. The first, and most important, is that CSS is a tool that allows you to easily apply page styling techniques to a whole web site from a single, text-based document. This means you can quickly change the visual layout of a page, selection of pages, or the entire site.

CSS as a Designer's Tools

The Web is not a forgiving place for a designer. By themselves, HTML elements on a page look boring. The World Wide Web Consortium (W3C) manages the Web's standards. Part of this management is the visual design and presentation of content using CSS. Without CSS, the Web would look very dull. See the example in Figure 2.1 of a page that has not been formatted with CSS.

CSS gives you the control you need to format content on the screen. Think of CSS as a set of instructions that explain how a document should be presented. Figure 2.2 is the same page from Figure 2.1, formatted with CSS.

CSS has been designed to be easily reused and shared throughout your web site. To this end, it is very easy to switch out design elements. Figure 2.3 is the same page illustrated in Figure 2.1 but with a new CSS design.

You, as a designer, now have much greater freedom in your design. The good news is that working with CSS is not too hard.

HTML5. doi: 10.1016/B978-0-240-81328-8.00007-0

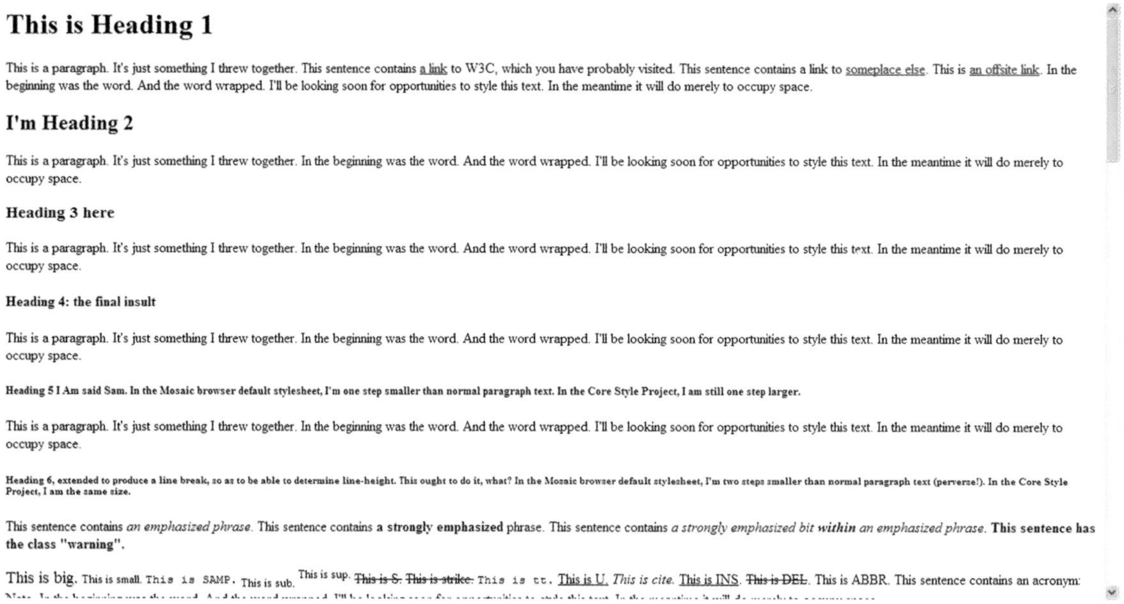

This is Heading 1

This is a paragraph. It's just something I threw together. This sentence contains a link to W3C, which you have probably visited. This sentence contains a link to someplace else. This is an offsite link. In the beginning was the word. And the word wrapped. I'll be looking soon for opportunities to style this text. In the meantime it will do merely to occupy space.

I'm Heading 2

This is a paragraph. It's just something I threw together. In the beginning was the word. And the word wrapped. I'll be looking soon for opportunities to style this text. In the meantime it will do merely to occupy space.

Heading 3 here

This is a paragraph. It's just something I threw together. In the beginning was the word. And the word wrapped. I'll be looking soon for opportunities to style this text. In the meantime it will do merely to occupy space.

Heading 4: the final insult

This is a paragraph. It's just something I threw together. In the beginning was the word. And the word wrapped. I'll be looking soon for opportunities to style this text. In the meantime it will do merely to occupy space.

Heading 5 I Am said Sam. In the Mosaic browser default stylesheet, I'm one step smaller than normal paragraph text. In the Core Style Project, I am still one step larger.

This is a paragraph. It's just something I threw together. In the beginning was the word. And the word wrapped. I'll be looking soon for opportunities to style this text. In the meantime it will do merely to occupy space.

Heading 6, extended to produce a line break, so as to be able to determine line-height. This ought to do it, what? In the Mosaic browser default stylesheet, I'm two steps smaller than normal paragraph text (perverse!). In the Core Style Project, I am the same size.

This sentence contains an emphasized phrase. This sentence contains a strongly emphasized phrase. This sentence contains a strongly emphasized bit within an emphasized phrase. This sentence has the class "warning".

This is big. This is small. This is SAMP. This is sub. This is sup. This is S. This is strike. This is tt. This is U. This is cite. This is INS. This is DEL. This is ABBR. This sentence contains an acronym: Note. In the beginning was the word. And the word wrapped. I'll be looking soon for opportunities to style this text. In the meantime it will do merely to occupy space.

Figure 2.1 CSS has not been used to format the design of this page.

This is Heading 1

This is a paragraph. It's just something I threw together. This sentence contains a link to W3C, which you have probably visited. This sentence contains a link to someplace else. This is an offsite link. In the beginning was the word. And the word wrapped. I'll be looking soon for opportunities to style this text. In the meantime it will do merely to occupy space.

I'm Heading 2

This is a paragraph. It's just something I threw together. In the beginning was the word. And the word wrapped. I'll be looking soon for opportunities to style this text. In the meantime it will do merely to occupy space.

Heading 3 here

This is a paragraph. It's just something I threw together. In the beginning was the word. And the word wrapped. I'll be looking soon for opportunities to style this text. In the meantime it will do merely to occupy space.

Heading 4: the final insult

This is a paragraph. It's just something I threw together. In the beginning was the word. And the word wrapped. I'll be looking soon for opportunities to style this text. In the meantime it will do merely to occupy space.

Heading 5 I Am said Sam. In the Mosaic browser default stylesheet, I'm one step smaller than normal paragraph text. In the Core Style Project, I am still one step larger.

This is a paragraph. It's just something I threw together. In the beginning was the word. And the word wrapped. I'll be looking soon for opportunities to style this text. In the meantime it will do merely to occupy space.

Heading 6, extended to produce a line break, so as to be able to determine line-height. This ought to do it, what? In the Mosaic browser default stylesheet, I'm two steps smaller than normal paragraph text (perverse!). In the Core Style Project, I am the same size.

This sentence contains an emphasized phrase. This sentence contains a strongly emphasized phrase. This sentence contains a strongly emphasized bit WITHIN an emphasized phrase. This sentence has the class "warning".

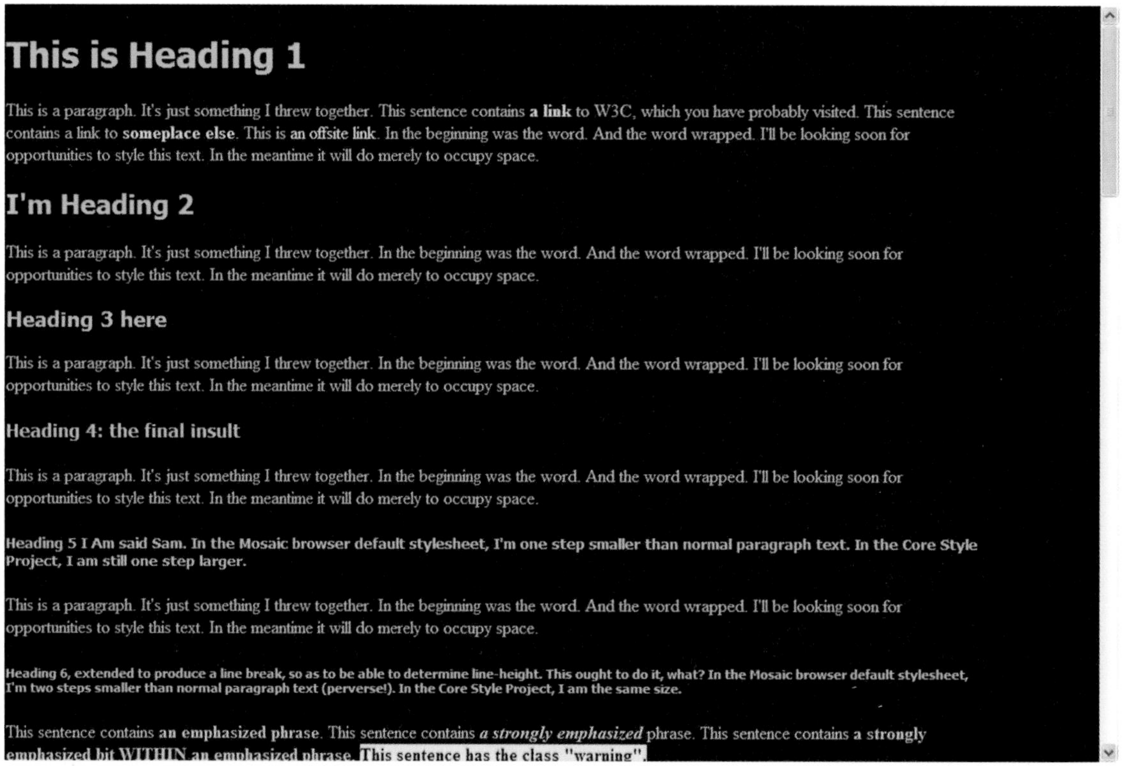

Figure 2.2 CSS is used to format the design of this page.

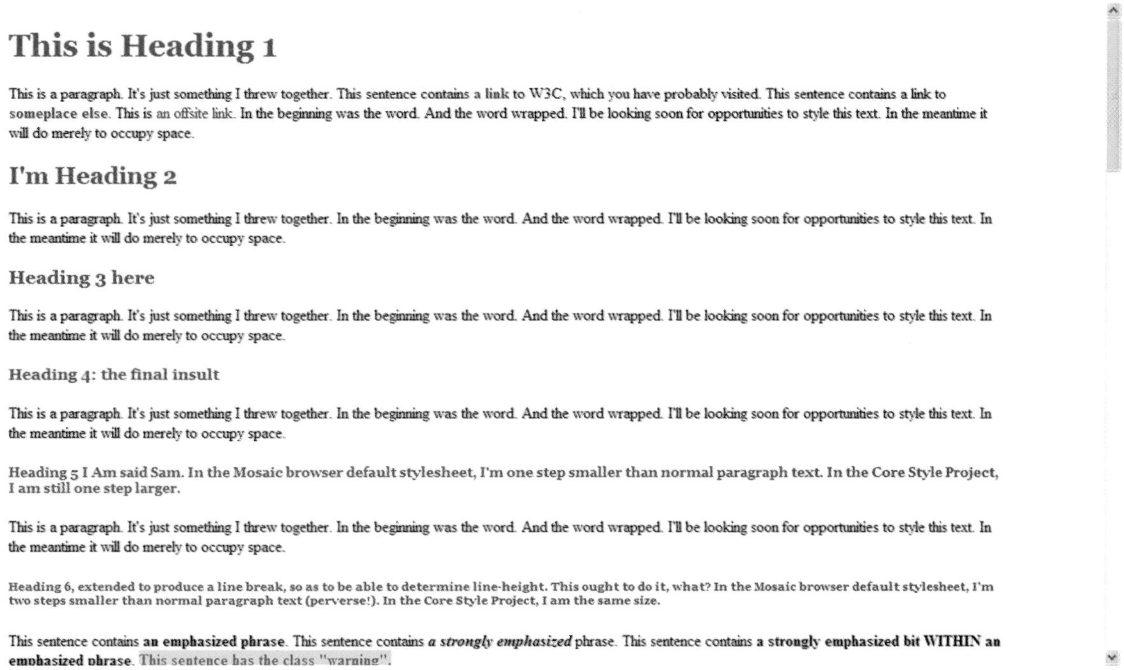

This is Heading 1

This is a paragraph. It's just something I threw together. This sentence contains a link to W3C, which you have probably visited. This sentence contains a link to someplace else. This is an offsite link. In the beginning was the word. And the word wrapped. I'll be looking soon for opportunities to style this text. In the meantime it will do merely to occupy space.

I'm Heading 2

This is a paragraph. It's just something I threw together. In the beginning was the word. And the word wrapped. I'll be looking soon for opportunities to style this text. In the meantime it will do merely to occupy space.

Heading 3 here

This is a paragraph. It's just something I threw together. In the beginning was the word. And the word wrapped. I'll be looking soon for opportunities to style this text. In the meantime it will do merely to occupy space.

Heading 4: the final insult

This is a paragraph. It's just something I threw together. In the beginning was the word. And the word wrapped. I'll be looking soon for opportunities to style this text. In the meantime it will do merely to occupy space.

Heading 5 I Am said Sam. In the Mosaic browser default stylesheet, I'm one step smaller than normal paragraph text. In the Core Style Project, I am still one step larger.

This is a paragraph. It's just something I threw together. In the beginning was the word. And the word wrapped. I'll be looking soon for opportunities to style this text. In the meantime it will do merely to occupy space.

Heading 6, extended to produce a line break, so as to be able to determine line-height. This ought to do it, what? In the Mosaic browser default stylesheet, I'm two steps smaller than normal paragraph text (perverse!). In the Core Style Project, I am the same size.

This sentence contains **an emphasized phrase**. This sentence contains *a strongly emphasized* phrase. This sentence contains **a strongly emphasized bit WITHIN an emphasized phrase**. This sentence has the class "warning".

Figure 2.3 CSS allows you to easily switch design elements.

Cascading Your Designs

There are three ways in which you can apply CSS to your HTML content:
- Directly within the HTML element.
- Locally on a web page.
- Externally using a special CSS file to manage your styles for an entire site.

Styles can be applied directly to an HTML element. This is done using the `style` attribute. The following is a section of basic HTML.

```
<h1>
This is Heading 1
</h1>
<p> It's just something I threw together. This
sentence contains <a href="http://www.w3.org/">a link</a>
to W3C, which you have probably visited. This sentence
contains a link to <a href="http://www.foo.net/">someplace
else</a>. This is <a href="http://www.htmlhelp.com/"
class="offsite">an offsite link</a>. In the beginning was
the word. And the word wrapped. I'll be looking soon for
opportunities to style this text. In the meantime it will
do merely to occupy space.
</p>
```

This is Heading 1

This is a paragraph. It's just something I threw together. This sentence contains a link to W3C, which you have probably visited. This sentence contains a link to someplace else. This is an offsite link. In the beginning was the word. And the word wrapped. I'll be looking soon for opportunities to style this text. In the meantime it will do merely to occupy space.

I'm Heading 2

This is a paragraph. It's just something I threw together. In the beginning was the word. And the word wrapped. I'll be looking soon for opportunities to style this text. In the meantime it will do merely to occupy space.

Figure 2.4 Unformatted HTML code.

```
<h2>
I'm Heading 2
</h2>
<p>
This is a paragraph. It's just something I threw
together. In the beginning was the word. And the word
wrapped. I'll be looking soon for opportunities to style
this text. In the meantime it will do merely to occupy
space.
</p>
```

Presented in a web page, Figure 2.4 shows how the HTML code looks.

The `style` attribute can now be used to format each element. Take, for instance, the first H1 element; the following style can be applied using CSS.

```
<h1 style="font-family: Verdana, Geneva, Tahoma,
sans-serif;font-size: 24px;color: #FF3300;font-weight:
bolder;">
This is Heading 1
</h1>
```

This is Heading 1

Figure 2.5 The `style` attribute is used to format the H1 element.

Figure 2.5 illustrates the change using the new style.

The challenge using the `style` attribute on a specific element is that the style cannot be easily shared with other elements on the page. There is a way to use CSS to format elements that are used frequently on a page. The CSS style definition for a page is located within the HEADER element. The following code shows where the CSS style is placed.

```
<head>
<meta content="text/html; charset=utf-8" http-
equiv="Content-Type"/>
<title>A sample CSS page</title>
<style type="text/css">
H1 {
    font-family: Verdana, Geneva, Tahoma, sans-serif;
    font-size: 24px;
```

```
        color: #FF3300;
        font-weight: bolder;
    }
    </style>
    </head>
```

This sample HTML code has moved the style definition for the H1 element into the style document. You can expand the document to format additional elements on the page. For instance, moving the CSS style definition to the top of the web page allows all of the P (paragraph) elements to look the same. The following CSS document placed in the HEAD section of the page will format all of the content on the screen.

```
    <head>
    <meta content="text/html; charset=utf-8" http-
equiv="Content-Type"/>
    <title>A sample CSS page</title>
    <style type="text/css">
    H1 {
        font-family: Verdana, Geneva, Tahoma, sans-serif;
        font-size: 24px;
        color: #FF3300;
        font-weight: bolder;
    }
    h2 {
        font-family: Verdana, Geneva, Tahoma, sans-serif;
        font-size: medium;
        color: #FF0000;
    }
    p {
        font-family: "Gill Sans", "Gill Sans MT", Calibri,
"Trebuchet MS", sans-serif;
        font-size: small;
    }
    body {
        margin: 2px}
    </style>
    </head>
```

Figure 2.6 shows that the two paragraphs now look the same.

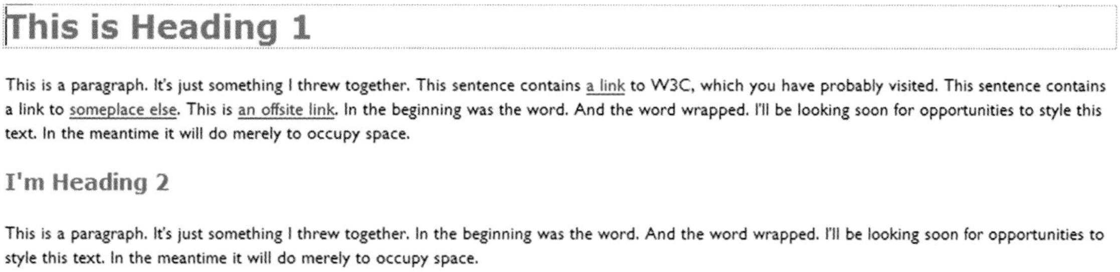

Figure 2.6 Placing the CSS style information within the HEAD element of a page allows elements to share the same design layout.

This is Heading 1

This is a paragraph. It's just something I threw together. This sentence contains a link to W3C, which you have probably visited. This sentence contains a link to someplace else. This is an offsite link. In the beginning was the word. And the word wrapped. I'll be looking soon for opportunities to style this text. In the meantime it will do merely to occupy space.

I'm Heading 2

This is a paragraph. It's just something I threw together. In the beginning was the word. And the word wrapped. I'll be looking soon for opportunities to style this text. In the meantime it will do merely to occupy space.

Cascading styles, however, have one additional trick up their sleeve. No web site is comprised of just one page. You have many, possibly hundreds or thousands, of pages in your web site. You do not want the burden of having to open each page and change the formatting each time you need to change the styles for your site.

Using CSS, you can now create a separate document in your site containing your style information and share it with all of your web pages. To create a shared CSS style document you need to create a text file with Notepad on a PC or TextEdit on a Mac. Copy your styles to the text file and save it to your site, naming the document with the extension .css. The final step is adding a line of code to the HTML that links to your web pages and points to the CSS document. The link is accomplished using the LINK element within the HEAD element in your web page. The following example is linking to a CSS document called "style.css."

```
<head>
<meta content="text/html; charset=utf-8"
http-equiv="Content-Type"/>
<title>A sample CSS page</title>
<link href="style.css" rel="stylesheet" type="text/css"/>
</head>
```

The result is that you can create multiple web pages that share the same look and feel, as shown in Figure 2.7.

CSS is a very flexible design tool you can use to control the presentation of your content in any web page.

Figure 2.7 Sharing a single CSS file allows the style formatting to be easily controlled over multiple web pages.

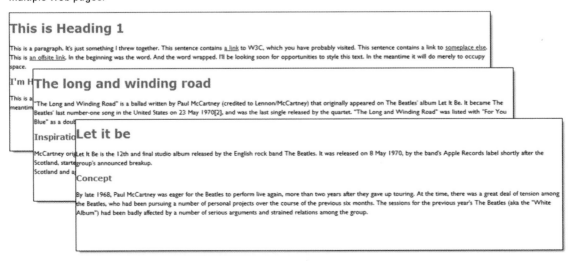

The Format of CSS

Cascading Style Sheets is essentially a document that lists the visual presentation of your content. You have seen that there are different places you can store CSS information. There are different ways in which the CSS style definition can be applied to elements.

Where to Get the Latest Information on CSS

The World Wide Web Consortium is the best place to go for the latest information on CSS. Check out the CSS Current Work Status page at *http://www.w3.org/Style/CSS/current-work*.

There are four main ways in which you can easily apply CSS to elements on a page:
- Modify an element's visual characteristics.
- Create a share class.
- Create a pseudo class.
- Create a pseudo element.

Modifying Elements with CSS

Elements can be formatted directly in your code using the `style` attribute. More likely you will want to share the style you create with other elements on the page or site. Earlier in the chapter an H1 and P element were modified with a custom style. To do this you should use the style sheet document.

You declare that you are going to modify an element in your style document by printing the element name. The following example demonstrates how to format a P element.

```
P {
}
```

The curly brackets following the P element identify where you can place the formatting elements for the P tag. The following example shows style information for the P element.

```
p {
    font-family: Arial, sans-serif;
    font-size: medium;
    color: #888;
    padding-left: 25px;
    padding-right: 50%;
}
```

Figure 2.8 illustrates how all of the P elements are modified by one style.

Lorem Ipsum Header

Lorem ipsum dolor sit amet, consectetur adipiscing elit. Etiam accumsan convallis odio, vitae semper mi pretium laoreet.

In vestibulum, ipsum consectetur cursus porttitor, mi tellus euismod purus, ac egestas nisl risus ac risus. Suspendisse a nisi mi, nec rutrum nisi. Suspendisse pretium aliquet convallis.

Aliquam sollicitudin elementum est, commodo gravida lorem imperdiet ac. Donec rhoncus turpis vitae risus commodo ac mollis ligula aliquam. Donec in mi arcu, id vulputate turpis. Nullam nunc dui, euismod vel lobortis nec, suscipit non velit. Aliquam ornare, nibh eget facilisis lobortis, ligula velit suscipit sem, id condimentum est turpis ut magna. Morbi vitae hendrerit nibh.

In hac habitasse platea dictumst. Suspendisse eleifend ligula quis massa porta rutrum. Praesent in dolor laoreet leo interdum pulvinar sit amet quis lectus.

Proin lobortis, justo et rhoncus porta, neque orci pellentesque enim, quis sollicitudin nisl lacus eu nisi.

Figure 2.8 A single P element style is shared by all P elements on the page.

Styles can be shared among several elements if you want them to have a common style. For instance, the following example lists five different elements that each have different styles but are all the same color and font-family.

```
<H1>Lorem Ipsum Header</H1>
<p>In vestibulum, ipsum consectetur cursus porttitor,
mi tellus euismod purus, ac egestas nisl risus ac risus.
Suspendisse a nisi mi, nec rutrum nisi. Suspendisse
pretium aliquet convallis. </p>
<h2>Lorem ipsum dolor sit amet</h2>
<p>Aliquam sollicitudin elementum est, commodo gravida
lorem imperdiet ac. Donec rhoncus turpis vitae risus commodo
ac mollis ligula aliquam. Donec in mi arcu, id vulputate
turpis. Nullam nunc dui, euismod vel lobortis nec, suscipit
non velit. Aliquam ornare, nibh eget facilisis lobortis,
ligula velit suscipit sem, id condimentum est turpis ut
magna. Morbi vitae hendrerit nibh. </p>
<h3>consectetur adipiscing elit</h3>
<p>In hac habitasse platea dictumst. Suspendisse
eleifend ligula quis massa porta rutrum. Praesent in dolor
laoreet leo interdum pulvinar sit amet quis lectus.</p>
<h4>Etiam accumsan convallis odio<h4>
<p>vitae semper mi pretium laoreet.</p>
```

The CSS is built up by applying first the shared styles between all five elements (H1, H2, H3, H4, and P). The first line in the style document lists all of the elements and then, between the curly brackets, the common font and color style is defined.

```
h1, h2, h3, h4, p{
    font-family: "Arial Narrow Bold", sans-serif;
    color: #CC3300;
}
```

Each element can now have its own style defined, as follows.

```
h1 {
    font-size: xx-large;
    font-weight: bolder;
}
h2 {
    font-size: medium;
}
h3 {
    font-size: small;
}
h4 {
    font-size: xx-small;
}
p {
    font-size: large;
    padding-left: 25px;
}
```

Figure 2.9 shows how the common styles can be shared among the different elements.

The good news is that you can apply CSS to any element on the screen, including new HTML5 elements such as ASIDE, HEADER, FOOTER, SECTION, ARTICLE, and DIALOG. The following HTML can be formatted with CSS.

```
<H1>Sample Header</H1>
<ASIDE>
<H1>The Headline is formatted with CSS</H1>
<P>The PARAGRAPH element inherits the font style
formatting from the ASIDE element.</P>
<P >A link to another web page is added <a
href="http://www.focalpress.com">here</a>.</P>
</ASIDE>
```

You can use the following style to format the presentation of the ASIDE element.

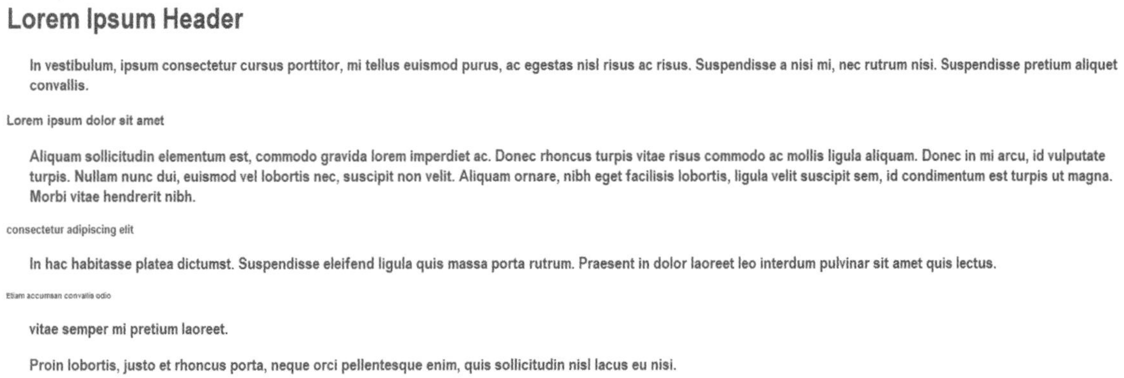

Figure 2.9 Common style definitions can be applied to many different elements at once.

Lorem Ipsum Header

In vestibulum, ipsum consectetur cursus porttitor, mi tellus euismod purus, ac egestas nisl risus ac risus. Suspendisse a nisi mi, nec rutrum nisi. Suspendisse pretium aliquet convallis.

Lorem ipsum dolor sit amet

Aliquam sollicitudin elementum est, commodo gravida lorem imperdiet ac. Donec rhoncus turpis vitae risus commodo ac mollis ligula aliquam. Donec in mi arcu, id vulputate turpis. Nullam nunc dui, euismod vel lobortis nec, suscipit non velit. Aliquam ornare, nibh eget facilisis lobortis, ligula velit suscipit sem, id condimentum est turpis ut magna. Morbi vitae hendrerit nibh.

consectetur adipiscing elit

In hac habitasse platea dictumst. Suspendisse eleifend ligula quis massa porta rutrum. Praesent in dolor laoreet leo interdum pulvinar sit amet quis lectus.

Etiam accumsan convallis odio

vitae semper mi pretium laoreet.

Proin lobortis, justo et rhoncus porta, neque orci pellentesque enim, quis sollicitudin nisl lacus eu nisi.

```
aside {
    margin: 2px;
    border-style: dashed;
    font-family: Verdana, Helvetica, Arial,
sans-serif;
    font-size: 18px;
    line-height: 1.2em;
    text-align: left;
    position: absolute;
    color: #999;
    background-color: ivory;
    position: absolute;
    left: 25px;
    top: 75px;
    width: 500px;
    height: 250px;
}
a {
    text-decoration: none;
    color: #0000FF;
}
h1 {
font-size: 20px;
}
p{
font-size: 12px;
}
```

Figure 2.10 shows the results.

The Headline is formatted with CSS

The PARAGRAPH element inherits the font style formatting from the ASIDE element.

A link to another web page is added **here**.

Figure 2.10 All HTML5 elements, including new elements like ASIDE, can be stylized with CSS.

Creating Class Styles

There are times when you do not want all of the elements on the page to look the same. In fact, there are a lot of times when you want to apply custom styles to sections of text or to whole sections. The CSS class definition is your assistant in these situations.

The CSS class works in a very similar way to the elements' style definition. You define the CSS class either in the style region within your HEAD element or in the CSS style document. The following is an example of a CSS class style.

```
.mainTitleStyle {
    font-family: Cambria, Cochin, Georgia, Times,
"Times New Roman", serif;
    font-size: 30px;
    font-weight: bolder;
    color: #008000;
}
```

As you can see, the main structure for defining the class style is the same as an element. The difference is that the class is identified by a leading period and the class name is all one word. You cannot use spaces in your class name.

After you have created your style you can apply it to any element in your web page. The element attribute `class` is used to associate the element with the CSS class. Here is an example.

```
<p class="mainTitleStyle">Lorem Ipsum Header</p>
<p>In vestibulum, ipsum consectetur cursus porttitor, mi
tellus euismod purus, ac egestas nisl risus ac risus. </p>
<p class="mainTitleStyle">Lorem ipsum dolor sit amet</p>
<p>Aliquam sollicitudin elementum est, commodo gravida
lorem imperdiet ac. </p>
<p class="mainTitleStyle">consectetur adipiscing elit</p>
<p >Lorem ipsum dolor sit amet</p>
```

You can see that the P element is used for each line of text. The titles for each section are highlighted using the `class` attribute. Figure 2.11 shows how the style looks in a web browser.

There is no limit to the number of CSS class style definitions you can have. Class styles are very flexible and are used in many

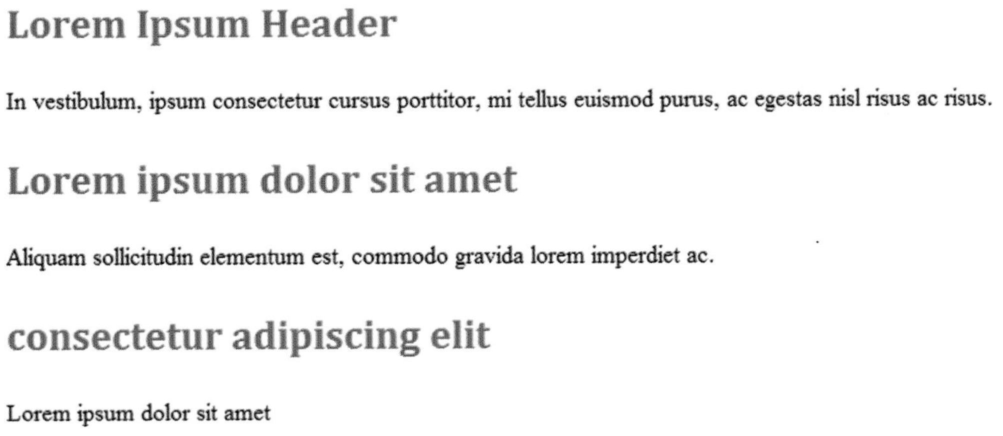

Figure 2.11 A custom CSS class is used to define the titles for each section.

Lorem Ipsum Header

In vestibulum, ipsum consectetur cursus porttitor, mi tellus euismod purus, ac egestas nisl risus ac risus.

Lorem ipsum dolor sit amet

Aliquam sollicitudin elementum est, commodo gravida lorem imperdiet ac.

consectetur adipiscing elit

Lorem ipsum dolor sit amet

web sites. Check out the CSS styles for sites such as *www.bbc.co.uk*, *www.cnn.com*, and *www.Google.com* for examples of the CSS class used to define sections of HTML.

Using Pseudo Class Styles

CSS gives you a third method for styling your content called a pseudo class, a special extension to the element style definition. The most common use for pseudo classes is with the ANCHOR element. The way an ANCHOR element, which identifies links on a web page, is defined in CSS is as follows.

```
a {
    text-decoration: none;
    color: #0000FF;
}
```

The ANCHOR element, however, completes several different activities. It has the default style, a different style when the link is being selected, a style for when the link has been visited, and a style for when you move your cursor over the link. Each of these different activities can be identified with pseudo classes. The following shows the pseudo class for a link that has been visited.

```
a:visited {
    color: #FF0000;
}
```

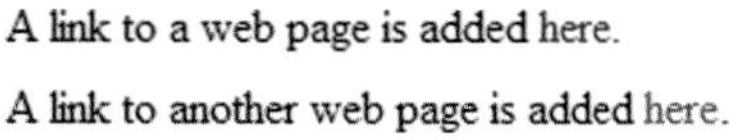

A link to a web page is added here.

A link to another web page is added here.

Figure 2.12 Pseudo classes can be used to control different states of the ANCHOR element.

The ANCHOR element is listed first in your style document and is followed by a colon with the special pseudo class name called `visited`. In your web page, the visited link will now have a different color, as shown in Figure 2.12.

The ANCHOR element has four pseudo classes: link, active, hover, and visited. The following style shows how you can define these four pseudo classes.

```
a{
    color: #0000FF;
}
a:link {
    text-decoration: none;
}
a:hover {
    text-decoration: underline;
}
a:active {
    text-decoration: line-through;
}
    a:visited {
    color: #FF0000;
}
```

The result is that you can now control the different actions of the ANCHOR tag.

CSS3 introduces additional pseudo class styles you can use. The complete list is:

- Active—the active element
- Focus—the element with focus
- Visited—a visited link
- Hover—the state when your cursor is over a link
- Link—an unvisited link
- Disabled—the state of an element when it has been disabled
- Enabled—the state of an element when it has been enabled
- Checked—a form element that has been checked
- Selection—when a user selects a range of content on the page
- Lang—the designer can choose which language is used for the style
- Nth-child(n)—an element that is a specified child of the first sibling
- Nth-last-child(n)—an element that is a specified child of the last sibling
- First-child—the first use of an element on the page
- Last-child—the last use of an element on the page
- Only-child—the only use of a element on the page

Using Pseudo Elements

New to CSS3 is a new extension called pseudo elements. A pseudo element allows you to control aspects of an element in the page. For instance, you may want special text treatment for the first letter of each paragraph you write. There are four pseudo elements you can use:

- First-letter
- First-line
- Before
- After

The definition for pseudo elements is very similar to pseudo classes. The following style applies first-letter pseudo element styles to the P element. Note that the pseudo element leads with two colons.

```
p::first-letter {
font-size: 60px;
}
```

Figure 2.13 illustrates how this is presented in the web browser.

Note how the leading letter of each line is much larger than the rest of the line. At this time there are few pseudo elements.

A link to a web page is added here.

A link to another web page is added here.

Figure 2.13 Pseudo elements modify specific parts of the element.

Designing Your Web Page with CSS

CSS is much easier to master than more complex parts of HTML5 such as Web Workers, Geo Location, and JavaScript. The basic premise for all CSS is that you have a definition that requires a value. For instance, if you want to define the size of a particular font, you write the correct CSS definition (font-size) and place a value; for example:

```
font-size: 60px;
```

There are four rules you must follow:
1. Use a valid CSS definition.
2. Place a colon after the definition.
3. Add a valid value for the definition.
4. Complete the statement with a semi-colon.

Follow these four rules and you are golden.

Tools to Help with Your CSS Designs

For basic CSS manipulation there are some great tools you can use. Adobe's Dreamweaver and Microsoft's Expression Web both support CSS2 design definition. Both of these tools offer visual editors you can easily use to write CSS. Unfortunately, your choices drop significantly when you start looking for more advanced CSS3 tools. This is in part due to the rapid development of CSS3. Check out *www.visualizetheweb.com* for the latest information on CSS3 tools.

When CSS was first released in 1997 there were about a dozen or so definitions to control visual aspects such as font size, color, and background color. Now there are hundreds of different definitions that can be used extensively with any element on the screen.

Controlling Font Display with CSS

One of the easiest places to start learning how to use CSS definitions is through font control. CSS1 and CSS2 support nine different definitions within the font-family:
- Font-family
- Font-size
- Color
- Text-shadow
- Font-weight
- Font-style
- Font-variant
- Text-transform
- Text-decoration

The font-family definition allows you to select a font for your design. Here is how to write the definition:

```
font-family: Arial;
```

The challenge in using the font-family definition is that the number of fonts you can select from is limited to the fonts installed on the computer of the person who is viewing your web page. Web browsers and operating systems install a core set of fonts that you can use in your designs. The list of fonts available that are "Web safe" include:

- Arial/Helvetica
- Times New Roman/Times
- Courier New/Courier
- Verdana
- Georgia
- Comic Sans MS
- Trebuchet MS
- Arial Black
- Impact
- Palatino
- Garamond
- Bookman
- Avant Garde

This list is not very exhaustive and you run into issues where the fonts will not match. For instance, you may select the font Tahoma and it will look great on Windows XP, Vista, and 7, but will not look the same on a Mac or iPhone. Often you will find that there are similar fonts on Windows and Mac computers, but they simply have different names. For instance, you can select the following font-family:

```
font-family: "Courier New", Courier, monospace;
```

This collection of fonts will allow the text to be presented correctly no matter the system viewing the page. In this instance, "Courier New" is the PC name for "Courier" on the Apple Mac; "monospace" is a Unix/Linux equivalent.

Here is a collection of safe font-family names you can use:

- Arial, Arial, Helvetica, sans serif
- Arial Black, Arial Black, Gadget, sans serif
- Comic Sans MS, Comic Sans MS, cursive
- Courier New, Courier New, Courier, monospace
- Georgia, Georgia, serif
- Impact, Impact, Charcoal, sans serif
- Lucida Console, Monaco, monospace
- Lucida Sans Unicode, Lucida Grande, sans serif
- Palatino Linotype, Book Antiqua, Palatino, serif
- Tahoma, Geneva, sans serif

- Times New Roman, Times, serif
- Trebuchet MS, Helvetica, sans serif
- Verdana, Verdana, Geneva, sans serif
- Wingdings, Zapf Dingbats (Wingdings, Zapf Dingbats)

Embedding Fonts Using CSS3

A way to get around the problems of creating font-family lists is to embed the font directly into the CSS. CSS3 finally allows you to do this across your web browsers. The technology for font embedding, however, is not new. Netscape Navigator 4 was the first web browser that allowed you to support font embedding using a plug-in technology called TrueDoc by Bitstream. To compete with Navigator 4, Microsoft released a "me too" technology called Embedded Open Type (EOT) in the Windows version of Internet Explorer 4. The technology has not been removed from the Microsoft browser and is still supported in Internet Explorer 8.

Embedded Open Type is a method of creating a file that can be downloaded to the web browser. The file is an EOT file. To protect the copyright of the original font developer the EOT file is created using a font outline of the original font. You can download the free Microsoft Web Embedding Font Tool (WEFT) from Microsoft to create your own EOT files (*http://www.microsoft.com/typography/web/embedding/*).

The EOT format is not an open format and has not been adopted by modern web browsers or embraced by W3C.

Without a shared standard for embedding fonts, designers have been forced to use other techniques to emulate font embedding. These have included creating JPEG images of text with custom fonts or using third-party plug-in technologies such as Adobe's Flash.

As you might expect, HTML5 has driven new technologies to enable true font embedding. Three standards are now recommended to embed fonts:

- TrueType
- OpenType
- Scalable vector graphic fonts

It is quite likely that you already have TrueType and OpenType fonts installed on your computer. They are, by default, the standard Windows font format. SVG fonts are more complex and will be covered in more detail in the Section 3 article, Rendering HTML5 Illustration.

Embedding a font into your CSS document is now very easy. Figure 2.14 shows text in a web page using a custom font.

To embed a font into a web page you need only two things: the font file and the definition in CSS linking to the font. The font BlackJar.ttf is used in Figure 2.14. Figure 2.15 shows you what the TrueType font looks like.

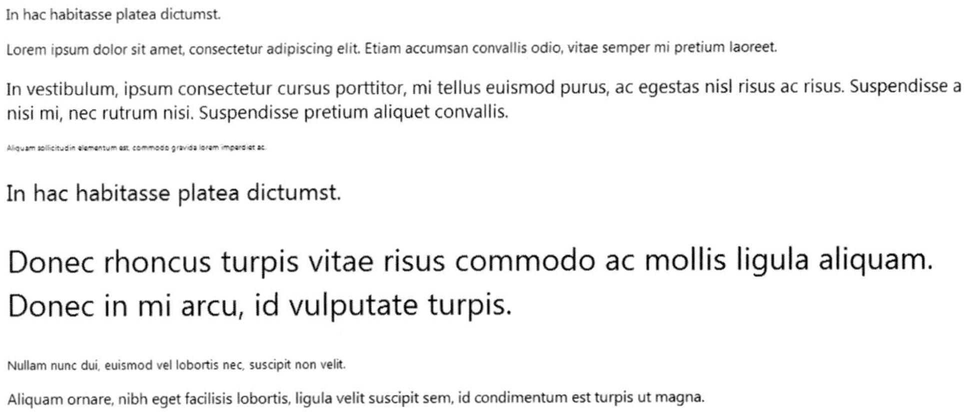

In hac habitasse platea dictumst.

Lorem ipsum dolor sit amet, consectetur adipiscing elit. Etiam accumsan convallis odio, vitae semper mi pretium laoreet.

In vestibulum, ipsum consectetur cursus porttitor, mi tellus euismod purus, ac egestas nisl risus ac risus. Suspendisse a nisi mi, nec rutrum nisi. Suspendisse pretium aliquet convallis.

Aliquam sollicitudin elementum est commodo gravida lorem imperdiet ac.

In hac habitasse platea dictumst.

Donec rhoncus turpis vitae risus commodo ac mollis ligula aliquam. Donec in mi arcu, id vulputate turpis.

Nullam nunc dui, euismod vel lobortis nec, suscipit non velit.

Aliquam ornare, nibh eget facilisis lobortis, ligula velit suscipit sem, id condimentum est turpis ut magna.

Figure 2.14 CSS3 now allows you to embed TrueType and OpenType fonts directly into your web pages.

You need to create a new font-family in your CSS document that links to the TrueType font. The following CSS code shows, in line 2, that you are creating a new font-family called "BlackJar" and, in line 3, you are linking to the font and identifying the type of font.

```
@font-face{
font-family: 'BlackJar';
src: url('BLACKJAR.ttf') format('truetype');
}
```

This text is an embedded font

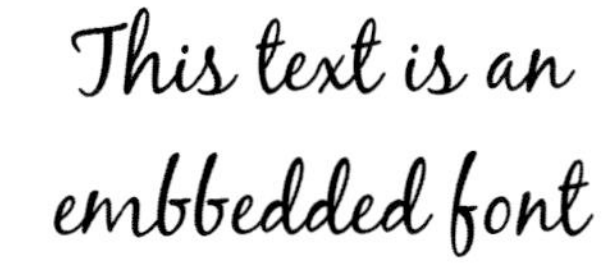

Figure 2.15 The TrueType font BlackJar.tff can now be embedded into a web page.

You now have a new font-family that you can reference in your normal CSS. Here, a P element is being formatted using the new font-family.

```
p {
text-align: center;
font-family: 'BlackJar';
font-size: 3cm;
}
```

You can now use the font within your page design. If you want to also use the font with Internet Explorer you can add the Embedded Open Type with your new font-family. You only need to modify the @font-face description as follows.

```
@font-face{
font-family: 'BlackJar';
src: url('BLACKJAR.ttf') format('truetype');
src: url('BLACKJAR.eot');
}
```

The fourth line links to an EOT version of the BlackJar font. You will notice that you do not need to add a format value for EOT fonts. Now your web pages will display correctly no matter what web browser is viewing your design. Font freedom has finally come to the Web!

Sizing Fonts with CSS Units of Measurement

After selecting a font-family for your text you will also want to select the size of the font. By default, all web browsers have a pre-installed definition for a standard font size. This font size is usually 12 point (pt). You can use this as a size for your fonts as they appear on the screen using the following CSS font-size definition:

```
font-size:medium;
```

If you want your font to appear smaller or larger on the screen you can use the following sizes for your fonts:
- Xx-small (approximately 7.5 pt)
- X-small (approximately 9 pt)
- Small (approximately 10 pt)
- Medium (approximately 12 pt)
- Large (approximately 14 pt)
- X-large (approximately 18 pt)
- Xx-large (approximately 24 pt)
- Smaller
- Larger

Each of these font sizes are relative to the core browser–defaulted font size. If the person who owns the web browser has changed that default, then the sizes will be dynamically changed.

As a designer you are limited by the default font-size list. The good news is that CSS allows you to leverage units of measurement to add precise size to your font. The following are all valid CSS units of measurement you can use:
- cm—centimeter
- in.—inch
- mm—millimeter
- pc—pica (1 pc = 12 pts)
- pt—point (1 pt = $^1/_{72}$ in.)
- px—pixels
- rem—font size of the root element

Using these different font sizes, the following styles are all valid.

```
.default {
    font-family: "Segoe UI", Tahoma, Geneva, Verdana;
    font-size: medium;
}
.px {
    font-family: "Segoe UI", Tahoma, Geneva, Verdana;
    font-size: 15px;
}
```

```
.cm {
    font-family: "Segoe UI", Tahoma, Geneva, Verdana;
    font-size: .5cm;
}
.mm {
    font-family: "Segoe UI", Tahoma, Geneva, Verdana;
    font-size: 2mm;
}
.inch {
    font-family: "Segoe UI", Tahoma, Geneva, Verdana;
    font-size: .25in;
}
.pica {
    font-family: "Segoe UI", Tahoma, Geneva, Verdana;
    font-size: 2pc;
}
.point {
    font-family: "Segoe UI", Tahoma, Geneva, Verdana;
    font-size: 10pt;
}
.rem {
    font-family: "Segoe UI", Tahoma, Geneva, Verdana;
    font-size: 1rem;
}
```

These font styles are applied to the following HTML code.

```
<p class="default">In hac habitasse platea dictumst.</p>
<p class="px">Lorem ipsum dolor sit amet, consectetur
adipiscing elit. Etiam accumsan convallis odio, vitae
semper mi pretium laoreet.</p>
<p class="cm">In vestibulum, ipsum consectetur cursus
porttitor, mi tellus euismod purus, ac egestas nisl
risus ac risus. Suspendisse a nisi mi, nec rutrum nisi.
Suspendisse pretium aliquet convallis.</p>
<p class="mm">Aliquam sollicitudin elementum est,
commodo gravida lorem imperdiet ac.</p>
<p class="inch">In hac habitasse platea dictumst.</p>
<p class="pica">Donec rhoncus turpis vitae risus
commodo ac mollis ligula aliquam. Donec in mi arcu, id
vulputate turpis.</p>
<p class="point">Nullam nunc dui, euismod vel lobortis
nec, suscipit non velit.</p>
<p class="rem">Aliquam ornare, nibh eget facilisis
lobortis, ligula velit suscipit sem, id condimentum est
turpis ut magna.</p>
```

Figure 2.16 shows how these fonts are presented in your web browser.

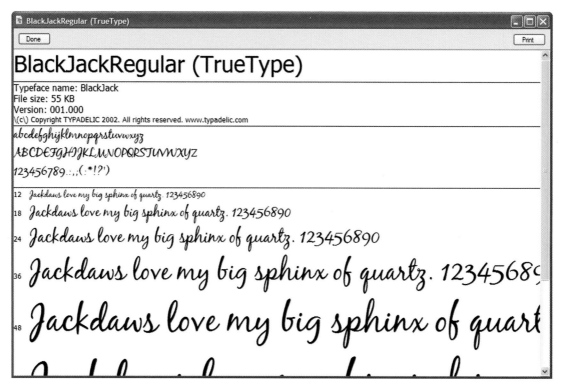

Figure 2.16 You have absolute control over your text using the many different units of measure available in CSS3.

Color Control for Fonts

As with size, color has many different units of measure. The default for Web design is hexadecimal, a combination of six letters and numbers. CSS3 provides a much broader palette of colors to choose from that include:

- Color name—you can create names for colors such as brown, black, red, or even cyan
- Full hexadecimal—a hexadecimal value comprised of six alpha-numeric values
- Short hexadecimal—a hexadecimal value comprised of three alpha-numeric values
- RGB—a combination of red, green, and blue values
- RGBA—a combination of red, green, and blue values with a transparency value (alpha)
- HSL—a combination of hue, saturation, and lightness
- HSLA—a combination of hue, saturation, and lightness with a transparency value (alpha)

The following CSS uses these values to show you can create the color red in several different ways.

```
.name {
color: red;
```

```
}
.fullHexVersion {
color: #FF0000;
}
.shortHexVersion {
color: #F00;
}
.rgb {
color: rgb(255,0,0);
}
.rgba {
color: rgba(255,0,0,100);
}
.hsl {
color: hsl(0%, 100%, 50%);
}
.hsla {
color: hsl(0%, 100%, 50%, 100%);
}
```

These different values are used in different places within the design community.

Adding Drop Shadow Text Effects

Love them or hate them, you cannot get away from the handy design technique of drop shadows. CSS3 now supports drop shadow effects and they are very easy to add to your designs.

There are four elements that you can use to control the drop shadow definition:

- horizontal-offset (length, required)
- vertical-offset (length, required)
- blur-radius (length, optional)
- shadow-color (color, optional)

The following CSS definition is an example of the use of drop shadow.

```
.dropShadow {
    font-family: "Segoe UI", Tahoma, Geneva, Verdana;
    font-size: medium;
    color: #CC3300;
    text-shadow: 0.25em 0.25em 2px #999;
}
```

The effect draws a light-gray drop shadow with a slight blur, as shown in Figure 2.17.

Different colors and units of measurement can be used with the drop shadow effect. The following CSS definition uses pixels and RGBA for the measurement and color.

In hac habitasse platea dictumst.

Figure 2.17 CSS now allows you to add drop shadows to your text.

```
.transparentDropShadow {
    font-family: "Segoe UI", Tahoma, Geneva, Verdana;
    font-size: 15px;
    color: rgba(255,0,0,1);
    text-shadow: 5px 5px 5px rgba(0, 0, 0, 0.5);
}
```

Finally, you can use the drop shadow effect to force a "cut-out" effect with your text. Apply the following CSS to text on the screen.

```
.cutout {
    font-family: "Segoe UI", Tahoma, Geneva, Verdana;
    font-size: 2pc;
    color: white;
    text-shadow: 0em 0em 2em black;
}
```

Figure 2.18 demonstrates the effect of the drop shadow as a cut out.

In hac habitasse platea dictumst.

Lorem ipsum dolor sit amet, consectetur adipiscing elit. Etiam accumsan convallis odio, vitae semper mi pretium laoreet.

Donec rhoncus turpis vitae risus commodo ac mollis ligula aliquam. Donec in mi arcu, id vulputate turpis.

Figure 2.18 You can use the drop shadow to create cut-out effects.

Additional Font Definitions

The remaining values within the font-family do not have ranges and can be summarized as:

- Font-weight—boldness value from 100–900, with 300 being normal
- Font-style—italic, normal, oblique
- Font-variant—normal, small caps
- Text-transform—capitalize, lowercase, normal

- Text-decoration—underline, overline, line-through, none, blinking

As you can see, CSS gives you an amount of control over how your text is displayed on the screen.

Working with Columns in CSS3

A challenge for any web page is to create content that is split over two or more columns on the page. Creating columns often requires using complex tables structured together. Though not strictly part of the text family of CSS definitions, the new multi-column layout is best at home when used with text on the screen.

The goal of the multicolumn definition is to allow your content to be spread evenly over two or more columns. There are three parts to a column layout:

- Number of columns
- Gap between the columns
- Column design (optional)

The following CSS demonstrates how you can set up multiple columns to display in Safari/Chrome and FireFox.

```
.simple {
    font-family: "Segoe UI", Tahoma, Geneva, Verdana;
    font-size: 12px;
    color: #444;
    text-align: justify;
    -moz-column-count: 4;
    -moz-column-gap: 1em;
    -webkit-column-count: 4;
    -webkit-column-gap: 1em;
}
```

In this example, the column count is four and the gap is 1em. Figure 2.19 shows how this is displayed in your web browser.

You can add a column design between each column. The structure is as follows.

```
-moz-column-rule: 1px solid #222;
-webkit-column-rule: 1px solid #222;
```

For each column design you can identify the width, border style, and color. You can use the standard measurement and color CSS formatting. The number of border styles you have to choose from is:

Figure 2.19 A simple, four-column layout.

Below is an example of a multi-column layout

Donec porta laoreet augue et tincidunt. Donec ac tempus neque. Aliquam pharetra sollicitudin felis sed tincidunt. Proin eleifend vestibulum urna mattis lacinia. Curabitur non augue quam, sed cursus erat. Suspendisse eu orci nunc. Sed volutpat, ipsum sed adipiscing tincidunt, neque ipsum dignissim dolor, sit amet mollis quam justo ut mi. In egestas vestibulum felis in aliquam. Ut a lectus non nisi molestie fringilla condimentum sed sem. Vivamus libero tortor, placerat in hendrerit sit amet, aliquet vitae turpis. Vivamus id convallis risus. Lorem ipsum dolor sit amet, consectetur adipiscing elit. Etiam accumsan convallis odio, vitae semper mi pretium laoreet. Donec rhoncus turpis vitae risus commodo ac mollis ligula aliquam. Donec in mi arcu, id vulputate turpis.

- None
- Hidden
- Dotted
- Dashed
- Solid
- Double
- Groove
- Ridge
- Inset
- Outset

Additional elements, such as the IMG, can be used with text content in the column layout. Figure 2.20 illustrates a complex use of a multicolumn layout.

The CSS to create this layout is as follows.

```
.complex {
    font-family: "Segoe UI", Tahoma, Geneva, Verdana;
    font-size: 1.2pc;
    color: #444;
    text-align: left;
    -moz-column-count: 3;
    -moz-column-gap: 1em;
    -moz-column-rule: 2px dotted #999;
    -webkit-column-count: 3;
    -webkit-column-gap: 1em;
    -webkit-column-rule: 2px dotted #999;
}
```

The style in this column layout is applied to a P element that contains both text and an IMG element. You should experiment with columns—they are certainly much easier to use than complex tables.

Figure 2.20 Columns can have decoration between each column.

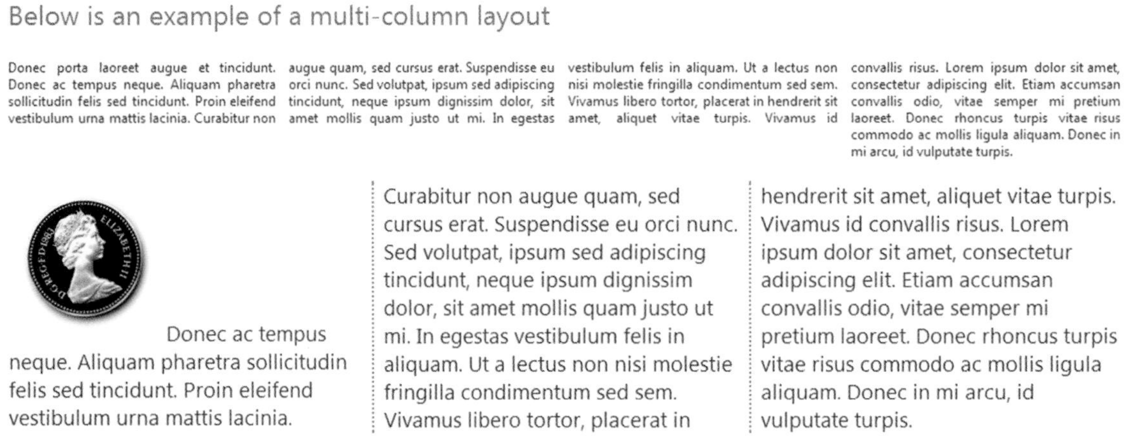

Below is an example of a multi-column layout

Donec porta laoreet augue et tincidunt. Donec ac tempus neque. Aliquam pharetra sollicitudin felis sed tincidunt. Proin eleifend vestibulum urna mattis lacinia. Curabitur non augue quam, sed cursus erat. Suspendisse eu orci nunc. Sed volutpat, ipsum sed adipiscing tincidunt, neque ipsum dignissim dolor, sit amet mollis quam justo ut mi. In egestas vestibulum felis in aliquam. Ut a lectus non nisi molestie fringilla condimentum sed sem. Vivamus libero tortor, placerat in hendrerit sit amet, aliquet vitae turpis. Vivamus id convallis risus. Lorem ipsum dolor sit amet, consectetur adipiscing elit. Etiam accumsan convallis odio, vitae semper mi pretium laoreet. Donec rhoncus turpis vitae risus commodo ac mollis ligula aliquam. Donec in mi arcu, id vulputate turpis.

Donec ac tempus neque. Aliquam pharetra sollicitudin felis sed tincidunt. Proin eleifend vestibulum urna mattis lacinia.

Curabitur non augue quam, sed cursus erat. Suspendisse eu orci nunc. Sed volutpat, ipsum sed adipiscing tincidunt, neque ipsum dignissim dolor, sit amet mollis quam justo ut mi. In egestas vestibulum felis in aliquam. Ut a lectus non nisi molestie fringilla condimentum sed sem. Vivamus libero tortor, placerat in

hendrerit sit amet, aliquet vitae turpis. Vivamus id convallis risus. Lorem ipsum dolor sit amet, consectetur adipiscing elit. Etiam accumsan convallis odio, vitae semper mi pretium laoreet. Donec rhoncus turpis vitae risus commodo ac mollis ligula aliquam. Donec in mi arcu, id vulputate turpis.

Using CSS3 to Control Visual Display

While most of your time working with CSS will be formatting text, CSS is not just the domain of text on the screen. Indeed, CSS is expanding in scope to allow you to control as much as possible on the screen. The final two sections look at CSS control over static and animated elements on the screen.

Positioning Design Elements with CSS

Have you used HTML tables to align elements in your web page? If so, it is a pain in the neck, isn't it? Using tables to control layout presents two key problems. First, the layout is flat with images "sliced" to fit correctly on the screen. Second, if you want to make a change to your design you need to relayout the whole table. Tables are simply not a sensible solution for design layout.

Fortunately, all web browsers now support positioning within CSS to give you absolute control over your design. The difference between using positioning in CSS to using HTML tables is dramatic. First, an element can be placed at any point on the screen using CSS positioning. There are no limitations. A second benefit is that you can layer elements on top of each other. If you are used to working with layers in PhotoShop or a similar graphics tool then you already understand the value of this feature. Layers allow you to segment regions of your design. When you need to make changes to your design, you only need to modify the layer with your content.

Use the following definitions to position an element on the screen:

- Position—values include absolute, relative, fixed, inherit
- Width—the width of the layer
- Height—the height of the layer
- Left—where from the left margin the layer starts
- Top—where from the top margin the layer starts
- Overflow—how to present content that goes beyond the scope of the layer
- Z-index—the stack order for layers on the screen

The following CSS can be applied to any HTML element to control the positioning of the element on the screen.

```
.firstLayer{
    Background-color: orange;
    position: absolute;
    width: 295px;
    height: 160px;
    z-index: 1;
    left: 439px;
    top: 28px;
    overflow
}
```

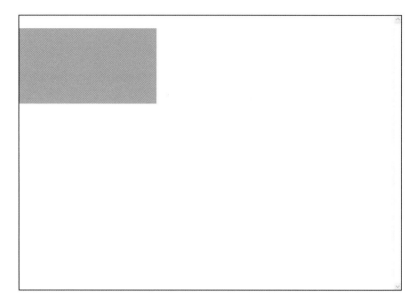

Figure 2.21 The positioning of the orange box is controlled using CSS positioning.

The following HTML code has the layer definition applied to it using a CSS class:

```
<article class="firstlayer"></article>
```

The orange box in Figure 2.21 is okay by itself, but what can you do with it? The position of any HTML element can be controlled with positioning. The orange box in this example is an HTML ARTICLE element. Any text, tables, graphics, or other HTML elements can be inserted into the ARTICLE. Figure 2.22 illustrates an image wrapped by text inside of an ARTICLE element positioned absolutely on the page.

Positioning is key to your design work in your web pages. With wide support of CSS positioning, you now have the control you need.

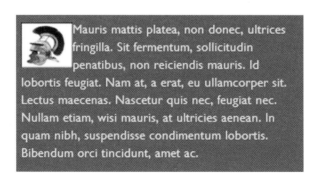

Figure 2.22 Content within a layered element inherits the positioning of the parent element.

Increase Control over Color

Control over the use of color has increased significantly with CSS3. You saw earlier that you can now use long hexadecimal, short hexadecimal, RGB, RGBA, HSL, and HSLA to have access to millions of colors. In addition to solid colors, CSS3 gives you the ability to add gradients.

You can currently create two different types of gradient: linear and radial, as shown in Figure 2.23.

The gradient definition is comprised of several key elements:

- Type—either radial or linear
- Point—two space-separated values that explain where the gradient starts (this can be achieved with a number, percentage, or using the keywords "top," "bottom," "left," and "right")
- Radius—the radius is a number that you only need to specify when you use the radial type
- Stop—the function of the stop value is to identify the blend strength as a percentage or number between 0 and 1 (such as 0.75 or 75%) and a color. You can use any CSS3-supported color.

Putting all of these together will give you a gradient. Gradients can be used with the following definitions:

- Background-image
- Border-image
- List-style-image
- Content property

The following example adds a gradient that goes from red to orange to orange to yellow.

```
body {
  background-image: -webkit-gradient(linear, left top,
left bottom, from(red), to(yellow), color-stop(0.5,
orange), color-stop(0.5, orange));}
```

As you can see, the gradient is substituting an image in the background-image definition. The first definition identifies the gradient as linear. The next definition explains the gradient is going to go from top to bottom. The two elected colors are red and yellow. The `stop` function has the colors blending halfway through to orange. The result is displayed in Figure 2.24.

A radial gradient is completed in a similar way. The following adds a radial gradient that moves from red to orange to yellow.

```
body {
  background-image: -webkit-gradient(radial, 45 45, 15, 100
100, 250, from(red), to(yellow), color-stop(50%, orange));}
```

In this instance, the numbers following the radial declaration determine the shape of the radius. The first two numbers dictate the angle of the ellipse in degrees. The third number dictates the size of the inner circle. The fourth and fifth numbers dictate the

(a)

(b)

Figure 2.23 You can create (a) linear and (b) radial gradients in CSS3.

Figure 2.24 Gradients can be used to create colored backgrounds.

Figure 2.25 The numbers determine the shape and size of the radius.

position of the gradient (left and top). The final number dictates the final size of the radius. Figure 2.25 is the result.

Currently, gradients are only supported in Safari and Chrome. This is expected to change with FireFox 4.0.

Multiple Background Objects

You quickly run into limitations when you can use only one background image. With CSS3 you can now run multiple background images. Any element that supports the background-image definition now supports multiple background images. Using background images is very easy. You can start by listing the images you want to use. Take for instance the following code.

```
background-image: url(http://upload.wikimedia.org/
wikipedia/commons/3/36/Team_Singapore_fireworks_display_
from_Singapore_Fireworks_Festival_2006.jpg), url(http://
upload.wikimedia.org/wikipedia/commons/b/b2/OperaSydney-
Fuegos2006-342289398.jpg);
```

You can specify where you want each background to appear on the screen using the background-position definition. The definition is paired for the position of the background:

```
background-position: bottom left, top right;
```

Figure 2.26 The two images are being used as background images

Figure 2.26 shows the end result.

As you might expect, you can mix gradients and multiple background images together. The following CSS blends a radial gradient with two background images.

```
<html>
<head>
<title>Multiple Backgrounds</title>
  <style>
    body {
      background-image:
url(http://upload.wikimedia.org/wikipedia/commons/3/36/
Team_Singapore_fireworks_display_from_Singapore_Fireworks_
Festival_2006.jpg), url(http://upload.wikimedia.org/
wikipedia/commons/b/b2/OperaSydney-Fuegos2006-342289398.
jpg), -webkit-gradient(radial, 45 45, 15, 100 100, 250,
from(gold), to(magenta), color-stop(50%, black));
background-repeat: no-repeat;
background-position: bottom left, top right;
      background-color:black;}
    </style>
</head>
<body>
</body>
</html>
```

Figure 2.27 shows the results.

Again, as with gradients, multiple backgrounds are not currently supported by FireFox.

Figure 2.27 Images and gradients can be mixed to create unique background images.

Adding Rounded Corners to Layers

Adding rounded corners is not a new technique for the Web. Many web sites use this technique. The effect, however, is created through using images and tables to create the illusion of rounded corners. Adding images to the pages ensures that the page takes longer to load and makes modifying the page later more complex.

A simpler approach is to use the proposed corner-radius CSS definition that is currently supported in FireFox 3.0, Safari 3.0, Mobile Safari on your iPhone/iPod Touch, and Google's Chrome. The corner-radius definition is a line you can add to your CSS style. The following HTML code has a style embedded that changes the presentation of the block of text to have rounded corners with a heavy, black outline.

```
<p style="-moz-border-radius: 10px;-webkit-
border-radius: 10px;border: 4px solid #FF0000;">
Lorem ipsum dolor sit amet, consectetur adipiscing elit.
Nam porta, lacus in cursus cursus, justo purus fringilla
nisi, quis cursus urna velit vel felis. Nulla ac mi.
Phasellus sodales dui vel tortor. Praesent dignissim.
Vestibulum vulputate nibh rutrum purus. Nulla ante. Sed
porta. Vestibulum commodo, mi nec tincidunt laoreet, urna
risus ornare libero, in imperdiet sapien enim vel nisi.</p>
```

The style description has been highlighted in bold. Your content will now look like Figure 2.28 in your web page.

As you can see, the block of text now has a solid red line with rounded corners. It is this style description that controls the size of the radius, not an image. You can then easily modify the description as shown in the following.

Lorem ipsum dolor sit amet, consectetur adipiscing elit. Nam porta, lacus in cursus cursus, justo purus fringilla nisi, quis cursus urna velit vel felis. Nulla ac mi. Phasellus sodales dui vel tortor. Praesent dignissim. Vestibulum vulputate nibh rutrum purus. Nulla ante. Sed porta. Vestibulum commodo, mi nec tincidunt laoreet, urna risus ornare libero, in imperdiet sapien enim vel nisi.

Figure 2.28 Layers can now have rounded corners.

```
-moz-border-radius: 10px
-webkit-border-radius: 10px
```

The standard is currently only in the proposal stage and has not been adopted by all web browsers. For this reason, you need to add two border-radius style descriptions: one for FireFox (-moz-border-radius), and one for Safari/Chrome (-webkit-border-radius). Changing the value of the border-radius will change the size of the border. For instance:

Figure 2.29 The border-radius controls how round the corners are.

```
Border-radius: 15 px
Border-radius: 25 px
Border-radius: 45 px
```

Figures 2.29 through 2.31 shows some border-radius examples.

As you increase the border-radius, you will also have to add additional styles, such as padding, to ensure that your border does not cut through the text as is shown in Figure 2.31 for the example of a 45-pixel border-radius. Here is how you can add padding to manage your style.

Figure 2.30 A border-radius of 25 pixels.

```
<p style="-moz-border-radius: 45px;-webkit-border-
radius: 45px;border: 4px solid #FF0000; padding:
12px;">Lorem ipsum dolor sit amet, consectetur adipiscing
elit. Nam porta, lacus in cursus cursus, justo purus
fringilla nisi, quis cursus urna velit vel felis. Nulla ac
mi. Phasellus sodales dui vel tortor. Praesent dignissim.
Vestibulum vulputate nibh rutrum purus. Nulla ante. Sed
porta. Vestibulum commodo, mi nec tincidunt laoreet, urna
risus ornare libero, in imperdiet sapien enim vel nisi.</p>
```

Figure 2.31 A border-radius of 45 pixels.

Figure 2.32 shows how the content looks.

Figure 2.32 The layer now looks like a rectangle with rounded corners.

Lorem ipsum dolor sit amet, consectetur adipiscing elit. Nam porta, lacus in cursus cursus, justo purus fringilla nisi, quis cursus urna velit vel felis. Nulla ac mi. Phasellus sodales dui vel tortor. Praesent dignissim. Vestibulum vulputate nibh rutrum purus. Nulla ante. Sed porta. Vestibulum commodo, mi nec tincidunt laoreet, urna risus ornare libero, in imperdiet sapien enim vel nisi.

The new border-radius style also has the option of allowing you to control which corner you want the border to appear on. This can be useful when you want to create tabs for your web page. For instance, the following style will add tabs to the top left and top right corners.

```
.standardTabEffect{
    font-family: Arial, Helvetica, sans-serif;
    font-size: 15px;
    background-color: #FFFF00;
    -moz-border-radius-topleft: 15px;
    -moz-border-radius-topright: 15px;
    -webkit-border-radius-topleft: 15px;
    -webkit-border-radius-topright: 15px;
    border: 4px solid #FF0000;
    padding: 10px;
    color: #FF0000;
    text-decoration: none;
    font-weight: bold;
}
```

This style can now be added to a central style sheet link to the content on your page. The content on your page can now reference the style. You can add the following HTML code to see this effect.

```
<a class="standardTabEffect" href="#">This is Tab 1
</a><a class="standardTabEffect" href="#">This is Tab 2
</a><a class="standardTabEffect" href="#">This is Tab 3</a>
```

Figure 2.33 shows how the HTML code will look when you view the page.

As you might imagine, you can inherit existing CSS formatting into your border-radius designs. For instance, you can add a simple rollover effect when you include the following style description. The important part is to add the :hover parameter. This instructs the web browser to only use this style when a user is rolling over the link with the mouse.

Figure 2.33 The border-radius is used to create tabbed buttons.

```
.standardTabEffect:hover{
    background-color: #FF0000;
    border: 4px solid #FFFF00;
    color: #FFFF00;
}
```

Figure 2.34 shows what the action looks like.

Without using complex images or tables, you have created a series of tabs that can be easily managed through CSS and HTML.

Figure 2.34 The hover pseudo class can add an effect as you move the mouse over a button.

Dazzling Your Audience with CSS3 Animation

CSS3 continues to expand what you can visually accomplish in your web pages. Animation is now also available to you as a design choice. Animation is split into two key parts: transitions and transforms.

- Transitions control the change of state for an element, such as text fading in or changing color.
- Transforms control the placement of an element.

The following two sections explain how you can control these two new animation techniques in your CSS designs.

Using Transitions in CSS

The transition effect is best used when you create a class and then a hover pseudo class to illustrate when the effect is to happen (i.e., when your cursor moves over the element). The transition itself is made of three parts:

- Property—the linked property between the two classes
- Duration—how long in seconds the transition will take
- Timing function
  The timing function keywords have the following definitions:
- Linear—the linear function just returns as its output the input that it received.
- Ease—the default function, ease, is equivalent to cubic-bezier (0.25, 0.1, 0.25, 1.0).
- Ease-in—the ease-in function is equivalent to cubic-bezier (0.42, 0, 1.0, 1.0).
- Ease-out—the ease-out function is equivalent to cubic-bezier (0, 0, 0.58, 1.0).
- Ease-in-out—the ease-in-out function is equivalent to cubic-bezier (0.42, 0, 0.58, 1.0)
- Cubic-bezier—specifies a cubic-bezier curve of which the P0 and P3 points are (0,0) and (1,1), respectively. The four values specify points P1 and P2 of the curve as (x1, y1, x2, y2).

The following example applies a transition effect on the color definition in the P element.

```
p {
    -webkit-transition: color 2s linear;
    font-size: medium;
    font-family: Arial, Helvetica, sans-serif;
    color: #FF0000;
}
p:hover {
    font-family: Arial, Helvetica, sans-serif;
    color: #0000FF;
}
```

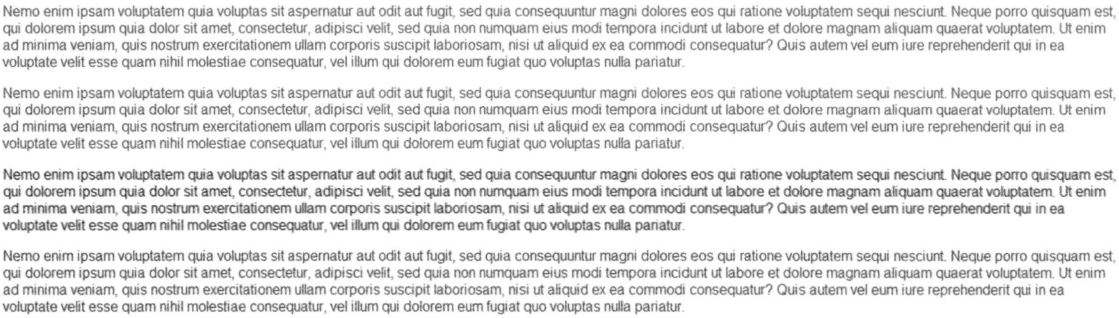

Nemo enim ipsam voluptatem quia voluptas sit aspernatur aut odit aut fugit, sed quia consequuntur magni dolores eos qui ratione voluptatem sequi nesciunt. Neque porro quisquam est, qui dolorem ipsum quia dolor sit amet, consectetur, adipisci velit, sed quia non numquam eius modi tempora incidunt ut labore et dolore magnam aliquam quaerat voluptatem. Ut enim ad minima veniam, quis nostrum exercitationem ullam corporis suscipit laboriosam, nisi ut aliquid ex ea commodi consequatur? Quis autem vel eum iure reprehenderit qui in ea voluptate velit esse quam nihil molestiae consequatur, vel illum qui dolorem eum fugiat quo voluptas nulla pariatur.

Nemo enim ipsam voluptatem quia voluptas sit aspernatur aut odit aut fugit, sed quia consequuntur magni dolores eos qui ratione voluptatem sequi nesciunt. Neque porro quisquam est, qui dolorem ipsum quia dolor sit amet, consectetur, adipisci velit, sed quia non numquam eius modi tempora incidunt ut labore et dolore magnam aliquam quaerat voluptatem. Ut enim ad minima veniam, quis nostrum exercitationem ullam corporis suscipit laboriosam, nisi ut aliquid ex ea commodi consequatur? Quis autem vel eum iure reprehenderit qui in ea voluptate velit esse quam nihil molestiae consequatur, vel illum qui dolorem eum fugiat quo voluptas nulla pariatur.

Nemo enim ipsam voluptatem quia voluptas sit aspernatur aut odit aut fugit, sed quia consequuntur magni dolores eos qui ratione voluptatem sequi nesciunt. Neque porro quisquam est, qui dolorem ipsum quia dolor sit amet, consectetur, adipisci velit, sed quia non numquam eius modi tempora incidunt ut labore et dolore magnam aliquam quaerat voluptatem. Ut enim ad minima veniam, quis nostrum exercitationem ullam corporis suscipit laboriosam, nisi ut aliquid ex ea commodi consequatur? Quis autem vel eum iure reprehenderit qui in ea voluptate velit esse quam nihil molestiae consequatur, vel illum qui dolorem eum fugiat quo voluptas nulla pariatur.

Nemo enim ipsam voluptatem quia voluptas sit aspernatur aut odit aut fugit, sed quia consequuntur magni dolores eos qui ratione voluptatem sequi nesciunt. Neque porro quisquam est, qui dolorem ipsum quia dolor sit amet, consectetur, adipisci velit, sed quia non numquam eius modi tempora incidunt ut labore et dolore magnam aliquam quaerat voluptatem. Ut enim ad minima veniam, quis nostrum exercitationem ullam corporis suscipit laboriosam, nisi ut aliquid ex ea commodi consequatur? Quis autem vel eum iure reprehenderit qui in ea voluptate velit esse quam nihil molestiae consequatur, vel illum qui dolorem eum fugiat quo voluptas nulla pariatur.

Figure 2.35 The transition effect allows you to move simple animation from one state to another.

As you move over any text using the P element the text will slowly change from red to blue. When you move away from the text it will change back. Figure 2.35 illustrates several paragraphs of text using the P element.

In the figure, the top paragraph is red, the third has transitioned to blue, and the fourth is transitioning from one color to the next. You can elect to have all of the properties be selected as part of the transition by changing the property value to `all` as in the following example.

```
p {
    -webkit-transition: all 2s linear;
    font-size: medium;
    font-family: Arial, Helvetica, sans-serif;
    color: #FF0000;
}

    p:hover {
    font-family: Arial, Helvetica, sans-serif;
    font-size: xx-large;
    color: #0000FF;
}
```

When a user interacts with the web page all the elements that can be transitioned are, as shown in Figure 2.36.

For quick, simple animation sequences, transitions are great.

Nemo enim ipsam voluptatem quia voluptas sit aspernatur aut odit aut fugit, sed quia consequuntur magni dolores eos qui ratione voluptatem sequi nesciunt. Neque porro quisquam est, qui dolorem ipsum quia dolor sit amet, consectetur, adipisci velit, sed quia non numquam eius modi tempora incidunt ut labore et dolore magnam aliquam quaerat voluptatem. Ut enim ad minima veniam, quis nostrum exercitationem ullam corporis suscipit laboriosam, nisi ut aliquid ex ea commodi consequatur? Quis autem vel eum iure reprehenderit qui in ea voluptate velit esse quam nihil molestiae consequatur, vel illum qui dolorem eum fugiat quo voluptas nulla pariatur.

Nemo enim ipsam voluptatem quia voluptas sit aspernatur aut odit aut fugit, sed quia consequuntur magni dolores eos qui ratione voluptatem sequi nesciunt. Neque porro quisquam est, qui dolorem ipsum quia dolor sit amet, consectetur, adipisci velit, sed quia non numquam eius modi tempora incidunt ut labore et dolore magnam aliquam quaerat voluptatem. Ut enim ad minima veniam, quis nostrum exercitationem ullam corporis suscipit laboriosam, nisi ut aliquid ex ea commodi consequatur? Quis autem vel eum iure reprehenderit qui in ea voluptate velit esse quam nihil molestiae consequatur, vel illum qui dolorem eum fugiat quo voluptas nulla pariatur.

Nemo enim ipsam voluptatem quia voluptas sit aspernatur aut odit aut fugit, sed quia consequuntur magni dolores eos qui ratione voluptatem sequi nesciunt. Neque porro quisquam est, qui dolorem ipsum quia dolor sit amet, consectetur, adipisci velit, sed quia non numquam eius modi tempora incidunt ut labore et dolore magnam aliquam quaerat voluptatem. Ut enim ad minima veniam, quis nostrum exercitationem ullam corporis suscipit laboriosam, nisi ut aliquid ex ea commodi consequatur? Quis autem vel eum iure reprehenderit qui in ea voluptate velit esse quam nihil molestiae consequatur, vel illum qui dolorem eum fugiat quo voluptas nulla pariatur.

Nemo enim ipsam voluptatem quia voluptas sit aspernatur aut odit aut fugit, sed quia consequuntur magni dolores eos qui ratione voluptatem sequi nesciunt. Neque porro quisquam est, qui dolorem ipsum quia dolor sit amet, consectetur, adipisci velit, sed quia non numquam eius modi tempora incidunt ut labore et dolore magnam aliquam quaerat voluptatem. Ut enim ad minima veniam, quis nostrum exercitationem ullam corporis suscipit laboriosam, nisi ut aliquid ex ea commodi consequatur? Quis autem vel eum iure reprehenderit qui in ea voluptate velit esse quam nihil molestiae consequatur, vel illum qui dolorem eum fugiat quo voluptas nulla pariatur.

Creating Animation with CSS3

For more complex animation you will want to use the new transform settings. The following HTML and CSS style allow you to add a bouncing text block to the screen.

Figure 2.36 All of the CSS definitions that support transitions can be animated.

```
<html>
  <head>
    <title>Bouncing Box example</title>
    <style type="text/css" media="screen">
      @-webkit-keyframes bounce {
        from {
          left: 0px;
        }
        to {
          left: 400px;
        }
      }
      .animation {
        -webkit-animation-name: bounce;
        -webkit-animation-duration: 2s;
        -webkit-animation-iteration-count: 4;
        -webkit-animation-direction: alternate;
        position: relative;
        left: 0px;
      }
    </style>
  </head>
  <body>
    <p class="animation">
      The text bounces back and forth
    </p>
  </body>
</html>
```

The animation is controlled through the use of the style sheet. There are two parts you need to control. The first sets up the type of animation you want to use. Here the setting is for an animation sequence named `bounce`. The animation and the movement will be from 0 px to the left 400 px.

```
@-webkit-keyframes bounce {
  from {
    left: 0px;
  }
  to {
  left: 400px;
  }
}
```

The next step is to define what gets animated. In this example you have a CSS class associated with the `bounce` animation. There are a couple of additional settings. The `duration` setting controls how long each animation sequence takes to play in seconds, and the `count` setting specifies how many times the animation plays. Together, it looks as follows.

```
.animation {
  -webkit-animation-name: bounce;
  -webkit-animation-duration: 2s;
  -webkit-animation-iteration-count: 4;
  -webkit-animation-direction: alternate;
  position: relative;
  left: 0px;
```

Currently, the examples above will only work in the latest versions of Safari and Google's Chrome. If, however, you have an iPhone or iPod Touch then your version of Safari already supports the new CSS animation sequences.

Delivering Solutions for the Mobile Market

Waiting for PC computers to catch up and support HTML5 may be eclipsed by the rapid adoption of smart phones and compact mobile devices spilling onto the market.

Smart mobile phones are receiving a lot of attention from the sheer power they pack. This power is extended to the mobile web browsers installed on these devices. The popular Apple iPhone runs Mobile Safari, a browser built from the open-source WebKit project. Google's Android mobile OS and Palm's Pre WebOS are also built from WebKit. Not to be out done, Mozilla and Opera have mobile browsers, too. All of these browsers run HTML5.

The problem is screen size. The real estate space for a Windows 7 PC can be ten times greater than the humble 480 × 320 space of the iPhone. To help you, CSS3 has a final trick up its sleeve.

The media definition in CSS allows you to identify different styles for different media types. Originally defined in CSS2, the CSS3 expands the functionality of the CSS2 version to allow you to specify any type of device.

The easiest place to use the media definition is right when you link to a CSS document in the head of the web page. Typically you will write the following code to link to a CSS document:

```
<link rel="stylesheet" type="text/css" href="style.css">
```

The media definition now allows you to specify a style to be associated with a device. Take, for instance, the following CSS link reference to two styles documents.

```
<link rel="stylesheet" type="text/css" media="screen"
href="screen.css">
<link rel="stylesheet" type="text/css" media="print"
href="print.css">
```

The first link uses the media definition to target a CSS document from the computer screen. The second CSS document targets how data are presented when the document is printed. Using this technique you can create two different presentation styles using the same content. One style is used for screen presentation and the other for print. Below is a list of the media names you can use:

- All—suitable for all devices
- Braille—intended for braille tactile feedback devices
- Embossed—intended for paged braille printers
- Handheld—intended for handheld devices (typically small screen, limited bandwidth)
- Print—intended for paged material and for documents viewed on screen in print preview mode
- Projection—intended for projected presentations (e.g., projectors)
- Screen—intended primarily for color computer screens
- Speech—intended for speech synthesizers
- tty—intended for media using a fixed-pitch character grid (such as teletypes, terminals, or portable devices with limited display capabilities)
- tv—intended for television-type devices (low resolution, color, limited-scrollability screens, sound available)

Having the names is great, but it does not help when there are so many different devices coming on to the market with different screen resolutions. To help with this, you can modify the media type to look for screen resolutions and deliver the appropriate style sheet. Using the property device-width you can specify a style sheet for a specific width.

```
<link rel="stylesheet" type="text/css" media="
(device-width: 3200px)" href="iphone.css">
```

Using CSS you can dynamically change the presentation of the content to best suite the device accessing the content.

What You Have Learned

CSS3 is an amazing advancement for Cascading Style Sheets. In this chapter you have seen how you have absolute control over your design using CSS to control placement of elements on the screen, the font structure, measurement, and color. CSS3 extends further from earlier versions of CSS to include basic and rich animation techniques and media management tools. Of all the technologies in HTML5, CSS is arguably receiving the most attention. The latest standards for CSS3 can be found at *http://www.w3.org/Style/CSS/current-work*.

PROJECT 2: APPLYING CSS3 TO YOUR WEB DESIGN

The goal of this project is to expand on the HTML5 pages you created in Project 1 by adding some color and flare. By themselves, HTML5 elements are not pretty. This is a good thing. Back in the days of HTML3.2, a nasty tool made itself available to web designs: the HTML FONT element. Brrr… I get shivers just thinking about. Today, Cascading Style Sheets (CSS) gives you greater flexibility to design your web sites.

To illustrate how powerful CSS is, let's take a look at the web site shown in Figure 2.1Proj with no styles applied to it.

Figure 2.1Proj HTML without CSS.

Figure 2.2Proj CSS is used to add style to the page.

Not pretty. You can even see that the design is confusing. Okay, now let's take a look at the site with CSS applied, as shown in Figure 2.2Proj.

Big difference, isn't it? CSS gives you the ability to dramatically change the position, style, and layout of your content. In this project you will develop a style sheet that will be applied to your HTML site.

Working with HTML5
You will want to use the HTML5 pages created in Project 1.

Linking to a Single CSS Document

There are several ways in which you can apply CSS to your site. You can place styles directly in line with your HTML elements as a `style` attribute or you can reference styles as `class` attributes defined in each web page or linked to a single CSS document. Linking to a single document allows you to use one file to manage the design for your entire site. You are going to use a link to a single style document for your site. Here's what you need to do:

1. Start by locating the HTML5 documents created in Project 1. You can also download them from *www.visualizetheweb.com*.
2. Place all of your HTML files into a single directory.
3. Open a text editor, such as Notepad or TextEdit, and create a new text document. Save the file as "style.css." Make sure to save the file with a CSS extension.

4. Open "default.html." You are now going to link the page to the CSS file you created with the following HTML placed in-between the HEAD elements:

```
<link rel="stylesheet" type="text/css"
href="style.css">
```

5. Repeat this for each document.

At this point you have linked all of your documents to a single style sheet. You can view the documents and you will see that nothing has changed visually at this time. From now on, all you need to do is modify the single CSS document in your text editor. Your edits will show in all of the web pages as you save your CSS file.

Embedding Fonts

Before jumping in and creating visual designs, let's think about fonts. It is true that the Web limits your use of fonts to a smattering of choices (Arial, Helvetica, Times, Times New Roman, Courier), but with CSS3 you can now embed almost any type of font into your web design.

The trick to embedding fonts is to understand which font-embedding technology to use with each web browser. For the most part you need to support the following font types:

- EOT (Embedded OpenType)
- TTF (TrueType Font)
- WOFF (Web Open Font Format)
- SVG

Included with the files on *www.visualizetheweb.com* are different formatted font files designed for use on the Web.

In this project you are going to use two fonts:

- ChunkFive
- Sansation

You need to copy the font files into the same directory as your HTML files.

Open the CSS document, and at the top of the page paste the following media definition for the ChunkFive font.

```
@font-face {
font-family: 'ChunkFiveRegular';
src: url('Chunkfive.eot');
src: local('ChunkFive'), local('ChunkFive'), url
('Chunkfive.woff') format('woff'), url('Chunkfive.ttf')
format('truetype'), url('Chunkfive.svg#ChunkFive')
format('svg');
}
```

You will see that the font is referenced as ChunkFiveRegular in the family name. This is a standard naming technique for fonts.

Embedding Fonts
The site *www.FontSquirrel.com* is a great online resource for downloading legally free fonts for your web pages.

The Sansation font has three types: regular, light, and bold. To differentiate the three, you need to add three new font media definitions with unique font-family names, as shown in the following.

```
@font-face {
font-family: 'SansationRegular';
src: url('Sansation_Regular.eot');
src: local('Sansation'), local('Sansation'),
url('Sansation_Regular.woff') format('woff'),
url('Sansation_Regular.ttf') format('truetype'),
url('Sansation_Regular.svg#Sansation') format('svg');
}
@font-face {
font-family: 'SansationLight';
src: url('Sansation_Light.eot');
src: local('Sansation'), local('Sansation-Light'),
url('Sansation_Light.woff') format('woff'), url
('Sansation_Light.ttf') format('truetype'), url('Sansation_
Light.svg#Sansation-Light') format('svg');
}
@font-face {
font-family: 'SansationBold';
src: url('Sansation_Bold.eot');
src: local('Sansation'), local('Sansation-Bold'), url
('Sansation_Bold.woff') format('woff'), url('Sansation_Bold.
ttf') format('truetype'), url('Sansation_Bold.svg#Sansation-
Bold') format('svg');
}
```

From now on, in your CSS, you can reference these new fonts by their font-family names.

Default Styles for Content

Now that you have created both your CSS file and defined two different fonts, it is time to use these tools to format the page. Again, Figure 2.3Proj is a screenshot of the site without any formatted CSS. It is still very dull.

So let's go ahead and format some basic styles on the page. There are three sets of elements that should be formatted for every project you work on: BODY, ANCHOR, and H1 to H3.

The BODY element assumes the defaults styles for the page. The following CSS class definition for the BODY uses SansationRegular as the font for the page.

```
body {
background-color: #EEEEEE margin: 0px;
        font-family: SansationRegular;
        font-size: 11px;
```

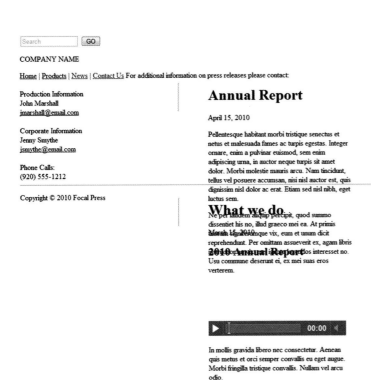

Figure 2.3Proj No CSS
formatting—very dull.

```
      line-height: 1.2em;
      text-align: left;
      position: absolute;
      color: #666666
}
```

You can see in Figure 2.4Proj that the Sansation font is now being used in the web design. Again, it is important to know that the font is only loaded into the web page as needed and is not being installed on your computer. This prevents copyright issues.

The next element to modify is the ANCHOR element, which is used to define links from one page to another. You can leverage pseudo class definitions for the AHCHOR element that allow different types of interaction from users with their mouses. In this instance, the two different types of action are when you actively select a link and when you move the cursor over the link (Figure 2.5Proj).

The following code forces all the links on the page to not have a line under them.

```
a:link {
      text-decoration: none;
      color: white;
}
```

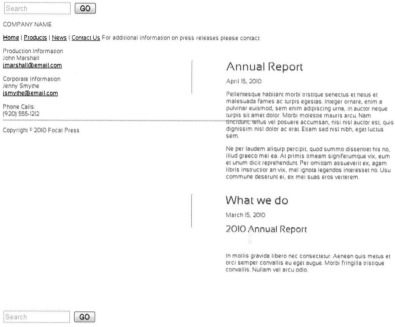

Figure 2.4Proj The embedded font Sansation is being used as the default font design for the page.

Figure 2.5Proj The ANCHOR element has a visual effect that shows when you are interacting with the element using your mouse.

The following CSS will show a line as you move your mouse over a link on the page.

```
a:hover {
        text-decoration: underline;
}
```

The following H1, H2, and H3 elements are used for formatting leading headlines in the text. As with other text elements on the page, you are using the embedded font-family Sansation.

```
h1 {
    font-size: 1.5em;
    font-family: SansationBold;
    font-weight: bold;
    text-align: left;
}
h2 {
    font-size: 1.3em;
    font-family: SansationBold;
    font-weight: bold;
    text-align: left;
}
h3 {
    font-size: 1.2em;
    font-family: SansationLight;
    font-weight: bold;
    text-align: left;
}
```

At this point you have created the main CSS design needed to control the font presentation. The next step is to block out where your content will appear on the page.

Applying Styles to Main Sections of Content

Content has to be placed onto your page. You may have done this in the past using complex table layouts. Nothing is easy about styling your pages using tables. The following three class definitions control where the main content for your site is placed on the page using CSS. CSS positioning is simple and easy to change.

The leftSection class outlines the left panel of the screen (Figure 2.6Proj).

```
.leftSection {
        border-style: solid;
        border-color: #333333;
        background-color: #333333;
        position: absolute;
        left: 0px;
        top: 0px;
        width: 230px;
        height: 100%;
        z-index: 1
}
```

The sectionOne class controls the main content of each page (Figure 2.7Proj).

Annual Report

April 15, 2010

Pellentesque habitant morbi tristique senectus et netus et malesuada fames ac turpis egestas. Integer ornare, enim a pulvinar euismod, sem enim adipiscing urna, in auctor neque turpis sit amet dolor. Morbi molestie mauris arcu. Nam tincidunt, tellus vel posuere accumsan, nisi nisl auctor est, quis dignissim nisl dolor ac erat. Etiam sed nisl nibh, eget luctus sem.

Ne per laudem aliquip percipit, quod summo dissentiet his no, illud graeco mei ea. At primis timeam signiferumque vix, eum et unum dicit reprehendunt. Per omittam assueverit ex, agam libris instructior an vix, mei ignota legendos interesset no. Usu commune deserunt ei, ex mei suas eros verterem.

What we do

March 15, 2010

2010 Annual Report

In mollis gravida libero nec consectetur. Aenean quis metus et orci semper convallis eu eget augue. Morbi fringilla tristique convallis. Nullam vel arcu odio.

Figure 2.6Proj The leftSection class controls how the left side of the screen is presented.

The Gizmo Product

The Gizmo Product varius viverra in a enim. Nulla varius pharetra luctus. Ut scelerisque consequat velit at accumsan.

Sed euismod eros The Gizmo Product egestas. Ut fringilla tincidunt ligula quis blandit. In et vestibulum orci.

Donec et metus sed purus ultrices interdum vel non purus. Nulla nisi velit, vulputate nec sodales The Gizmo Product quis odio. Praesent malesuada pulvinar leo, vel ultricies metus eleifend at.

Another Product

Another Product Main Features:

- Nunc ultrices adipiscing elit, eu fermentum lacus consequat in.
- Nam laoreet aliquam mi, at feugiat urna tempus non.
- Vestibulum nec dui magna, sit amet ullamcorper libero.

Another Product Support

Phasellus dictum elementum erat. Another Product tellus imperdiet ac. Sed quis porttitor eros.

How to service Another Product

Etiam gravida dui a purus sollicitudin tempus blandit sem pulvinar.

Figure 2.7Proj The main content for each page will be formatted with the sectionOne class.

```
.sectionOne {
        position: absolute;
        left: 355px;
        top: 105px;
        width: 1px;
        height: 60px;
        z-index: 3;
}
```

The FOOTER element is placed at the bottom of the page. A CSS class is used to define the FOOTER element. You can use a footer style class definition in your CSS document, however, the same styling will be used on all FOOTER elements you have on a page if you have two or more (Figure 2.8Proj). Using a CSS class allows you to control where the style is applied to your elements.

```
.footerStyle {
        font-family: SansationLight;
        position: absolute;
        left: 415px;
        top: 620px;
        width: 400px;
        height: 40px;
        z-index: 5;
}
```

Figure 2.8Proj The FOOTER element now has its own CSS style.

At this point you have the core styles needed for your pages. The next area you will style is the main navigation.

Applying Styles to the Navigation Elements

CSS gives you the ability to control the position of content on the screen and, when using CSS3 features, you can add new attributes such as advanced color technique, embedded fonts, and transformations.

The project you are working on has a particularly interesting use of CSS3 in the navigation block. There are three elements that form the navigation class style: the default design, specific ANCHOR element formatting, and pseudo class style for the ANCHOR element.

The following definition controls the overall style of the navigation. There are two key elements you should notice: use of the ChunkFiveRegular embedded font and the forced transformation of the navigation to 270 degrees (Figure 2.9Proj).

Figure 2.9Proj The navigation section uses CSS3 transformation to rotate the text 270 degrees.

```
.navigationStyle {
        color: #CCCCCC;
        font-family: ChunkFiveRegular;
        font-size: 16px;
        font-weight: bolder;
        line-height: 35px;
        letter-spacing: normal;
        position: absolute;
        left: -1px;
        top: 150px;
        width: 450px;
        height: 80px;
        z-index: 4;
        -webkit-transform: rotate(270deg);
        -moz-transform: rotate(270deg);
}
```

There are links to different parts of your web site placed within the navigation. Below is a specific style that targets just the ANCHOR element within your navigation style definition. By default, the ANCHOR style definition inherits all of the CSS definitions created in the `navigationStyle` class and is then able to add specific styles for the ANCHOR element.

```
.navigationStyle a {
        color: #CCCCCC;
        text-decoration: none;
}
```

Finally, a pseudo class style extends the ANCHOR element within the `navigationStyle` class to add an underline as you move your cursor over any links.

```
.navigationStyle a:hover {
        text-decoration: underline;
}
```

You can see in this section how you can create a core class in CSS and then extend it to different elements—in this case the ANCHOR element—and pseudo characteristics within each element.

Applying Styles to the Form Elements

There is no need for you to have ugly forms (Figure 2.10Proj). CSS gives you the control to build forms that look beautiful. The key to working with forms is to understand the element that controls the data captured in the form: the INPUT element.

Following is a simple CSS style that changes the presentation of all INPUT elements (Figure 2.11Proj).

Figure 2.10Proj A web form that does not use CSS styles.

Figure 2.11Proj By adding a few lines of CSS, the form looks very different.

110

```
INPUT {
        font-family: SansationLight;
        font-size: 9pt;
        font-weight: bold;
        background-color: #336699;
        border-color: #336699;
        border-style: solid;
        border-width: 2px;
        color: gray;
        height: 20px
        -moz-border-radius: 10px;
        -webkit-border-radius: 10px;
}
```

Notice that the style in the figure embeds a font into the INPUT element. This means that you will be using the new font when you type into the form fields. Also, you now have rounded corners, colored text, and colored form fields. The end result is a very different looking form field. Gone are the days of boring forms.

Additional Styles

There are a number of additional visual elements that require styling. A feature that is present on each page is the company name. A unique style is applied to the company name. As with the navigation class you defined earlier, you will see that the company NameStyle class uses an embedded font and rotates the text 270 degrees.

```
.companyNameStyle {
        color: #FFFFFF;
        font-family: ChunkFiveRegular;
        font-size: 45px;
        font-weight: bolder;
        line-height: 35px;
        letter-spacing: normal;
        position: absolute;
        left: -50px;
        top: 150px;
        width: 450px;
        height: 80px;
        z-index: 4;
        -webkit-transform: rotate(270deg);
        -moz-transform: rotate(270deg);
}
```

The news page has a section that is used for the ASIDE element. A specific style is used to present the ASIDE on the screen. Below is the CSS style used in the presentation. It is worth noting that the space occupied by the ASIDE is defined in the CSS along with rounded corners and an embedded font.

```
aside {
        position: absolute;
        left: 740px;
        top: 200px;
        width: 150px;
        height: 190px;
        z-index: 6;
        background-color: #808080;
        color: #FFFFFF;
        -moz-border-radius: 10px;
        -webkit-border-radius: 10px;
        padding: 5px;
        font-family: SansationLight;
}
```

Advanced CSS Execution

Up to this point you have been controlling the layout of the site with CSS. However, CSS does give you additional control. With a little work you can make the CSS used in the site interactive. You are going to add an interactive menu to the site and include a timeline tool, all developed with CSS.

There are distinct advantages to using CSS for simple, interactive content in your site. The first is ease of execution. CSS is not like JavaScript. It is, relatively speaking, a simple language to learn. A second reason is portability: CSS is designed to be shared across your site.

Up to this point, you have been creating a simple web site. For this design it has been okay to keep all of the files in the same folder of the site. This does, however, lead to problems when you start creating larger sites. Now is the time to do a little housekeeping. Open up the folder structure and let's move a few files around.

1. Open up the folder you have been storing all of your web files to. Create the following folders: CSS, Products, and News. See Figure 2.12Proj.

Figure 2.12Proj A little housekeeping in your folder structure will help with future site enhancements.

Documents library
HTML Files

Name	Date modified	Type	Size
css	4/3/2010 9:41 AM	File folder	
images	4/3/2010 8:34 AM	File folder	
news	4/3/2010 9:29 AM	File folder	
products	4/3/2010 9:31 AM	File folder	
contactUs.html	4/3/2010 9:28 AM	HTML Document	4 KB
default.html	4/3/2010 9:33 AM	HTML Document	4 KB
menu.html	4/3/2010 9:28 AM	HTML Document	2 KB

2. Now, drag the CSS file "style.css" to the CSS folder.
3. Open up your web pages and change the link to the CSS file to the following:

```
<link href="css/style.css" rel="stylesheet" type="text/
css"/>
```

4. Open the new CSS folder. Create a subfolder and name it Fonts. Drag your fonts into the new Fonts folder; this keeps all of your fonts collected together. You will need to update your references of the fonts. Open up "style.css" and change the URL source to point to the Fonts subfolder. You can see the changes added to the following CSS.

```
@font-face {
font-family: 'ChunkFiveRegular';
src: url('fonts/Chunkfive.eot');
src: local('ChunkFive'), local('ChunkFive'),
url('fonts/Chunkfive.woff') format('woff'), url('fonts/
Chunkfive.ttf') format('truetype'), url('fonts/Chunkfive.
svg#ChunkFive') format('svg');
    }
@font-face {
font-family: 'SansationRegular';
src: url('fonts/Sansation_Regular.eot');
src: local('Sansation'), local('Sansation'),
url('fonts/Sansation_Regular.woff') format('woff'),
url('fonts/Sansation_Regular.ttf') format('truetype'),
url('fonts/Sansation_Regular.svg#Sansation')
format('svg');
    }
@font-face {
font-family: 'SansationLight';
src: url('Sansation_Light.eot');
src: local('Sansation'), local('Sansation-Light'),
url('fonts/Sansation_Light.woff') format('woff'), url('fonts/
ansation_Light.ttf') format('truetype'), url('fonts/
Sansation_Light.svg#Sansation-Light') format('svg');
    }
@font-face {
font-family: 'SansationBold';
src: url('Sansation_Bold.eot');
src: local('Sansation'), local('Sansation-Bold'),
url('fonts/Sansation_Bold.woff') format('woff'),
url('fonts/Sansation_Bold.ttf') format('truetype'),
url('fonts/Sansation_Bold.svg#Sansation-Bold')
format('svg');
    }
```

5. Save the "style.css" file.

This little bit of housework will help keep your site more organized as you add more content.

Creating a Menu with CSS

Having a menu system is a common feature for all web sites. For your new HTML5 web site there is no reason why you, too, cannot have a cool menu system. The current navigation uses just text, but with a little more effort we can create an elegant CSS solution. The screenshot in Figure 2.13Proj shows what the new menu will look like.

Figure 2.13Proj A 100% CSS menu system.

The new menu is now more graphically pleasing and comes with submenus that can link to different web sites. Believe it or not, this menu is not created with JavaScript or Flash. It is all CSS.

There are three main elements to this menu:

- HTML content
- Images to create the button effects
- Lots of CSS

Let's start by looking at the HTML. The current menu looks as follows.

```
<navigation id="NavigationLink" style="" class=
"navigationStyle">
<a href="default.html">Home</a>|<a href="products/
products.html">Products</a>|<a href="news/news.
html">News</a>|<a href="contactUs.html">Contact Us</a>
</navigation>
```

You cannot add submenus to this structure. To add submenus you need to control how the content is listed on the page. Fortunately, HTML has the LIST element that allows you to easily indent lists. Using CSS you will see how to show and hide top- and second-level list elements (Figure 2.14Proj). Your new HTML will look like the following.

```
<navigation id="NavigationLink" style="" class=
"navigationStyle">
    <section class="menu">
        <ul>
            <li><a class="left_nosub" href="default.
html">Home</a></li>
            <li><a class="center_hassub" href="products/
products.html">Products</a>
                <ul>
                  <li><a href="products/project.html">Current
Projects</a></li>
                    <li><a href="products/clients.html">Clients</a></li>
                    <li><a href="products/archives.html">Archives</a></li>
                    <li><a href="products/ideas.html">Submit An
Idea</a></li>
                </ul>
            </li>
            <li><a class="center_hassub" href="news/news.
html">News</a>
                <ul>
                  <li><a href="news/article.html">Articles</a></li>
                    <li><a href="news/timeline.html">Timeline</a></li>
                </ul>
            </li>
            <li><a class="right_nosub" href="contactUs.
html">Contact Us</a></li>
        </ul>
    </section>
</navigation>
```

- Home
- Products
    - Current Projects
    - Clients
    - Archives
    - Submit An Idea
- News
    - Articles
    - Timeline
- Contact Us

Figure 2.14Proj The new menu will start as a list with sublists.

The new menu you will be creating will have a significant amount of CSS. To keep your design workspace clutter free let's go ahead and create a second CSS file. The great thing with HTML is that you can have multiple CSS files in a single web page.

Add the file "menu.css" to the CSS folder. Open "default.html" and add the following link below your current "style.css" link:

```
<link href="css/menu.css" rel="stylesheet" type="text/css">
```

The next step is to create the images you will need in your menu. Figure 2.15Proj shows a screenshot of the images and an explanation for each image is as follows (see also Figure 2.16Proj):
1. center.png—center background image
2. center_hassub.png—center background image when you roll cursor over it
3. left.png—left background image

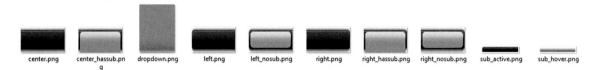

Figure 2.15Proj Here is the collection of PNG files you need in your menu.

Figure 2.16Proj Here is how the PNG files are used in the menu structure.

4. left_hassub.png—left background image when you roll cursor over it with a subimage
5. left_nosub.png—left background image when you roll cursor over it with no subimage
6. right.png—right background image
7. right_hassub.png—right background image when you roll cursor over it with a subimage
8. right_nosub.png—right background image when you roll cursor over it with no subimage
9. dropdown.png—gray background when dropdown menu appears
10. sub_active.png—background image for submenu options
11. sub_hover.png—highlighted background when cursor hovers over a submenu

Up to this point you have the HTML and images needed to create your menu. The final step is to add the CSS. Looking at the HTML above you will see that there are four main CSS class references defined. Each reference refers to an HTML LIST on the page.

• The SECTION element has the class reference "menu."
• The first LIST ITEM has the class reference "left_nosub."
• The last LIST ITEM has the reference "right_nosub."
• The middle LIST ITEMs have the reference "center_hassub."

These references are used in the CSS file "menu.css" to create your design.

1. Open up "menu.css" and start adding CSS to build out the menu. Begin by adding the reference to an embedded font.

```
@font-face {
font-family: 'SansationRegular';
src: url('fonts/Sansation_Regular.eot');
src: local('Sansation'), local('Sansation'),
url('fonts/Sansation_Regular.woff') format('woff'),
url('fonts/Sansation_Regular.ttf') format('truetype'),
url('fonts/Sansation_Regular.svg#Sansation') format('svg');
}
```

2. The first class you need to define is the menu class. This forms the basis for all of your definitions. The default is to apply the font-family SansationRegular with the font size of 11 points. The outline of the menu has a zero margin, and is positioned relative to the placement of the SECTION elements on the page with a z-index of 1000. The z-index is important, as it forces the submenu items to be in front of any content on the screen.

```
.menu {
        font-family: SansationRegular;
        position: relative;
        font-size: 11px;
        margin: 0;
        z-index: 1000;
}
```

3. The next step is to add the default style that will apply to all elements—in this case the UNORDERED, LIST ITEM, and ANCHOR elements. You will see a default font color (#f0f0f0) is applied to all text items and all text is now centered. The "center.png" image is now being used as the background image to all items (you will see how to override this in a moment) and all items have a default width and height. It is important to add the width and height properties, otherwise the width and height are defined by the text elements. Forcing a width and height allows you to create a buttonlike effect.

```
.menu ul li a {
        display: block;
        text-decoration: none;
        color: #f0f0f0;
        font-weight: bold;
        width: 81px;
        height: 42px;
        text-align: center;
        border-bottom: 0;
        background-image: url('../images/black/center.
png');
        line-height: 48px;
        font-size: 11px;
        overflow: hidden;
        padding-left: 1px;
}
```

4. Because you are using CSS you can override elements. The following CSS adds custom left and right end caps to the menu. At this point you can choose to up the ante by using the rounded corners and gradients colors now supported in CSS. However, to illustrate how PNG files can also be used, we will use images.

```
.menu .left_nosub {
        background-image: url('../images/black/left.
png');
        padding-left: 1px;
        margin-right: -1px;
}
.menu .right_nosub {
        background-image: url('../images/black/right.
png');
}
```

5. The next step is to add the default presentation for UL elements that are contained within the menu class. Controlling elements within classes is one of the strengths of CSS.

```
.menu ul {
        padding: 0;
        margin: 0;
        list-style: none;
}
.menu ul li {
        float: left;
        position: relative;
}
.menu ul li ul {
        display: none;
}
```

6. The next step is to add functionality as you move the cursor over a link. The top-level navigation elements change the color of the text and the background image as you move the cursor over them. The following CSS does this for you.

```
.menu ul li:hover a {
        color: #000;
        background: url('../images/black/center_
hassub.png');
}
.menu ul li:hover ul li a.center_hassub {
        background: #6a3;
        color: #000;
}
.menu ul li:hover ul li:hover a.center_hassub {
        background: #6fc;
        color: #000;
}
.menu ul li:hover ul li ul {
        display: none;
}
```

7. The background image for the far-left and far-right buttons will also be swapped out with the following.

```
.menu ul li:hover .left_nosub {
        color: #000;
        background: url('../images/black/left_nosub.png');
}
.menu ul li:hover .right_hassub {
        color: #000;
        background: url('../images/black/right_hassub.png');
}
.menu ul li:hover .right_nosub {
        color: #000;
        background: url('../images/black/right_nosub.png');
}
```

8. This menu structure is exciting because you can add submenus. The following CSS controls how the submenus appear on the screen. You will see a `display` property is forcing the objects in the submenu to flow down in a block format and formats each object into a fixed area. As with the main heading items, forcing the area of the item gives you the illusion of a button effect.

```
.menu ul li:hover ul li a {
        background-image: none;
        display: block;
        height: 28px;
        line-height: 26px;
        color: #000;
        width: 142px;
        text-align: left;
        margin: 0;
        padding: 0 0 0 11px;
        font-weight: normal;
}
```

9. The background image to each dropdown item is gray. The following CSS controls the presentation of the dropdown image.

```
.menu ul li:hover ul {
        margin: 0 0 0 3px;
        padding: 0;
        background-image: url('../images/black/
dropdown.png');
        background-repeat: no-repeat;
        background-position: bottom left;
}
```

10. As you move the cursor over each item in the submenu, the button effect changes to a different background. This is achieved with a PNG file called "sub_hover." The following CSS applies the hover effect.

```
.menu ul li:hover ul li a:hover {
        color: #000 !important;
        background-image: url('../images/black/sub_
hover.png');
}
.menu ul li:hover ul li:hover ul {
        display: block;
        position: absolute;
        left: 105px;
        top: 0;
}
.menu ul li:hover ul li:hover ul.left {
    left: -105px;
}
```

11. The final CSS definition changes the background image as you click on the item selected.

```
.menu ul li:hover ul .sub_active {
        background-image: url('../images/black/sub_
active.png');
        margin-right: 1px;
}
```

12. At this point you will want to save "menu.css" and preview your page.

You now have a 100% CSS menu structure. Again, you will see there is no JavaScript here.

Designing with CSS3

The improvements in CSS3 give you more opportunities for creativity. This can be clearly seen in the final step of this project: adding a timeline to your page. Each timeline item in the following figure will now change as your roll your cursor over it.

Figure 2.17Proj CSS3 techniques and advanced CSS class and element control were used to create this timeline.

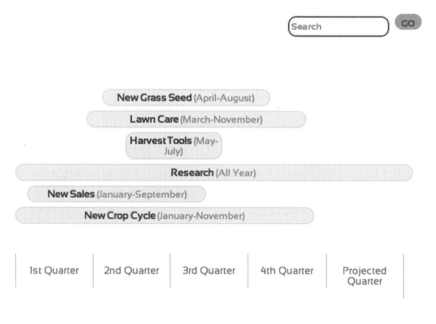

Unlike the menu system created before, you will create the whole timeline using just HTML and CSS, as follows. No stinking images here!

1. Let's start with creating a new web page. In the News folder, add a file named "timeline.html." You can also save one of your files with a new name.

2. Open "timeline.html" and locate the ARTICLE element with the ID "article_one." Delete any content in the ARTICLE so you have a clean page. Also remove any inline CSS style in the ARTICLE element. The HTML for the ARTICLE should look as follows.

```
<article id="article_one">
</article>
```

3. Go ahead and add a SECTION element inside of the ARTICLE, as follows.

```
<article id="article_one">
<section>
</section>
</article>
```

4. At this point you have created the placeholder for your content. The content itself is, as with the navigation, controlled using LI elements. The timeline is actually created using two lists. The first list is used for the highlighted elements and the second is used to show the different milestone markers. Both lists are placed within the SECTION element.

5. The first list uses the following code.

```
<ul>
  <li>New Grass Seed
    <time>(April-August)</time>
  </li>
  <li>Lawn Care
    <time>(March-November)</time>
  </li>
  <li>Harvest Tools
    <time>(May-July)</time>
  </li>
  <li >Research
    <time>(All Year)</time>
  </li>
  <li>New Sales
    <time>(January-September)</time>
  </li>
  <li>New Crop Cycle
    <time>(January-November)</time>
  </li>
</ul>
```

- New Grass Seed (April-August)
- Lawn Care (March-November)
- Harvest Tools (May-July)
- Research (All Year)
- New Sales (January-September)
- New Crop Cycle (January-November)

- 1st Quarter
- 2nd Quarter
- 3rd Quarter
- 4th Quarter
- Projected Quarter

Figure 2.18Proj The lists do not look like the timeline, yet!

Notice that the TIME element is being used to highlight the months.

6. The second list is used to define the quarters. Following is the HTML code to create the second list below the first list.

```
<ul>
  <li>1st Quarter</li>
  <li>2nd Quarter</li>
  <li>3rd Quarter</li>
  <li>4th Quarter</li>
  <li>Projected Quarter</li>
</ul>
```

Figure 2.18Proj shows the lists currently. Now you are ready to crack open your CSS skills and turn the lists into art.

7. Start by creating a new CSS file named "timeline.css" and save it to your CSS folder.

8. Open "timeline.html" and add a reference to "timeline.css." You need to modify the link because the "timeline.html" file is in its own subfolder. The following code will point to the file. You will see that there are leading ".." in front of the file. This tells the HTML to load a file from a folder above the folder you are currently in.

```
<link href="../css/style.css" rel="stylesheet"
type="text/css" />
  <link href="../css/menu.css" rel="stylesheet"
type="text/css">
  <link href="../css/timeline.css" rel="stylesheet"
type="text/css">
```

9. The easiest section of the timeline to create is the markers along the bottom. You will see that the markers are all equally spaced. This is controlled through a class file called "intervals." The intervals class modifies the UL element. The following removes the standard bullet point used in an unordered list.

```
ul.intervals {
        list-style-type: none;
        padding: 0;
        display: block;
    }
```

10. The timeline code is extendable, so you can add it to any page. For this reason, a percentage is used to control the width of the items. The width depends on the number of intervals. For example, 100/5 = 20%; then subtract a little bit of room for the borders. In this case you will see that the width is set to 19.5%. Many of the pages font settings identified in the CSS document "style.css" are inherited. For this reason, the font

SansationRegular is used as the default font-family. Other properties are overridden in the following definition.

```
ul.intervals li {
        background: #fff;
        border-right: 1px solid #ccc;
        color: #999;
        float: left;
        font-size: 1.2em;
        margin: 0;
        padding: 15px 0;
        text-align: center;
        width: 19.5%;
}
```

11. You need to modify the HTML elements so that they can display the CSS correctly. Below is the list with a reference to the intervals class.

```
<ul class="intervals">
<li>1st Quarter</li>
<li>2nd Quarter</li>
<li>3rd Quarter</li>
<li>4th Quarter</li>
<li>Projected Quarter</li>
</ul>
```

12. When you test your page you will notice that all of the LI elements are equally spaced across the screen. What would tidy up the design, however, is a gray border on the left side of the first element. CSS allows you to inherit styles. Go ahead and add a class to the first element in the list; name the class "first."

```
<li class="first">1st Quarter</li>
```

13. In your "timeline.css" file, add the following CSS definition.

```
ul.intervals li.first {
        border-left: 1px solid #ccc;
}
```

14. It is very interesting what is happening here. You are referencing a class called "first" that is associated with the LI element, but it must also be contained within the class called "intervals" in the UL element. Figure 2.19Proj shows you how it all looks when packaged together.

15. The next step is to create the items in the timeline. The items use two CSS techniques to define the content. The first is to create the general presentation of each item; the second is to finely tweak the presentation of each item. Let's get started by adding a new class to the leading UL element in the list. Name the new class `events` as shown in the following.

- New Grass Seed (April-August)
- Lawn Care (March-November)
- Harvest Tools (May-July)
- Research (All Year)
- New Sales (January-September)
- New Crop Cycle (January-November)

Figure 2.19Proj The intervals defining each quarter are added to the bottom of the HTML.

1st Quarter	2nd Quarter	3rd Quarter	4th Quarter	Projected Quarter

```
<ul class="events">
    <li>New Grass Seed
      <time>(April-August)</time>
    </li>
    <li>Lawn Care
      <time>(March-November)</time>
    </li>
    <li>Harvest Tools
      <time>(May-July)</time>
    </li>
    <li>Research
      <time>(All Year)</time>
    </li>
    <li>New Sales
      <time>(January-September)</time>
    </li>
    <li>New Crop Cycle
      <time>(January-November)</time>
    </li>
</ul>
```

16. Open the "timeline.css" file. The following CSS changes the presentation of the UL with the class name events to have no formatting.

```
ul.events {
        list-style-type: none;
        margin: 0;
        padding: 0 0 20px 0;
}
```

17. The next style defines how the events class will look like on the page. It will come as no surprise that the border-radius is being used to create the rounded corners of the rectangles. The text color, padding, and alignment are modified, but the font-family style is inherited from the main page.

```
ul.events li {
        -webkit-border-radius: 11px;
        -moz-border-radius: 11px;
        border-radius: 11px;
        background: #eee;
        border: 1px solid #ddd;
```

```
                color: #707070;
                font-size: 1.2em;
                font-weight: bold;
                margin-bottom: 6px;
                padding: 3px 0;
                position: relative;
                text-align: center;
        }
```

18. Save your files. When you preview your web page you will see that each item now has rounded corners (Figure 2.20Proj).

19. Inline styles within each list item can be used to control the width and starting point from the left. The following HTML code now includes the inline style you can use to format each item (see also Figure 2.21Proj).

```
<li style="width: 42%; left: 22%;">New Grass Seed
    <time>(April-August)</time>
</li>
<li style="width: 55%; left: 18%;">Lawn Care
    <time>(March-November)</time>
</li>
```

New Grass Seed (April-August)

Lawn Care (March-November)

Harvest Tools (May-July)

Research (All Year)

New Sales (January-September)

New Crop Cycle (January-November)

| 1st Quarter | 2nd Quarter | 3rd Quarter | 4th Quarter | Projected Quarter |

Figure 2.20Proj Each item in the timeline now has rounded corners.

New Grass Seed (April-August)

Lawn Care (March-November)

Harvest Tools (May-July)

Research (All Year)

New Sales (January-September)

New Crop Cycle (January-November)

| 1st Quarter | 2nd Quarter | 3rd Quarter | 4th Quarter | Projected Quarter |

Figure 2.21Proj The events in the timeline are now spaced correctly.

```
<li style="width: 404%; left: 28%;">Harvest Tools
  <time>(May-July)</time>
</li>
<li style="width: 100%; left: 0%;">Research
  <time>(All Year)</time>
</li>
<li style="width: 45%; left: 3%;">New Sales
  <time>(January-September)</time>
</li>
<li style="width: 75%; left: 0;">New Crop Cycle
  <time>(January-November)</time>
</li>
```

20. There are a few minor CSS styles you can apply to format the content further. Each item listed contains a TIME element. The following will format text in the TIME element.

```
ul.events li time {
        color: #aaa;
        font-weight: normal;
        font-size: 0.9em;
}
```

21. The final effect you can apply is some simple animation. As you move the cursor over each item in the timeline, you can transition the styles from one format to another. To do this you need to modify ul.events li and add a hover pseudo type by adding the transition property.

```
ul.events li {
        -webkit-border-radius: 11px;
        -moz-border-radius: 11px;
        border-radius: 11px;
        -webkit-transition: all 0.5s linear;
        -moz-transition: all 1s linear;
        transition: all 1s linear;
        background: #eee;
        border: 1px solid #ddd;
        color: #707070;
        font-size: 1.2em;
        font-weight: bold;
        margin-bottom: 6px;
        padding: 3px 0;
        position: relative;
        text-align: center;
}
```

22. The following is the hover pseudo class. Three properties are highlighted. The transition will happen over 0.5 seconds with just these properties, leaving the remainder intact.

```
ul.events li:hover {
        background: #707070;
```

```
        border: 1px solid #ddd;
        color: #eee;
    }
```

23. The final step is to place the whole timeline content onto the web page. The following HTML modifies the leading ARTICLE element to place everything on to the page.

```
<article id="article_one" style="position: absolute;
left: 300px; top: 100px; width: 500px; z-index: 2;">
```

24. Save your content and view your cool, interactive timeline as shown in Figure 2.22Proj.

Figure 2.22Proj You can now move the cursor over each item, triggering a subtle transition.

It is important to recognize that the effects you have accomplished in this chapter do not require JavaScript. This is all 100% CSS.

Summary

Cascading Style Sheets are a powerful way to control the presentation of content in your web pages. HTML5 introduces CSS3 embedded fonts, rounded corners, transformation, and animation. The project you have created here illustrates how you can easily add these complex technologies.

Advanced CSS solutions, such as the menu and timeline tool, do take more time to create, but illustrate how flexible CSS is becoming. You can, of course, extend the styles and create additional styles to format specific areas of content. This is just a springboard to launch your creativity.

At this time you have all core styles needed for the site. Save your style sheet and view your web site. It looks different, doesn't it?

RENDERING HTML5 ILLUSTRATION

Tags are used in HTML5 to place and organize content at a level that is descriptive. This does not mean that the page will look good. Presentation of content on the page is controlled using Cascading Style Sheets Level 3, or CSS3, in HTML5.

There are times, however, when you need to present graphics, too. Typically, HTML has only provided support for pixel-based images in JPEG and GIF image format. With HTML5, you can now create mathematically generated images. The new formats are scalable vector graphics (SVG) and CANVAS. The difference between the two is that SVG is an XML-based language that describes how an image should be displayed in two-dimensional (2D) constructs. The CANVAS tag also describes 2D images, but it does so using JavaScript. The CANVAS tag also allows you to easily integrate interactivity within it using JavaScript.

In this article you will learn the following:
- The new image formats available in HTML5.
- How to draw using SVG.
- How to draw with CANVAS.
- How to add interactivity to CANVAS using JavaScript.

The goal at the end of this article is that you will understand how you can use the image formats in HTML5.

The Tale of Web Image Formats

The Web is not a friendly place for a designer. For many years you have been limited to the number of file formats you can use. There are two predominant file formats used on the Web for creating graphics: JPEG and GIF.

HTML5. doi: 10.1016/B978-0-240-81328-8.00008-2

131

Figure 3.1 This image is in JPEG format. The right side shows the pixel-by-pixel construction of the image.

Figure 3.2 The GIF image is using a Web-safe color palette of 256 colors. You can see by the grainy texture that the image is not photorealistic.

Figure 3.3 PNG graphics allow you to have the best of JPEG and GIF technologies in a single format.

Bitmap Images: Using JPEG, GIF, and PNG Images on the Web

Both JPEG and GIF image formats are raster images created from pixels of individual color. Both have positives and negatives. JPEG images are an open standard managed by the Joint Photographers Expert Group. The JPEG file format allows you to create photorealistic images (Figure 3.1). A great place to go to view millions of JPEG images is Yahoo's Flickr. A JPEG image is identified with the extension of either JPEG or JPG.

The second file format used widely on the Internet is GIF, graphics interchange format. Unlike JPEG, which support millions of colors, the GIF file format only allows you to create images that support a color palette of 256 colors (Figure 3.2). On the face of it, the GIF format appears to be inferior to the JPEG format. However, the GIF format does have two features the JPEG format does not: setting transparency as a color and sequencing a series of images together to play back as a simple animation.

Both JPEG and GIF image formats, however, are now being superseded by a more sophisticated image format: PNG. Portable network graphics (PNG) are a raster-based file format that gives the best of both JPEG and GIF and a little more (Figure 3.3). A PNG image format will support 32-byte images for photorealistic presentation. Additionally, like GIF images, backgrounds in PNG images can be set to be transparent.

While PNG, GIF, and JPEG images are all great, it is difficult to programmatically change the graphical display of the images. For instance, you cannot create a bar chart using JPEG images that change as new data come in. HTML5 introduces two solutions that address this problem: SVG and CANVAS.

The CANVAS HTML5 element allows you to create bitmap images programmatically using JavaScript as the designer. Through this technique, complex animations and interactive solutions can be created. Google has established ChromeExperiments. com (*http://www.chromeexperiments.com/*) to demonstrate powerful CANVAS and JavaScript experiments (Figure 3.4).

The second technology, SVG (scalable vector graphics), is a vector-based technology that enables you to create images and animation using XML syntax similar to HTML. SVG started as an open standard in 1999. The support for SVG started out patchy, but, with the release of FireFox, that all changed. FireFox 1.5 introduced support for SVG, with other competing browsers such as Chrome and Safari rapidly adopting the standard

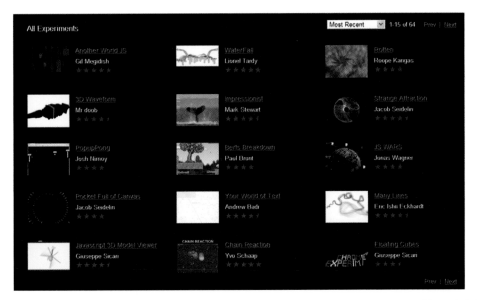

Figure 3.4 ChromeExperiments. com showcases how far you can take technologies such as SVG and CANVAS.

through support of the WebKit Web Browser project. SVG as an alternative vector graphics technology is being widely adopted. As an example, Wikipedia.org has over 250,000 SVG images on its site.

Creating SVG Graphics

If you are comfortable working with HTML code then you will feel comfortable working with SVG. SVG is an XML-based drawing language that allows you to describe your drawing using standard XML elements. For instance, the following code is describing how to create a star shape. Figure 3.5 shows the resulting SVG drawing.

```
<?xml version="1.0" standalone="yes"?>
<svg version="1.1"
viewBox="0.0 0.0 720.0 540.0"
fill="none" stroke="none"
stroke-linecap="square"
stroke-miterlimit="10"
xmlns="http://www.w3.org/2000/svg"
xmlns:xlink="http://www.w3.org/1999/xlink">
<path
d="M240 148L298 148L316 96L334 148L392 148L345
180L363 232L316 200L269 232L287 180Z"
fill-rule="nonzero"
fill="#ff9900"
stroke="#ff0000"
```

Figure 3.5 A star drawn using SVG XML syntax.

```
stroke-width="2.0"
stroke-linejoin="round"
stroke-linecap="butt">
</path></svg>
```

If you want to change the fill color inside of the star, you only need to change the value of the `fill` property to a new color. Say you would prefer a red star; simply change the fill value to red, as follows:

```
fill=red
```

Figure 3.6 shows that the star is now red.

Allowing the browser to control the color, shape, and visual elements of the SVG image allows you to write programs that dynamically control the SVG illustrations.

SVG comes with some fundamental benefits:
- Images scale easily.
- SVG is accessible.
- Search engines can easily read and understand SVG images.

These benefits make using SVG very compelling.

Figure 3.6 Any element used to build an SVG drawing can be easily edited.

The Fundamentals of Creating SVG Images and Adding Them to Your Web Pages

Unlike traditional drawing, SVG can be "drawn" all in code. You can use your favorite text editor to create any type of SVG illustration. The easiest way to manage SVG drawings is to save each illustration to a text file with the extension SVG. You can then treat your SVG drawings as if they are image files like JPEG or PNG files.

All SVG files will start with a line declaring the document is an XML file. The following line should be placed at the start of all your SVG documents:

```
<?xml version="1.0" standalone="yes"?>
```

Following the XML declaration is some information explaining the SVG document. The first line specifies which version of SVG you are using. The most commonly adopted version is 1.1:

```
<svg version="1.1"
```

The `viewBox` property identifies the size of the canvas you are working with. The `viewBox` is constructed of four properties that identify the X and Y coordinates of the `viewBox` and width and height.

```
viewBox="0.0 0.0 300.0 800.0"
```

You can specify drawing attributes that should be used for all objects in the image in the opening SVG properties. Here all objects in the illustration will, by default, have no fill or stroke, and a square line will be used to draw images with a stroke miter of 5.

```
fill="none"
stroke="none"
stroke-linecap="square"
stroke-miterlimit="5"
```

The final two attributes provide links to the SVG namespace standard.

```
xmlns="http://www.w3.org/2000/svg"
xmlns:xlink="http://www.w3.org/1999/xlink">
```

Drawing is managed through a number of elements, with PATH being the main one. The role of the PATH element is to draw out the specific coordinates of an image point by point. In the following example, a single line is drawn.

```
<path d="M8 16L776 0" fill-rule="nonzero" stroke="blue"
stroke-width="5" stroke-linejoin="round" stroke-
linecap="butt">
</path>
</svg>
```

A closing SVG element completes your code. Your drawing can now be saved and added to a web page.

When you have completed an SVG drawing there are several ways in which you can add SVG images to your web page. Unlike JPEG, GIF, and PNG files, you cannot use the IMG element to add an SVG drawing to your web page. You do, however, have three alternative methods.

The first is to use the OBJECT element:

```
<object data="star.svg" width="300" height="800"/>
```

The OBJECT tag has several attributes. The most important is the `data` attribute that references the location of the SVG file. The `width` and `height` attributes define the space used on the screen for the SVG drawing.

A second method you can use to add SVG images to your web page is through the use of the IFRAME element. Typically, you use the IFRAME element to load an external web page, but you can also load an SVG image directly into your web page. Here is an example:

```
<iframe src="star.svg" width="300" height="800"></iframe>
```

These two methods for embedding SVG images into your web page are relatively easy to use and are not much more complicated to use than the IMG element.

The third method of adding SVG images to a web page is to insert the SVG XML directly into the HTML code itself. The following code is HTML saved as a web page. There is no need to use separate SVG files in this example.

```
<html>
  <head>
    <title>SVG embedded inline in XHTML</title>
  </head>
  <body>
    <h1>SVG embedded inline in XHTML</h1>
    <svg xmlns="http://www.w3.org/2000/svg" width="300"
height="800">
    <path
    d="M240 148L298 148L316 96L334 148L392 148L345 180L363
232L316 200L269 232L287 180Z"
    fill-rule="nonzero"
    fill="#ff9900"
    stroke="#ff0000"
    stroke-width="2.0"
    stroke-linejoin="round"
    stroke-linecap="butt">
    </path> </svg>
  </body>
</html>
```

Adding the SVG coded directly to a web page only requires that you use SVG element tags inside of your HTML.

At the end of the day, it is really up to you as to how you want to add SVG images to your web pages.

Understanding the Basics of Creating Shapes

As with HTML, SVG is built of elements. The difference between SVG and HTML is that the elements in SVG are used to construct images. The main elements you will use in building your drawings are:

- LINE—for defining lines
- POLYLINE—for defining shapes constructed of lines
- RECT—for defining rectangles
- CIRCLE—for defining circles
- ELLIPSE—for defining ellipses

- POLYGON—for defining polygons
- PATH—for defining arbitrary paths

The most basic drawing element for SVG is a line. To define a straight line you need to declare where in the `viewBox` property the line starts on the X and Y axes and where the line ends on the X and Y axes. This is referred to as X1, Y1 and X2, Y2. Here is an example of a straight line.

```
<?xml version="1.0" standalone="no"?>
<!DOCTYPE svg PUBLIC "-//W3C//DTD SVG 1.1//EN"
"http://www.w3.org/Graphics/SVG/1.1/DTD/svg11.dtd">
<svg width="100%" height="100%" version="1.1"
xmlns="http://www.w3.org/2000/svg">
<line x1="25" y1="150" x2="300" y2="150"
style="stroke:red;stroke-width:10"/>
```

In this example the line starts 25 pixels in from the left side of the browser window, the line is 300 pixels long, and the line is horizontal along the Y axis. Figure 3.7 is how it looks in your web browser with additional CSS styling to emphasize the line.

Figure 3.7 A line is drawn in SVG using the LINE element.

You can easily modify the settings for the X and Y axes to change the position of your line. In the following SVG code, the line is changed to run vertically.

```
<?xml version="1.0" standalone="no"?>
<!DOCTYPE svg PUBLIC "-//W3C//DTD SVG 1.1//EN"
"http://www.w3.org/Graphics/SVG/1.1/DTD/svg11.dtd">
<svg width="100%" height="100%" version="1.1"
xmlns="http://www.w3.org/2000/svg">
<line x1="300" y1="310" x2="300" y2="10"
style="stroke:red;stroke-width:10"/>
</svg>
```

Figure 3.8 shows the results and how the line is displayed.

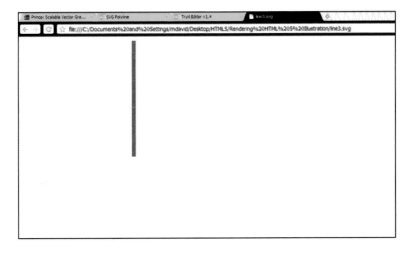

Figure 3.8 Changing the XML element values changes the display of the line.

The POLYLINE element extends the functionality of the LINE element to enable you to build drawings created with lines. The construction is created through valued pairs of X and Y coordinates using POLYLINE's `point` attribute. Here is an example of creating a square shape using the POLYLINE element.

```
<?xml version="1.0" standalone="no"?>
<!DOCTYPE svg PUBLIC "-//W3C//DTD SVG 1.1//EN"
"http://www.w3.org/Graphics/SVG/1.1/DTD/svg11.dtd">
<svg width="100%" height="100%" version="1.1"
xmlns="http://www.w3.org/2000/svg">
<polyline points="5,5 5,150 150,150 150,5 5,5"
style="fill:white;stroke:red;stroke-width:2"/>
</svg>
```

Figure 3.9 shows the final drawing.

You can create more complex shapes with the POLYLINE element. In this example a set of stairs is created. All you have to remember is that the first value in the value pair is the X axis and the second value is the Y axis. Figure 3.10 shows the results.

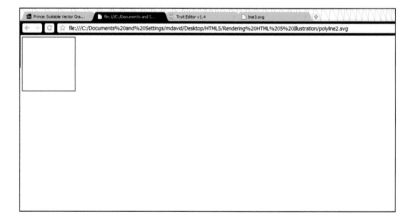

Figure 3.9 The POLYLINE element can be used to draw images with straight lines. In this case a square is drawn.

Figure 3.10 A drawing created of straight lines can be created using the POLYLINE element.

```
<?xml version="1.0" standalone="no"?>
<!DOCTYPE svg PUBLIC "-//W3C//DTD SVG 1.1//EN"
"http://www.w3.org/Graphics/SVG/1.1/DTD/svg11.dtd">
<svg width="100%" height="100%" version="1.1"
xmlns="http://www.w3.org/2000/svg">
<polyline points="5,0 5,40 40,40 40,80 80,80 80,120"
style="fill:white;stroke:red;stroke-width:2"/>
</svg>
```

Rectangle shapes can be created in SVG using the RECT element. The RECT element has two attributes, `width` and `height`. The following SVG adds a rectangle of width 400 pixels and height 400 pixels. Additional styling using CSS has been added to the drawing so you can see it. The results are shown in Figure 3.11.

```
<?xml version="1.0" standalone="no"?>
<!DOCTYPE svg PUBLIC "-//W3C//DTD SVG 1.1//EN"
"http://www.w3.org/Graphics/SVG/1.1/DTD/svg11.dtd">
<svg width="100%" height="100%" version="1.1"
xmlns="http://www.w3.org/2000/svg">
<rect width="400" height="400"
style="fill:red;stroke-width:5;
stroke:yellow"/>
</svg>
```

Creating circles is similar to creating rectangles in SVG. The difference is you use the CIRCLE element. At its most basic, the CIRCLE element only requires that you define the radius of the circle using an `r` attribute. The following SVG code draws a circle with a radius of 150 pixels.

Figure 3.11 The RECT element allows you to easily create rectangle shapes such as this square.

```
<?xml version="1.0" standalone="no"?>
<!DOCTYPE svg PUBLIC "-//W3C//DTD SVG 1.1//EN"
"http://www.w3.org/Graphics/SVG/1.1/DTD/svg11.dtd">
<svg width="100%" height="100%" version="1.1"
xmlns="http://www.w3.org/2000/svg">
<circle r="150" stroke="yellow"
stroke-width="5" fill="red"/>
</svg>
```

Figure 3.12 shows the results of the CIRCLE element in more detail.

Figure 3.12 The CIRCLE element allows you to draw circles on the screen.

As you can see in the figure, defining only the radius forces most of the circle to drop off the top left corner of the browser window. To correct this you can use two additional, optional attributes, cx and cy, to define the X and Y axes positions of the circle on the screen.

```
<?xml version="1.0" standalone="no"?>
<!DOCTYPE svg PUBLIC "-//W3C//DTD SVG 1.1//EN"
"http://www.w3.org/Graphics/SVG/1.1/DTD/svg11.dtd">
<svg width="100%" height="100%" version="1.1"
xmlns="http://www.w3.org/2000/svg">
<circle cx="160" cy="160" r="150" stroke="yellow"
stroke-width="5" fill="red"/>
</svg>
```

Figure 3.13 shows the use of these attributes.

The ELLIPSE element extends the functionality of the CIRCLE element by allowing you to control the radius along the X and Y axes using the rx and ry attributes. You will see in the following code that the ELLIPSE element also leverages the CIRCLE element's cx and cy attributes to position the ellipse in the web browser. Figure 3.14 shows the results

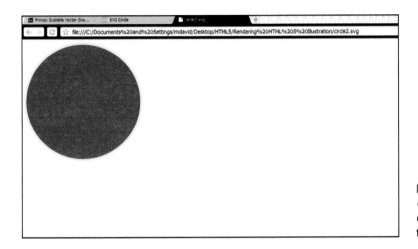

Figure 3.13 Using the cx and cy attributes enables you to control where on the screen the CIRCLE element is placed.

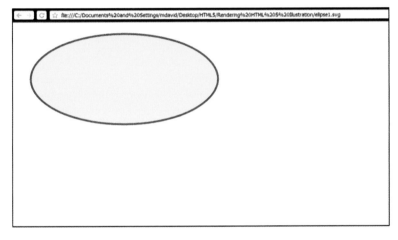

Figure 3.14 An ellipse can be created using the ELLIPSE element.

```
<?xml version="1.0" standalone="no"?>
<!DOCTYPE svg PUBLIC "-//W3C//DTD SVG 1.1//EN"
"http://www.w3.org/Graphics/SVG/1.1/DTD/svg11.dtd">
<svg width="100%" height="100%" version="1.1"
xmlns="http://www.w3.org/2000/svg">
<ellipse cx="300" cy="150" rx="250" ry="120"
style="fill:yellow;
stroke:red;stroke-width:5"/>
</svg>
```

A POLYGON shape is similar to the POLYLINE element. Using X and Y value pairs you can draw whole polygon shapes. The following is an example of a triangle. Figure 3.15 shows the results.

```
<?xml version="1.0" standalone="no"?>
<!DOCTYPE svg PUBLIC "-//W3C//DTD SVG 1.1//EN"
"http://www.w3.org/Graphics/SVG/1.1/DTD/svg11.dtd">
<svg width="100%" height="100%" version="1.1"
xmlns="http://www.w3.org/2000/svg">
```

Figure 3.15 A triangle is created using the POLYGON element.

```
<polygon points="220,100 290,220 150,220"
style="fill:yellow;
stroke:red;stroke-width:5"/>
</svg>
```

The most complex drawing element you will create using SVG is the PATH element. Each drawing you create with the PATH element is built using a series of special codes that explain where the line is supposed to move to on the screen. Those codes are:

- M = move to
- L = line to
- H = horizontal line to
- V = vertical line to
- C = curve to
- S = smooth curve to
- Q = quadratic Belzier curve to
- T = smooth quadratic Belzier curve to
- A = elliptical arc to
- Z = close path to

The following code creates a smiley face illustration using the PATH element and the codes above to create the drawing. Figure 3.16 shows the results from the code.

Figure 3.16 The POLYLINE element allows you to create complex images such as this smiley face.

```
<?xml version="1.0" standalone="yes"?>
<svg version="1.1" viewBox="0.0 0.0 1152.0 864.0"
fill="none" stroke="none" stroke-linecap="square"
stroke-miterlimit="10" xmlns="http://www.w3.org/2000/svg"
xmlns:xlink="http://www.w3.org/1999/xlink">
<path d="M56 108L56 108C56 66 92 32 136 32C180 32 216
66 216 108C216 150 180 184 136 184C92 184 56 150 56 108Z"
fill-rule="nonzero" fill="#ffff00"></path>
<path d="M102 85C102 81 106 77 110 77C115 77 119 81
119 85C119 90 115 93 110 93C106 93 102 90 102 85M153
85C153 81 157 77 162 77C166 77 170 81 170 85C170 90 166
93 162 93C157 93 153 90 153 85" fill-rule="nonzero"
fill="#cccc00" stroke="#ff0000" stroke-width="2.0"
stroke-linejoin="round" stroke-linecap="butt"></path>
<path d="M93 141Q136 169 179 141" fill-rule=
"nonzero" stroke="#ff0000" stroke-width="2.0" stroke-
linejoin="round" stroke-linecap= "butt"></path>
<path d="M56 108L56 108C56 66 92 32 136 32C180 32 216
66 216 108C216 150 180 184 136 184C92 184 56 150 56 108Z"
fill-rule="nonzero" stroke="#ff0000" stroke-width="2.0"
stroke-linejoin="round" stroke-linecap="butt"></path>
</svg>
```

As you can see, it is quite complex to create PATH-defined illustrations. For this reason, it is recommended that you use an SVG drawing tool to create PATH-based illustrations (more on that later).

Adding CSS-Based Color

SVG is a technology that allows you to create drawings. To add color to those drawings, however, you leverage Cascading Style Sheets. There is no need to use a different technology for applying color, as CSS and SVG are partners in HTML5. Both have strengths that can be enhanced with each other.

To provide an example, let's look back at the ellipse drawing created earlier (see Figure 3.14).

```
<?xml version="1.0" standalone="no"?>
<!DOCTYPE svg PUBLIC "-//W3C//DTD SVG 1.1//EN"
"http://www.w3.org/Graphics/SVG/1.1/DTD/svg11.dtd">
<svg width="100%" height="100%" version="1.1"
xmlns="http://www.w3.org/2000/svg">
<ellipse cx="300" cy="150" rx="250" ry="120"
style="fill:yellow;
stroke:red;stroke-width:5"/>
</svg>
```

After the ellipse image is drawn there is a `style` attribute. The `style` attribute in SVG allows you to add a CSS style to the image. In HTML you have a `style` attribute that behaves exactly the same.

Modifying the `style` attribute will visually change the presentation of the ellipse. The following example changes the fill to blue and the stroke color to gray. Figure 3.17 shows the results.

Figure 3.17 CSS is used to set the visual appearance of an SVG drawing.

```
<?xml version="1.0" standalone="no"?>
<!DOCTYPE svg PUBLIC "-//W3C//DTD SVG 1.1//EN"
"http://www.w3.org/Graphics/SVG/1.1/DTD/svg11.dtd">
<svg width="100%" height="100%" version="1.1"
xmlns="http://www.w3.org/2000/svg">
<ellipse cx="300" cy="150" rx="250" ry="120"
style="fill:blue;
stroke:gray;stroke-width:5"/>
</svg>
```

Both the `fill` and `stroke` properties control the color of the inside of an image. In this example a CSS color name is used, but you can use any of the color formats you use to control CSS, including the following:

- Color name—you can have names for colors such as brown, black, red, or cyan.
- Full hexadecimal—a hexadecimal value comprised of six alpha-numeric values.
- Short hexadecimal—a hexadecimal value comprised of three alpha-numeric values.
- RGB—a combination of red, green, and blue values.
- RGBA—a combination of red, green, and blue values with a transparency value (alpha).
- HSL—a combination of hue, saturation, and lightness.

- HSLA—a combination of hue, saturation, and lightness with a transparency value (alpha).

In addition to using CSS colors you can use any of the following measurements:

- cm—centimeter
- in. —inch
- mm—millimeter
- pc—pica (1 pica = 12 points)
- pt—point (1 point = $\frac{1}{72}$ inch)
- px—pixels

Through leveraging CSS you can change the stroke of the ellipse using short hexadecimal and the measurement in CM.

```
<?xml version="1.0" standalone="no"?>
<!DOCTYPE svg PUBLIC "-//W3C//DTD SVG 1.1//EN"
"http://www.w3.org/Graphics/SVG/1.1/DTD/svg11.dtd">
<svg width="100%" height="100%" version="1.1"
xmlns="http://www.w3.org/2000/svg">
<ellipse cx="300" cy="150" rx="250" ry="120"
style="fill:blue;
stroke:#999;stroke-width:1cm"/>
</svg>
```

Figure 3.18 shows how CSS colors and measurements can be used.

To add a linear of radial gradient to an SVG drawing you need to use specific SVG gradient elements.

Figure 3.18 Standard CSS colors and measurements can be used to control the presentation of a drawing.

Applying Gradients to SVG Images

SVG employs a great technique that allows you to reuse a gradient definition over one or more images in your SVG illustration. This is done using either the LINEARGRADIENT or RADIALGRADIENT element types. Both gradients allow you to define the horizontal and vertical colors and direction of the gradient.

Let's look first at linear gradients. The LINEARGRADIENT element is constructed by five different attributes that define over a linear direction how the gradient will behave. The first attribute you need to provide information for is the `id` attribute, which allows you to give your gradient a name you can use to reference from your drawing.

For a linear gradient you can draw your gradient moving over an X–Y axis direction. To determine the direction of the gradient you have to specify the start and end X and start and end Y axes points. The following illustrates a left–right gradient:

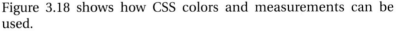

```
<linearGradient x1="0%" y1="0%" x2="100%" y2="0%">
```

To create a vertical gradient you change the Y and X axes to:

```
<linearGradient x1="0%" y1="100%" x2="0%" y2="0%">
```

You can see the difference between the two numbers is changing the X or Y axis to 100%. See Figure 3.19.

Changing the X and Y axes percentages will change how the gradient is drawn. Adding color to the gradient is the next step. To do this, you create a list of two or more colors using the STOP element. For instance, to create a simple yellow-to-red gradient color change you will add two STOP elements as shown in the following.

```
<stop offset="0%" style="stop-color:yellow;
stop-opacity:1"/>
    <stop offset="100%" style="stop-color:red;
stop-opacity:1"/>
```

Figure 3.19 Linear gradients can be applied in SVG images using the LINEARGRADIENT element.

The `offset` attribute dictates where in the drawing the gradient starts. The example above draws a smooth gradient color change over the space of the image. The `style` attribute allows you to list any CSS-specific color. You can add the two colors to the LINEARGRADIENT in the following example.

```
<?xml version="1.0" standalone="no"?>
<!DOCTYPE svg PUBLIC "-//W3C//DTD SVG 1.1//EN"
"http://www.w3.org/Graphics/SVG/1.1/DTD/svg11.dtd">
<svg width="100%" height="100%" version="1.1"
xmlns="http://www.w3.org/2000/svg">
<defs>
<linearGradient id="yellow_red" x1="0%" y1="100%"
x2="0%" y2="0%">
<stop offset="0%" style="stop-color:yellow;
stop-opacity:1"/>
    <stop offset="100%" style="stop-color:red;
stop-opacity:1"/>
</linearGradient>
</defs>
<rect width="400" height="400"
style="fill:url(#yellow_red);
stroke:yellow"/>
</svg>
```

You can see that the rectangle image uses a URL string to find the style called #yellow_red. The `yellow_red` color style is the name of the gradient. See Figure 3.20.

Radial gradients are similar to linear gradients. The difference is that you define essentially two circles—an outer and inner circle—with the radial gradient. As with linear gradients, the RADIALGRADIENT element requires a valid ID name to identify the gradient. Following that, you have five attributes to define the inner and outer circle and radius. Following is an example where the `cx` and `cy` attributes are the outer circle, the `r` attribute is the radius, and the `fx` and `fy` attributes are the inner circle.

```
<radialGradient id="yellow_red" cx="50%" cy="50%" r="50%"
fx="50%" fy="50%">
```

Figure 3.20 Linear gradients can be drawn horizontally.

The colors for the gradient are defined using a STOP list. The following code shows the radial gradient applied to a rectangle.

```
<?xml version="1.0" standalone="no"?>
<!DOCTYPE svg PUBLIC "-//W3C//DTD SVG 1.1//EN"
"http://www.w3.org/Graphics/SVG/1.1/DTD/svg11.dtd">
<svg width="100%" height="100%" version="1.1"
xmlns="http://www.w3.org/2000/svg">
<defs>
<radialGradient id="yellow_red" cx="50%" cy="50%"
r="50%"
fx="50%" fy="50%">
<stop offset="0%" style="stop-color:yellow;
stop-opacity:1"/>
<stop offset="100%" style="stop-color:red;
stop-opacity:1"/>
</radialGradient>
</defs>
<rect width="400" height="400"
style="fill:url(#yellow_red);
stroke:yellow"/>
</svg>
```

Figure 3.21 shows the results.

Both the linear and radial gradients can have more than two colors. The following code (see Figure 3.22) has four colors.

```
<stop offset="0%" style="stop-color:yellow;
stop-opacity:1"/>
<stop offset="25%" style="stop-color:red;
stop-opacity:1"/>
<stop offset="50%" style="stop-color:blue;
stop-opacity:1"/>
<stop offset="100%" style="stop-color:black;stop-
opacity:1"/>
```

In addition, you can link multiple images to a single gradient. The following SVG code links a circle and rectangle to the same gradient.

```
<?xml version="1.0" standalone="no"?>
<!DOCTYPE svg PUBLIC "-//W3C//DTD SVG 1.1//EN"
"http://www.w3.org/Graphics/SVG/1.1/DTD/svg11.dtd">
<svg width="100%" height="100%" version="1.1"
xmlns="http://www.w3.org/2000/svg">
<defs>
<radialGradient id="yellow_red" cx="50%" cy="50%"
r="50%"
fx="50%" fy="50%">
<stop offset="0%" style="stop-color:yellow;
stop-opacity:1"/>
<stop offset="25%" style="stop-color:red;
stop-opacity:1"/>
```

Figure 3.21 A radial gradient applied to a rectangle shape.

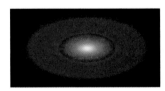

Figure 3.22 Multiple colors can be created to change the gradient.

```
   <stop offset="50%" style="stop-color:blue;
stop-opacity:1"/>
   <stop offset="100%" style="stop-color:black;
stop-opacity:1"/>
   </radialGradient>
   </defs>
   <rect width="500" height="250"
   style="fill:url(#yellow_red);
   stroke:yellow"/>
   <circle cx="250" cy="250" r="180" stroke="black"
   stroke-width="2" fill="url(#yellow_red)" />
   </svg>
```

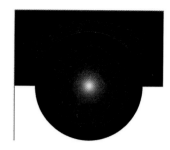

Figure 3.23 Gradient color definitions can be shared among shapes.

The results are shown in Figure 3.23.

Adding Text to Your SVG Drawings

Text can be added to your SVG drawings using the TEXT element. At its most basic, all you need to do is add the TEXT element to your SVG document, as shown in the following code and Figure 3.24.

```
<svg xmlns="http://www.w3.org/2000/svg"
    xmlns:xlink="http://www.w3.org/1999/xlink">
    <text x="100" y="40">It was the best of times</text>
</svg>
```

The x and y attributes specify where on the screen the text will appear. Formatting of the text is controlled using CSS in the style attribute. Text can have the following styles applied to it:

- Font-family—the name of the font
- Font-size—the size of the font
- Kerning—the space between letters
- Stroke—the outside color of a font
- Fill—the inside color of a font
Following is an example SVG code showing text formatting.

```
<svg xmlns="http://www.w3.org/2000/svg"
    xmlns:xlink="http://www.w3.org/1999/xlink">
    <text x="100" y="40"
        style="font-family: Arial;
            font-size: 24pt;
            stroke: red;
            fill: yellow;
            kerning: 3; "
    >It was the best of times</text>
</svg>
```

It was the best of times

Figure 3.24 Text can be easily inserted into an SVG drawing use the TEXT element.

Figure 3.25 shows the results of the code.

Text is treated as simply another image type in SVG. This allows you to add some additional visual effects. As an example, you can use a gradient as the FILL style for your text. The following SVG code exaggerates the size of the text to show a gradient fill (see Figure 3.26).

Figure 3.25 Formatted SVG text.

It was the best of times

Figure 3.26 Both linear and radial gradients can be used to style text.

It was the best

```
<svg xmlns="http://www.w3.org/2000/svg"
     xmlns:xlink="http://www.w3.org/1999/xlink">
<radialGradient id="yellow_red" cx="50%" cy="50%"
r="50%"
   fx="50%" fy="50%">
<stop offset="0%" style="stop-color:yellow;
stop-opacity:1"/>
<stop offset="25%" style="stop-color:red;
stop-opacity:1"/>
<stop offset="50%" style="stop-color:blue;
stop-opacity:1"/>
<stop offset="100%" style="stop-color:black;
stop-opacity:1"/>
</radialGradient>
  <text x="100" y="140"
        style="font-family: Arial;
               font-size  : 96pt;
               stroke     : red;
               fill       : url(#yellow_red);
        "
   >It was the best</text>
</svg>
```

SVG supports a method where you can embed a font into the document. Embedding a font in SVG is, however, tricky. The challenge is that to embed a font you must specify the exact shape of each font glyph you use. A glyph is a shape matched to a key on your keyboard. Figure 3.27 is a glyph of the letter "A."

SVG's GLYPH element draws the outline of the font and ties it to a character. This can get complex very quickly. The following is an example of what you will need to duplicate just the letter "a" as a reusable glyph in SVG.

Figure 3.27 A glyph of the letter "A."

```
<glyph unicode="a" glyph-name="a" horiz-adv-x="577"
d="M595 -324H-36V898H595V-324ZM117 27Q123 25 130 20T146
29Q154 41 159 59T166 86Q169 96 167 103T172 113Q181 115
```

```
185 106T202 97Q213 97 227 102T273 108Q306 108 320 105T347
109Q359 115 370 123T387
    127Q388 126 393 118T403 101T412 82T417 67Q420 57 426
41T451 23Q471 19 477 25T486 47Q491 60 478 71T460 96Q457
102 448 126T426 178T404 235T387 279Q382 296 372 321T351
371T332 416T321 443Q318 448 317 460T313 485T307 510T297
528Q291 533 284 528T271
    516T261 500T254 485Q253 473 257 464T261 448Q261 442 255
434T245 414Q241 405 240 397T238 381Q238 373 220 338T189
265Q177 230 176 217T172 194Q171 186 166 169T151 138Q147
128 138 112T120 78T110 44T117 27ZM366 235Q375 218 377
201T376 169Q375 163
    368 162T351 163T329 168T310 171Q280 171 269 176Q265
180 256 176T228 165Q208 158 201 159T187 164Q183 165 186
172T195 189T207 208T215 228Q217 237 224 257T240 299T255
337T261 355Q261 359 256 362T245 369Q242 370 249 377T262
392Q269 402 271 408T282
    411Q286 409 298 385T324 330T351 271T366 235ZM243
222L250 238Q254 246 257 253T261 264Q267 272 268 284Q269
292 272 302Q267 298 262 285T253 256Q247 238 243 222ZM294
186Q292 193 288 201T277 207Q272 205 265 205H257L294
186ZM201 78L340 83Q328 86 306
    86T260 83Q231 82 201 78ZM194 70Q190 60 188 53Q181
36 176 30Q172 27 169 25T165 18Q162 15 162 12Q175 23 181
31Q196 52 194 70ZM491 126Q494 122 489 136T475 174T452
232T424 303Q390 388 344 496Q383 394 414 314Q429 278 442
245T465 187T481 144T491 126Z"/>
```

To use a full alphabet you will need to create the lowercase and uppercase for each character on the keyboard. Your files for a simple font will get very large, very quickly.

Adding Interactivity and Javascript to Your SVG Drawings

You can use JavaScript to add interactivity to your SVG illustrations. You do this using the SCRIPT element in your SVG document. The following example adds a JavaScript that changes the color of a rectangle shape each time you click on it.

```
<?xml version="1.0" encoding="UTF-8" standalone="no"?>
<!DOCTYPE svg PUBLIC "-//W3C//DTD SVG 1.0//EN"
"http://www.w3.org/TR/2001/REC-SVG-20010904/DTD/svg10.
dtd">
<svg xmlns="http://www.w3.org/2000/svg"
xmlns:xlink="http://www.w3.org/1999/xlink" width="800"
height="800">
   <script type="text/ecmascript">
   <![CDATA[
     function randomColor(evt) {
     var red = Math.round(Math.random() * 255);
```

```
        var green = Math.round(Math.random() * 255);
        var blue = Math.round(Math.random() * 255);
        evt.target.setAttributeNS(null,"fill","rgb("+ red
+","+ green+","+blue+")");
        }
    ]]>
    </script>
      <rect id="myBlueRect" width="600" height="600"
x="40" y="20" fill="orange" onClick="randomColor (evt)"/>
    </svg>
```

You can see that the JavaScript is wrapped in a CDATA element. This allows the script to be correctly interpreted by the JavaScript engine running in the web browser. The `onClick` event attribute links the name of the JavaScript function with the rectangle.

Through using JavaScript you can do a lot with SVG. Some great sites that push the interactive limits of JavaScript and SVG integration are:

- *http://raphaeljs.com/*
- *http://svgkit.sourceforge.net/*
- *http://www.liquidx.net/plotkit/*
- *http://www.lutanho.net/svgvml3d/index.html*
- *http://code.google.com/p/svgweb/*

Each of these sites gives you libraries of JavaScript code that allow you to complete complex, interactive SVG presentations.

Leveraging SVG Drawing Tools

If you have gotten this far then you have realized that drawing with SVG is complex. There are, unfortunately, very few illustration tools you can use to create SVG drawings. Fortunately, the few tools that are on the market just happen to be very good.

Adobe's Illustrator has supported, since CSS2, the ability to export any illustration in SVG format. This is great news, as you can take complex drawings and import them directly to SVG.

While Illustrator will export to SVG, the open-source project InkSpace will save and edit SVG files directly. InkSpace is not as easy to use as Illustrator, but it is free, and it is certainly easier to create SVG illustrations with InkSpace than by scratch.

Sketsa is a Java-based SVG drawing tool. The tool itself is quite basic, but, again, it is better than nothing.

Finally, if you use Google's Docs to create documents online then you will be interested to know that the Insert Image feature uses SVG to create the images. Additionally, if you use a text, then Google uses the complex Glyph editor to embed the fonts for you.

The good news is that there are tools you can use to create SVG illustrations. The bad news is that there are few tools you can use to visually apply interactivity to your SVG drawings. With SVG becoming more popular for sites such as Google Maps and Wikipedia and now as a first-class citizen in HTML5, we should expect SVG authoring tools to become more common.

Adding the CANVAS Element to Your Web Page

There is a royal battle happening in the Web-o-sphere between technologies that enable you to create cool, interactive animations online. The current "king" is Adobe's Flash, with Microsoft's SilverLight coming in guns blazing. The "black horse" contender is the emerging HTML5 standard. Baked into HTML5 is a new element called CANVAS. Not sure what CANVAS is? Do you own a Mac? Most of the widgets you run on your dashboard are built with HTML5's CANVAS element.

The CANVAS element gives you the ability to build Adobe Flash–like applications without having to use Flash. It is in the early stages of development, but some of the things you can already accomplish are very impressive. If you are running Google's Chrome, FireFox, or Safari, then you will want to check out *http://www.chromeexperiments.com/*, a site that pushes the capabilities of what can be done in your browser (Figure 3.28). In particular, look at the CANVAS experiments. Is it me, or do they look very Flash-like?

In many ways, CANVAS looks and feels very similar to SVG. The very valid question is: Why two technologies that are the same? There is a fundamental difference between CANVAS and SVG. SVG is a drawing technology that creates vector images. CANVAS, on the other hand, dynamically creates bitmap images.

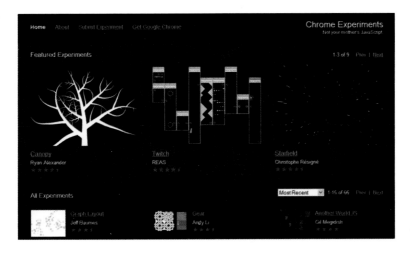

Figure 3.28 Google's ChromeExperiments.com web site showcases some of the best CANVAS solutions on the Web.

You can think of CANVAS as a programmable version of JPEG/PNG images.

Unlike SVG, a technology that has been maturing for a decade as a separate standard and only recently became included as part of HTML5, CANVAS was created as part of HTML5. The CANVAS technology was originally created by Apple to help in the creation of desktop widgets for the Mac OSX operating system. The technology was quickly included into WebKit, the technology Apple leverages to power its Safari web browser, and CANVAS has been adopted by Mozilla's FireFox, Opera's Browser, and Google's Chrome. CANVAS is a powerful drawing tool that aligns with competing technologies such as Adobe's Flash and Microsoft's SilverLight.

The only browser that currently does not support CANVAS is Microsoft's Internet Explorer. You can, however, add CANVAS support to Internet Explorer through a plug-in called ExplorerCanvas, which can be downloaded at *http://excanvas.sourceforge.net/*.

At the end of the end day, SVG is a good solution, whereas CANVAS is an exciting emerging solution. A lot of technology from Google, Apple, Opera, and Mozilla is being invested into expanding the functionality of CANVAS.

Starting with the Basics

There are two parts you need to create a visual element using CANVAS. The first is the CANVAS element itself used in your HTML. In many ways, the CANVAS element is very much the same as any other element used in HTML. Here is an example:

```
<canvas id="myCanvas" width="640" height="480">
</canvas>
```

The tag uses the new HTML5 element CANVAS as the opening and closing tag. The `width` and `height` attributes specify the size of the CANVAS space on the screen. It is the ID that is important. Here the ID is named `myCanvas`.

Using JavaScript, you can now program the illustration that will appear in the CANVAS tag. The following example creates a black, outlined square that appears in your web page using JavaScript and Canvas.

```
<html>
  <head>
    <title>Basic Canvas Drawing</title>
    <script type="text/javascript">
      function draw(){
        var canvas = document.getElementById ('myCanvas');
```

```
        if (canvas.getContext){
            var ctx = canvas.getContext('2d');
         }
        }
      </script>
      <style type="text/css">
        canvas { border: 1px solid black; }
      </style>
    </head>
    <body onLoad="draw();">
        <canvas id="myCanvas" width="150" height="150">
  </canvas>
      </body>
    </html>
```

Figure 3.29 The CANVAS element draws a simple rectangle.

Figure 3.29 shows the end result.

Stepping through the code you will see that the CANVAS element has not changed. What is modified is how the object in the CANVAS element is presented. Using JavaScript, you start a new function named `draw`. The `draw` function is constructed of a variable called `myCanvas`. The `myCanvas` variable declares that the CANVAS element is a 2D object. The distinction of 2D is important, as it is expected that a three-dimensional (3D) definition will be added to the CANVAS element as part of the WebGL 3D program.

You use Cascading Style Sheets to define the color and border thickness for the drawing. In this instance, the drawing is black with a solid 1-pixel outline.

The `onLoad` event in the BODY element triggers when the CANVAS illustration is drawn.

Controlling Shapes

The CANVAS element does not have the same rich collection of primitive drawing objects you find in SVG. The only primitive drawing object is a rectangle. This does not limit what you can draw, as CANVAS leverages an alternative, rich collection of path drawing functions that allow you to create complex paths, arcs, Bezier curves, and quadratic curves that you can use as the basis of your illustrations.

The rectangle shape is built of four basic parts:
- X—starting position of the rectangle along the X axis
- Y—starting position of the rectangle along the Y axis
- Width—width of the rectangle
- Height—height of the rectangle

The following is an example of a solid rectangle shape:

```
myRectangle.fillRect(15,15,100,100);
```

This description places the rectangle as starting 15 pixels in from the left side of the CANVAS element (the X axis), 15 pixels from the top of the CANVAS element (the Y axis), and with a width and height of 100 pixels each. You need to add the following HTML to view the rectangle.

```
<html>
  <head>
    <title>Basic Canvas Drawing</title>
<script>
    function draw(){
    var canvas = document.getElementById ('myCanvas');
    if (canvas.getContext){
      var myRectangle = canvas.getContext('2d');
        myRectangle.fillRect(15,15,100,100);
      }
    }
</script>
        <style type="text/css">
          canvas { border: 1px solid black; }
        </style>
  </head>
  <body onLoad="draw();">
        <canvas id="myCanvas" width="150" height="150">
</canvas>
      </body>
    </html>
```

The code describing the rectangle must be placed in the SCRIPT section of your HTML page. Below you will see that a variable called `myRectangle` is declared on line 6. Line 7 describes what the variable `myRectangle` will look like. The CANVAS element in the HTML body illustrates where the rectangle will be drawn.

There are three different types of rectangle primitive you can draw. The previous example demonstrates how to use the `fillRect` shape. You can also draw `clearRect` and `strokeRect`.

- `clearRect` draws a transparent rectangle on the screen.
- `strokeRect` draws only the outline of the rectangle on the screen.

Following is how you write the JavaScript describing how to draw the three different rectangle primitives.

```
myRectangle.fillRect(15,15,100,100);
myRectangle.clearRect(20,20,60,60);
myRectangle.strokeRect(25,25,50,50);
```

All three rectangles can be combined with JavaScript and presented within your web page, as follows.

```
<html>
  <head>
    <title>Basic Canvas Drawing</title>
<script>
    function draw(){
```

```
      var canvas = document.getElementById('myCanvas');
      if (canvas.getContext){
        var myRectangle = canvas.getContext('2d');
        myRectangle.fillRect(15,15,100,100);
        myRectangle.clearRect(20,20,60,60);
        myRectangle.strokeRect(25,25,50,50);
      }
    }
  </script>
      <style type="text/css">
        canvas { border: 1px solid black; }
      </style>
    </head>
    <body onLoad="draw();">
      <canvas id="myCanvas" width="150" height="150">
</canvas>
    </body>
    </html>
```

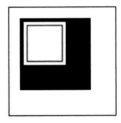

Figure 3.30 There are three different types of rectangle primitive you can draw using the CANVAS element.

See Figure 3.30 for how the rectangles appear. All other drawings are created from paths you must describe.

Drawing Simple Shapes

Shapes are described in JavaScript and presented in the CANVAS element. The structure for describing a shape takes the following basic methods:

- beginPath
- moveTo
- closePath
- fill

The role of the beginPath method is to declare the start of the shape. Following the beginPath method is where you start drawing your shape. The moveTo method is used to describe that you have moved your virtual pen and are starting to draw a new shape. Following the moveTo method is where you describe the structure of the shape. The following code demonstrates how a triangle is started and drawn.

```
myShape.beginPath();
myShape.moveTo(750,500);
myShape.lineTo(1000,750);
myShape.lineTo(1000,250);
```

The first line declares the start of the shape. The second line is the moveTo method stating that the drawing will start at 750 pixels from the left (X axis) and down 500 pixels (Y axis).

The triangle itself is a closed shape. By default you do not need to use the closePath method. You use the closePath method to close a shape when it is not clear where the closure for the shape is.

Figure 3.31 A simple triangle is drawn using the CANVAS element.

The final method is the fill method. Together, the code looks as follows, and Figure 3.31 shows the end result.

```
<html>
  <head>
    <title>Basic Canvas Drawing</title>
<script>
    function draw(){
    var canvas = document.getElementById ('myCanvas');
    if (canvas.getContext){
       var myShape = canvas.getContext('2d');
myShape.beginPath();
myShape.moveTo(750,500);
myShape.lineTo(1000,750);
myShape.lineTo(1000,250);
myShape.fill();
    }
}
</script>
  </head>
  <body onLoad="draw();">
    <canvas id="myCanvas" width="1500" height="1500">
</canvas>
  </body>
</html>
```

The `lineTo` property describes the shape. There are four tools you can use to describe your shape:
- Lines
- Arcs
- Bezier curves
- Quadratic curves

These four shape drawing tools allow you to create any type of shape.

Drawing Lines

The most simple path to describe is the line. Using the `lineTo` property you describe the starting and ending X and Y axes positions. For instance, the following code describes a basic rectangle.

```
myTriangle.beginPath();
myTriangle.moveTo(10, 10);
myTriangle.lineTo(500, 10);
myTriangle.lineTo(10, 500);
myTriangle.lineTo(10, 10);
```

The `lineTo` property describes the three lines used to create position:

```
myTriangle.lineTo(500, 10);
myTriangle.lineTo(10, 500);
myTriangle.lineTo(10, 10);
```

Figure 3.32 shows what the triangle will look like.

The following code shows how to present the triangle shape in your web browser.

```
<!DOCTYPE html> <html lang="en">
  <head> <meta charset="utf-8">
    <title>Drawing a Rectangle</title>
    <script type="text/javascript"><!--
window.addEventListener('load', function () {
  var elem = document.getElementById('myCanvas');
  if (!elem || !elem.getContext) {
    return;
  }
  var myTriangle = elem.getContext('2d');
  if (!myTriangle) {
    return;
  }
  myTriangle.fillStyle = "orange";
  myTriangle.strokeStyle = "yellow";
  myTriangle.lineWidth = 7;
  myTriangle.beginPath();
  myTriangle.moveTo(10, 10);
  myTriangle.lineTo(500, 10);
  myTriangle.lineTo(10, 500);
  myTriangle.lineTo(10, 10);
  myTriangle.fill();
  myTriangle.stroke();
  myTriangle.closePath();
}, false);
    // --></script>
  </head> <body style="background-color:#000;">
<canvas id="myCanvas" width="500" height="500">
</canvas>
    </body> </html>
```

Figure 3.32 The lineTo method allows you to draw lines in a CANVAS image.

Using the `lineTo` property allows you to draw simple, line-based shapes.

Creating Arcs

When you want to draw a circle you use the Arc method. An arc is drawn with six different properties:

- `x`—the coordinates for the circle's center along the X axis.
- `y`—the coordinates for the circle's center along the Y axis.
- `radius`—the size of the circle.
- `startAngle`—the start point of the arc.
- `endAngle`—the end point of the arc.
- `anticlockwise`—a Boolean value that dictates the direction the circle is drawn.

The following code describes the structure of an arc:

```
context.arc(260,260,250,0,7,true);
```

Figure 3.33 The Arc method allows you to draw circles.

Figure 3.33 shows the circle as it is drawn on the page.

The following code embeds the Arc method and instructions into a CANVAS drawing.

```
<!DOCTYPE html>
<html>
  <head>
    <title>Canvas - Creating a Circle</title>
    <script type="text/javascript">
      window.onLoad = function() {
        var drawingCanvas = document.getElementById
('myCircle');
        if(drawingCanvas && drawingCanvas.getContext) {
          var context = drawingCanvas.getContext('2d');
          context.strokeStyle = "yellow";
          context.fillStyle = "red";
          context.lineWidth = 20;
          context.beginPath();
          context.arc(260,260,250,0,Math.PI*2,true);
          context.closePath();
          context.stroke();
          context.fill();
        }
      }
    </script>
  </head>
  <body>
    <canvas id="myCircle" width="550" height="550">
    </canvas>
  </body>
</html>
```

Figure 3.34 The Arc method can be controlled visually with the same controls you use for other CANVAS drawing methods.

Figure 3.34 illustrates how you can add color to your circles.

In addition to the Arc method you also can add Bezier and quadratic curves, both of which are mathematical calculations for creating an image. Bezier curves were developed by French mathematician Pierre Bezier in 1962. A Bezier curve is calculated from a parametric curve describing a parabola. Figure 3.35 shows the four points used to create a Bezier curve.

A quadratic curve is based on the Bezier curve. The difference is that the quadratic curve is constructed of three points of definition instead of just one. It can be difficult to draw complex, Bezier curve images in CANVAS for a single, simple reason: There are no visual drawing tools, such as Adobe Illustrator, that export images that can be read by the CANVAS element.

Adding Color

So you now have basic shapes on the page. Big deal, right? Using JavaScript you can now begin to programmatically

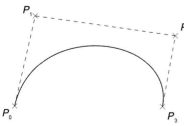

Figure 3.35 A Bezier curve.

paint your objects. The following shows two semitransparent intersecting squares. You will see that the fill color is a CSS style.

```
<html>
  <head>
    <script type="application/x-javascript">
    function draw() {
      var canvas = document.getElementById ("myCanvas");
        if (canvas.getContext) {
        var ctx = canvas.getContext("2d");
        ctx.fillStyle = "rgb(0,0,500)";
        ctx.fillRect (10, 10, 150, 150);
        ctx.fillStyle = "rgba(0, 300, 0, 0.5)";
        ctx.fillRect (75, 75, 150, 150);
        }
      }
  </script>
</head>
<body onLoad="draw();">
    <canvas id="myCanvas" width="300"
    height="300"></canvas>
  </body>
</html>
```

The fillStyle method allows you to apply CSS style formatting. Leveraging CSS increases the amount of visual control you have on your drawings on the screen. As with SVG you can use any of the CSS color naming formats such as Hex and RGB.

Linear and radial gradients can also be applied to CANVAS images. As with SVG, the linear and radial gradients inherit how CSS implements gradients. The gradient construction is developed by first creating a shape, giving the gradient a name, defining the gradient, and then applying the gradient.

The first step is to create a shape. The following is a simple CANVAS rectangle:

```
myRectangle.fillRect(10,10,650,650);
```

The next step is to create a new variable that declares a new gradient. The following line creates a new gradient that is named verticalGradient. The name is arbitrary; what is not arbitrary is the description of the gradient type that follows the name.

```
var verticalGradient = myRectangle.createLinearGradient
(0,0,0,650);
```

Here you are associating the gradient with the CANVAS object myRectangle. At this point the gradient will not paint the image that comes later—the code at this point merely associates the gradient and the image. The property createLinearGradient dictates where the gradient will paint an object. The values in the parenthesis are the X and Y axes and height and width.

A gradient must have at least two colors. The following will paint a gradient color that starts red and then transitions 50% through the image to yellow.

```
verticalGradient.addColorStop(0, 'red');
verticalGradient.addColorStop(0.5, 'yellow');
```

The final step is to use the `paintStyle` property to paint the gradient into the rectangle:

```
myRectangle.fillStyle = verticalGradient;
```

The whole CANVAS script looks as follows.

```
<html>
  <head>
    <title>Linear Gradient</title>
    <script type="application/x-javascript">
      function draw() {
        var myRectangle = document.getElementById
('myCanvas').getContext('2d');
        var verticalGradient = myRectangle.
createLinearGradient(0,0,0,650);
        verticalGradient.addColorStop(0, 'red');
        verticalGradient.addColorStop(0.5, 'yellow');
        myRectangle.fillStyle = verticalGradient;
        myRectangle.fillRect(10,10,650,650);
      }
    </script>
  </head>
  <body onLoad="draw();">
      <canvas id="myCanvas" width="800" height="800">
</canvas>
    </body>
</html>
```

Figure 3.36 Linear gradients can be applied to CANVAS images.

Figure 3.37 A radial gradient applied to a CANVAS image.

See Figure 3.36 for an example image.

As with the linear gradient, the radial gradient is painted onto an image and the gradient must be constructed of at least two colors. As with SVG, the radial gradients require starting and stopping radius definitions, size, and position. The following creates a radial gradient called `myRadialGradient` with three colors: red, yellow, and blue.

```
var myRadialGradient = myCircle.
createRadialGradient(0,150,150,0,140,90);
  myRadialGradient.addColorStop(0, 'red');
  myRadialGradient.addColorStop(0.9, 'yellow');
  myRadialGradient.addColorStop(1, 'blue');
```

You need to add the gradient to your CANVAS description, as follows. See also Figure 3.37.

```
<html>
  <head>
    <title>A canvas radialGradient example</title>
    <script type="application/x-javascript">
      function draw() {
        var myCircle = document.getElementById
('myCanvas').getContext('2d');
        var myRadialGradient = myCircle.
createRadialGradient(0,150,150,0,140,90);
        myRadialGradient.addColorStop(0, 'red');
        myRadialGradient.addColorStop(0.9, 'yellow');
        myRadialGradient.addColorStop(1, 'blue');
        myCircle.fillStyle = myRadialGradient;
        myCircle.fillRect(0,0,450,450);
      }
    </script>
  </head>
  <body onLoad="draw();">
    <canvas id="myCanvas" width="500" height="500">
</canvas>
  </body>
</html>
```

Gradients are useful for creating depth on an object. Careful use of gradients can simulate a 3D environment.

Adding Animation to CANVAS Images

Animation can be added to CANVAS images. As you can imagine, animation requires additional work. To make your life easier there is a great JavaScript library called CAKE (Canvas Animation Kit Experiment) that you can download at *http:// code.google.com/p/cakejs/*. Using the CAKE library you can easily create CANVAS-based animation. The following code will create a pulsing blue circle.

```
window.onLoad = function()
{
    var CAKECanvas = new Canvas(document.body, 600, 400);
    var myCircle = new Circle(100,
        {
            id: 'myCircle',
            x: CAKECanvas.width/3,
            y: CAKECanvas.height/2,
            stroke: 'blue',
            strokeWidth: 20,
            endAngle: Math.PI*2
        }
    );
```

```
myCircle.addFrameListener(
  function(t, dt)
    {
          this.scale = Math.sin(t/1000);
    }
);
CAKECanvas.append(myCircle);
};
```

The final step you need to take to ensure that your animation works is to download the CAKE library files to your web site. The files can be downloaded at *http://glimr.rubyforge.org/cake/*. You will need to save the CAKE JS library to your web site. In the HEAD section of your web page you will need to make a linked reference to the CAKE library. It will look like this:

```
<script type="text/javascript" src="cake.js">
</script>
```

To accomplish the animation use the Scale method. The effect is very similar to Adobe's Flash, but with the benefit of running correctly on web browsers found on mobile devices such as the iPhone, MyTouch, and Palm Pre.

The introduction of CANVAS and SVG gives you great opportunities to create complex and compelling illustrations programmatically inside of your HTML5 web pages. It is fair to say that CANVAS is still growing in technical scope. Expect additions and changes to the technology over the next few years. A big addition will be the inclusion of 3D within CANVAS.

What You Have Learned

This article introduced you to scalable vector graphics (SVG) and the CANVAS element. These two technologies enable you to programmatically build images inside your web pages without needing graphic tools such as Adobe Illustrator, Flash, or PhotoShop.

PROJECT 3: INSERTING VIDEO INTO YOUR WEB DESIGN

There is no doubt that video is a central player in HTML5. Sites such as Hulu, YouTube, and Vimeo serve millions of customers every day. The new VIDEO element allows you to easily add video to your web site. The focus of this project chapter is to take a Microsoft PowerPoint slideshow, convert it into a video, and place it in your web site using the new VIDEO element.

You will be building on to the web site you started with the previous two projects. Files for the project can be downloaded from *www.visualizetheweb.com*.

Creating the Video

The first step is to create the video you will be using in the project site. For this project you will be taking an existing PowerPoint slideshow and converting it to video.

The PowerPoint slideshow is a basic, three-slide presentation (Figure 3.1Proj). Open up the document "2010 Report.pptx" to view the presentation.

Creating Video

There are many ways in which you can create video. Some tools that you can use include Windows Live Movie Maker, iMovie, and Premiere.

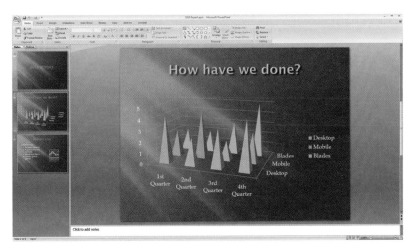

Figure 3.1Proj The PowerPoint slideshow that will be used in your web site.

HTML5. doi: 10.1016/B978-0-240-81328-8.00003-3

Figure 3.2Proj E.M. PowerPoint Converter.

There are many tools you can use to convert PowerPoint to video. For this presentation I have used E.M. PowerPoint Convertor (Figure 3.2Proj). The free version will allow you to convert PowerPoint to AVI, WMV, and MPEG video.

To save you time, you will find a video that has been created in AVI format included with the files for this project (Figure 3.3Proj). Currently, AVI is a very popular format for creating videos. It is very likely that this is a format you are using.

Converting the Video to Ogg Format

After you download the video you need to convert it into a format that will be readable in HTML5. There are two formats you can choose: Ogg and MPEG4. The tool you are going to use to create the Ogg Theora video is Firefogg.

To use Firefogg you must have FireFox 3.5 or later installed. If you do, then go to *www.firefog.com*, where you will be asked to install a plug-in (Figure 3.4Proj). When you have installed the plug-in, your browser will ask you to restart—go ahead and do that. Now, go to *http://firefogg.org/make/index.html* to start the process of converting the video (Figure 3.5Proj).

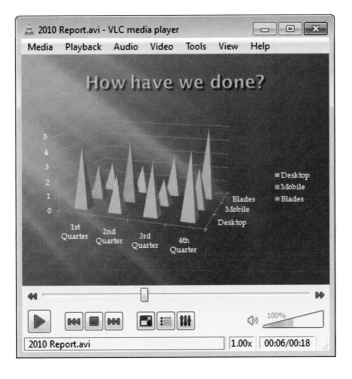

Figure 3.3Proj The video is now in an AVI file format.

Figure 3.4Proj Firefogg is a web site that uses a plug-in in FireFox to convert videos into Ogg Theora format.

Press the button to select a file. A window will open allowing you to search through your hard drive. Select the AVI file you created earlier.

To keep things simple, we are going to use just the basic settings for converting your video, which means, at this point,

Figure 3.5Proj Creating an Ogg Theora video at Firefogg is completed within the web page.

all you need to do is select the Save Ogg button to create the Ogg Theora video. The final result is a video packaged with the file name "2010 report.ogv." See Figures 3.6Proj through 3.8Proj.

The next step is to embed the video file directly into your web page.

Figure 3.6Proj Firefogg gives you the opportunity to modify many settings before you create the Ogg Theora video.

Figure 3.7Proj A progress bar tells you how long the video conversion process will take.

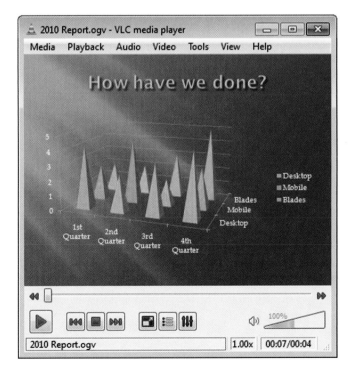

Figure 3.8Proj The Ogg Theora–encoded video is identical in quality to the original AVI file.

Embedding the Video into the Web Page

Inserting the Ogg Theora video into your web page is very easy to do with HTML5. Let's go ahead and add the code you need.

Open the file "news.html" and locate the code for the second headline. Change the headline to read:

```
<H2>2010 Annual Report</H2>
```

Now, let's go ahead and insert the HTML code that will allow the Ogg Theora video you created earlier to play back correctly (Figure 3.9Proj).

```
<video controls>
<source src='2010 Report.ogv'>
</video>
```

Figure 3.9Proj The Ogg Theora is now embedded into your web page.

You can now save your web page and view it in FireFox or Chrome. The video you created is now embedded into your web page with standard playback controls. It's that easy.

The challenge that you are now faced with is getting your video to play back on Apple's Safari and Microsoft's IE9. Both browsers *do not* support Ogg Theora. Arghh! Split standards.

Past battles between competing technologies such as Real-Networks versus Microsoft's media formats require that you write complex scripts to detect which plug-in was installed. This is no problem for the new VIDEO element.

To support accurate playback of video on Safari and IE9 you need to use the other media standard: MPEG4. The first step you need to take is to convert the original AVI video file into an MPEG4. As with your Ogg Theora conversion, there is a Web solution for that, as follows.

1. Go to *www.media-convert.com* (Figure 3.10Proj).
2. The default setting is Local File Conversion. In the top left corner you can choose a file from your hard drive. Select the AVI file used in the Ogg Theora conversion.
3. The Input Format tool allows you to pick the file type you are uploading. This helps with the conversion process. You will see that there are dozens of file types you can choose from (Figure 3.11Proj). Select the AVI format.
4. The Convertor tool is as easy to use as it looks. What is amazing is the ever-increasing number of file formats you can convert too. In the Output section of the page, choose which file type you would like to convert to—there are 20 different types (Figure 3.12Proj). You want to select MPEG4.

Figure 3.10Proj The *www. media-convert.com* online service will convert video from one format to another.

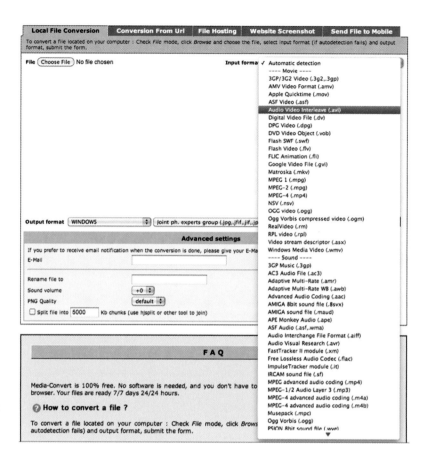

Figure 3.11Proj You can upload almost any type of video and audio file.

5. Enter your email address into the Email form field. Select the OK button to start the video conversion process. An email will be sent to your inbox when the file is converted from AVI to MPEG4. The link allows you to download the file.

6. Save the new MPEG4 file to the same folder with the Ogg Theora video file. Now you need to add one line of code as follows to the VIDEO element to include the new MPEG video file. The second source reference will play a file if the browser does not support the first source.

```
<video controls>
<source src='2010 Report.ogv'>
<source src='2010 Report.mp4'>
</video>
```

So, this is all great, but the user interface controls are not consistent from one web browser to another. This can all be changed with a little JavaScript and CSS3 magic.

Let's start with the JavaScript. You can do a lot with JavaScript, but in this example you are going to add a simple Play/Pause

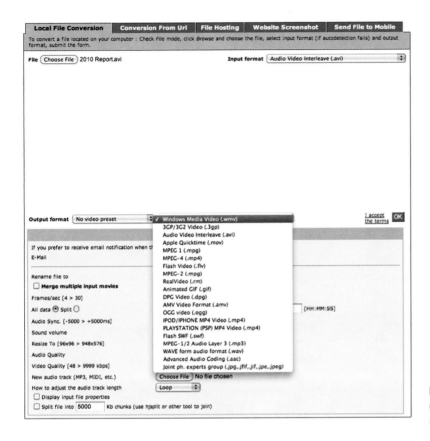

Figure 3.12Proj There are 20 different output formats you can use to convert the AVI file.

button. The following example will look for an element on the screen using the VIDEO element. When it does, it will use the VIDEO DOM objects `play` and `pause`. Enter the following script into the HEAD element of the web page.

```
<script>
function playPauseVideo() {
  var myVideo = document.getElementsByTagName('video')
[0];
  if (myVideo.paused)
    myVideo.play();
  else
    myVideo.pause();
}
</script>
```

Under the VIDEO element in the web page you are now going to add the Play/Pause button. When you press the button the video will either play or pause.

```
<a href="#" onClick="playPauseVideo()"
class="mediaButtons">Play/Pause</a>
```

You can, at this point, leave the design. But, this is HTML5. You can dress up the button with a little CSS3. Place the following CSS into the HEAD element of your page.

```
<style>
.mediaButtons {
    background: #999;
    margin-left: 10px;
    display: inline;
    border: 4px solid #CCC;
    display: block;
    line-height: 32px;
    color: #fff;
    font-family: arial, sans-serif;
    font-size: 14px;
    font-weight: bold;
    float: left;
    text-decoration: none;
    padding: 0 10px;
    text-shadow: -1px -1px 6px rgba(0, 0, 0, 0.6), -1px
-1px 1px #000;
    -moz-border-radius: 10px;
    -webkit-border-radius: 10px;
    border-radius: 10px;
    -moz-box-shadow: 0px 10px 20px rgba(0, 0, 0, 0.5);
    -webkit-box-shadow: 0px 10px 20px rgba(0, 0, 0, 0.5);
    box-shadow: 0px 10px 20px rgba(0, 0, 0, 0.5);
    background-image: -webkit-gradient(linear, left top,
left bottom, from(rgba(255, 255, 255, 0.8)), to(rgba(255,
255, 255, 0)), color-stop(30%, rgba(255, 255, 255, 0.4)),
color-stop(50%, rgba(255, 255, 255, 0.2)));
    background-image: -moz-linear-gradient(-90deg,
rgba(255, 255, 255, 0.8), rgba(255, 255, 255, 0.4) 30%,
rgba(255, 255, 255, 0.2) 50%, rgba(255, 255, 255, 0));
    }
</style>
```

Finally, you will want to remove the automatic controls from the video. The VIDEO element should now look like this with no controls attribute (Figure 3.13Proj).

```
<video>
    <source src='../media/2010 Report.ogv'>
    <source src='../media/2010 Report.mp4'>
</video>
```

Using CSS has two benefits on this page: First, the playback design is consistent from one browser to another; second, you can use the same CSS styles with the AUDIO element.

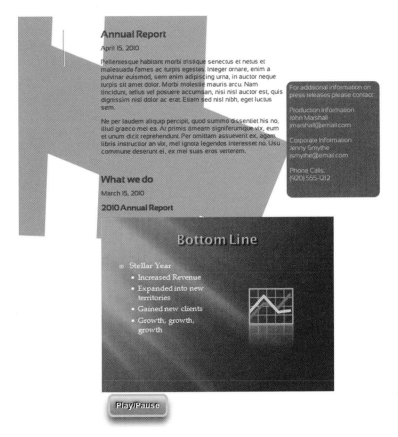

Figure 3.13Proj CSS is used to create a stylized Play/Pause button.

Adding Audio to Your Web Page

Audio is added to HTML in almost exactly the same way as video. Also, as with video, there is a conflict of audio standards between Ogg Vorbis and MPEG4. Again, as with the VIDEO element, you can use the `source` attribute to link different media types.

Interestingly, even though MP3 is supported on almost all computers, FireFox does not play back MP3 audio. You have to use Ogg Theora audio. The *www.media-convert.com* web site allows you to convert an audio file from MP3 to Ogg Theora.

Add the following code below your video for an audio broadcast.

```
<audio controls>
<source src='2010AudioReport.oga'>
<source src='2010AudioReport.mp3'>
</audio>
```

How easy is that? Including the `controls` attribute also adds the default controls to allow you to play and stop the audio file. However, do not use the default audio controls. You want to use controls that look the same as the VIDEO element.

Add the following button below the audio file.

```
<a href="#" onClick="playPauseAudio()"
class="mediaButtons">Play/Pause</a>
```

The button is very similar to the button that plays the video. You can see that the button uses the same CSS file to help style it. The difference is the reference to a new function, the `playPauseAudio` function. The function to play audio is very similar to video. The difference with the following script is that you are referencing the AUDIO element.

```
function playPauseAudio() {
  var myAudio = document.getElementsByTagName('audio')
[0];
  if (myAudio.paused)
  myAudio.play();
  else
  myAudio.pause();
}
```

At this point you can save your work and view your new web page. You have easily added audio and video to your web site.

Summary

As you can see from this project, the code needed to add video to your web page is not very complicated. The hardest part is the actual creation of the video in the first place. This is the objective of HTML5 video support. You should not be distracted by the complexities of inserting video into a web page; your focus should be on the creation of the content.

As with video, audio is now becoming much easier to work with. Also, as with video, the challenge you have is the two different audio CODECs being supported by the different browsers: Ogg and MPEG4. The good news is that you can use the new `source` attribute with your VIDEO or AUDIO element to target different file types supported by Mozilla's FireFox, Google's Chrome, Apple's Safari, or Microsoft's Internet Explorer 9.

Rich media is prevalent on the Web. Adding it to your web site is now as easy as inserting an image.

HTML5 RICH MEDIA FOUNDATION

In the last five years, high-speed Internet connections have become the norm for residential users and businesses across the globe. It is even expected that mobile phones can receive high-speed data feeds. Gone are the days of dial-up Internet.

The ability to push more data down Internet "pipes" now enables you to access richer content online above and beyond text and images. Two formats that benefit from higher bandwidth rates are audio and video. To this end, HTML5 is now making video and audio elements first-class citizens alongside the IMG element for images and text on your web page.

In this article you will find out how to use the VIDEO and AUDIO elements in your web pages, how to create content that will play back through your web pages, and how to add interactivity via JavaScript to the new elements.

Working with VIDEO and AUDIO Tags

There are two parts to controlling rich media content: the client and the server. In this section you will learn the details of how to control the client piece, the HTML5 VIDEO and AUDIO tags, and review the different ways media can be delivered by servers.

Unless you have not noticed, there is a lot of video on the Internet. From sites such as Hulu to Vimeo to the massive YouTube, video is the centerpiece to our digital world (Figure 4.1). To address this demand, HTML5 includes support for two new elements: VIDEO and AUDIO.

Today, the centerpiece technology for delivering media online is Adobe's Flash. Adobe has done a very good job of being a good Internet citizen in providing a technology that is easy to use and easy to consume. The challenge you have is that adding Flash-based video to your web page is still hard to complete. To add Flash-based media content yourself you need three things:

HTML5. doi: 10.1016/B978-0-240-81328-8.00009-4

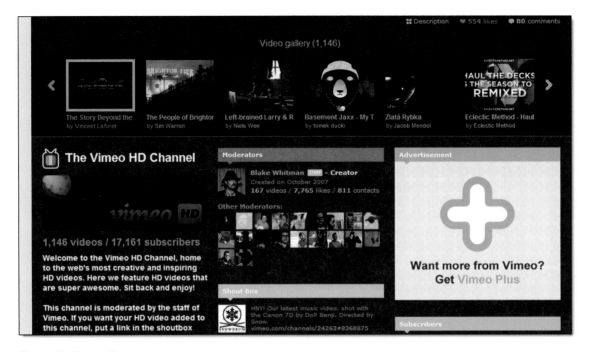

Figure 4.1 Vimeo allows uploading and broadcasting videos online.

- Video or audio files
- Flash authoring tool
- Some HTML expertise with Flash

As an example, to create a video that is embedded in Flash you need to take the following steps:

1. Open a Flash authoring tool (such as CS4 or CS5).
2. Import a digital version of your video.
3. Use the Adobe video conversion wizard and convert the video to a format that will play back in Flash.
4. Publish your Flash movie (you now have two files: a video file and a Flash SWF file).
5. Upload both files to your server.
6. Add the correct HTML to your web page.

Adding the HTML is the hard part with Flash. Following is an example of how complex it can be to add a Flash video to your web page.

```
<div id="flashContent">
<object classid="clsid:d27cdb6e-ae6d-11cf-
96b8-444553540000" width="550" height="400"
id="FlashVideo" align="middle">
    <param name="movie" value="FlashVideo.swf"/>
    <param name="quality" value="high"/>
    <param name="bgcolor" value="#ffffff"/>
    <param name="play" value="true"/>
    <param name="loop" value="true"/>
    <param name="wmode" value="window"/>
```

```
<param name="scale" value="showall"/>
<param name="menu" value="true"/>
<param name="devicefont" value="false"/>
<param name="salign" value=""/>
<param name="allowScriptAccess" value= "sameDomain"/>
<!--[if !IE]>-->
<object type="application/x-shockwave-flash"
data="FlashVideo.swf" width="550" height="400">
<param name="movie" value="FlashVideo.swf"/>
<param name="quality" value="high"/>
<param name="bgcolor" value="#ffffff"/>
<param name="play" value="true"/>
<param name="loop" value="true"/>
<param name="wmode" value="window"/>
<param name="scale" value="showall"/>
<param name="menu" value="true"/>
<param name="devicefont" value="false"/>
<param name="salign" value=""/>
<param name="allowScriptAccess" value="sameDomain"/>
<!--<![endif]-->
<a href="http://www.adobe.com/go/getflash">
<img src="http://www.adobe.com/images/shared/download_
buttons/get_flash_player.gif" alt="Get Adobe Flash player"/>
</a>
<!--[if !IE]>-->
</object>
<!--<![endif]-->
</object>
</div>
```

In contrast to using Flash CS4 to create the video you can also use web sites such as Vimeo to convert the video. Following is an example of the HTML code that Vimeo generates to enable you to syndicate your media content.

```
<object width="400" height="300"><param
name="allowfullscreen" value="true"/><param
name="allowscriptaccess" value="always"/>
<param name="movie" value="http://vimeo.com/moogaloop.
swf?clip_id=8341236&amp;server=vimeo.com&amp;show_
title=1&amp;show_byline=1&amp;show_ portrait=0&amp;color=&
amp;fullscreen=1"/>
<embed src="http://vimeo.com/moogaloop.
swf?clip_id=8341236&amp;server=vimeo.com&amp;show_
title=1&amp;show_byline=1&amp;show_portrait=0&amp;col
or=&amp;fullscreen=1" type="application/x-shockwave-
flash" allowfullscreen="true" allowscriptaccess="always"
width="400" height="300"></embed>
</object>
```

Both services generate complex code. HTML5 addresses this problem dramatically. The native Flash authoring tool generates over 30 lines of code to embed a Flash movie that, in turn, embeds a video file. In HTML5 all you need is a video file and one line of code using the new VIDEO element, as follows:

```
<video src="videoFile.mp4"></video>
```

Yes, it really is that simple.

Using HTML5 Rich Media Tags

HTML5 wants to make it easier for you to add video and audio using the new VIDEO and AUDIO elements. The two new elements are supported by the following web browsers:

- FireFox 3.5, 3.6+
- Google Chrome
- Apple's Safari 3.0, 4.0+
- Opera Web Browser 10.5+

As you can see, there is no support for the VIDEO and AUDIO elements in Internet Explorer. If you have already read the previous articles in this book, then Microsoft's lack of support for HTML5 will come as no shock.

Controlling Video with VIDEO Tags

Using the VIDEO element is as easy as follows:

```
<video src="myMovie.ogg"></video>
```

That's it. There is no need to add complex OBJECT elements and parameters. If you want to get crazy you can use the following different attributes for the VIDEO element:

- `autoplay`—the video will play immediately if already downloaded in your cache
- `controls`—a simple playback head will be added with VCR-like Play/Pause controls
- `height` and `width`
- `loop`—you can loop the video

To get the most out of your video playback you will want to use some of these attributes. For instance, if you want your video to start playing when the web page has finished loading you will want to use the `autoplay` attribute as follows:

```
<video src="google_main.mp4" autoplay></video>
```

The video will not automatically play if you do not include it. A second useful attribute to add is the `controls` attribute, as follows:

```
<video src="google_main.mp4" autoplay controls></video>
```

You will notice that the `controls` attribute looks different in each browser. Figure 4.2 shows the `controls` attribute used in

Google Chrome, Figure 4.3 shows the attribute in Apple's Safari, and Figure 4.4 shows the attribute in FireFox.

Each browser uses a different playback video engine, and each engine has its own default control style. This can become a problem when it comes to presenting a video playback experience that is consistent from one browser to another. There is a way to override this issue.

Figure 4.2 The playback video controls in Google Chrome.

Figure 4.3 The playback video controls in Apple's Safari.

Figure 4.4 The playback video controls in FireFox.

The VIDEO and AUDIO elements can be controlled with JavaScript. This means you can control your media using your own custom controls. As an example, the following steps will allow you to add a custom Play/Pause button to your video.

You have to start with a blank HTML5 page as follows.

```
<!DOCTYPE HTML>
<html>
<head>
<title>Video in HTML5</title>
</head>
<body>
</body>
</html>
```

In the BODY element section add the VIDEO element and link to a video file as follows.

```
<video autoplay>
  <source src="google_main.mp4">
</video>
```

You can see here that the video file does not have any attributes. These you will add programmatically with JavaScript.

Next, add an ANCHOR tag.

```
<a href="#">Play/Pause</a>
```

The tag uses the # to create a fake link. Selecting this link will not do anything.

Now, the next piece is to add the JavaScript to allow the Play/Pause text to control the video. After the VIDEO element add the following JavaScript.

```
<script>
  var video = document.getElementsByTagName ('video')[0];
</script>
```

This script gives the VIDEO element a name that you can reference. The final step is to add a script to the ANCHOR tag.

```
<a href="#" onClick="if (video.paused) video.play();
else video.pause()">Play/Pause</a>
```

The ANCHOR element uses an `onClick` event to trigger an if/else JavaScript command. Simply put, if the button is pressed and the video has not been played, then the video will start to play. Otherwise, if the video is playing and the button is selected it will pause the video. All together your code will look as follows.

```
<!DOCTYPE HTML>
<html>
<head>
<title>Video in HTML5</title>
</head>
<body>
<video autoplay>
  <source src="google_main.mp4">
</video>
  <script>
    var video = document.getElementsByTagName ('video')[0];
    </script>
  <br/>
  <a href="#" onClick="if (video.paused) video.play();
else video.pause()">Play/Pause</a>
  </p>
</body>
</html>
```

As Figure 4.5 shows, the custom control does not look too fancy, but what you have is a control that is consistent from browser to browser. See also Figure 4.6.

An additional benefit to using JavaScript to control the presentation of your controls is that you can use CSS to style the controls (Figure 4.7). The following code is a basic style applied to our video controls.

Figure 4.5 Creating a custom
video playback control using
JavaScript previewed in Google
Chrome.

Figure 4.6 The custom
JavaScript control looks the
same in Apple's Safari.

Figure 4.7 Using CSS to control the presentation of the Play/Pause controls.

```
<!DOCTYPE HTML>
<html>
<head>
<title>Video in HTML5</title>
<style type="text/css">
a {
    font-family: "Franklin Gothic Medium", "Arial
Narrow", Arial, sans-serif;
    font-size: large;
    text-decoration: none;
    color: #C0C0C0;
}
h1 {
    font-family: "Franklin Gothic Medium", "Arial
Narrow", Arial, sans-serif;
    font-size: 24pt;
    color: #C0C0C0;
}
body {
    background-color: #000000;
}
</style>
</head>
<body>
<h1 align="center">Video with Custom JavaScript
Controls</h1><p align="center">
<video autoplay>
  <source src="google_main.mp4">
</video>
<script>
  var video = document.getElementsByTagName ('video')[0];
</script>
```

```
<br/>
<a href="#" onClick="if (video.paused) video.play();
else video.pause()"> Play/Pause</a>
</p>
</body>
</html>
```

There are other controls you can add to your VIDEO element. For instance, you can add a playback head to track where you are in the video, fast forward, and rewind as well. You can see an example of HTML5 video support with custom controls at YouTube (*http://www.youtube.com/html5*; see also Figure 4.8).

There is no doubt that, as the HTML5 VIDEO element matures, tools to quickly create skins and themes for video players will be developed.

Figure 4.8 YouTube's experimental HTML5 video page.

Controlling Audio with AUDIO Tags

Audio can be controlled in exactly the same way as video in HTML5. Leveraging the new AUDIO element, you can embed audio files directly into your web page. Again, as with the VIDEO element, the process of embedding audio into your web page is very easy. In order to embed audio into your web page you need either an MP3/AAC or Ogg Theora–formatted audio file.

```
<audio autoplay controls>
  <source src="sample.mp3">
</audio>
```

Figure 4.9 The playback controls for AUDIO are the same as those for VIDEO.

In the previous code, the AUDIO element has the `autoplay` and `controls` attributes added. You will see in Figure 4.9 that the controls are stripped-down versions of the AUDIO element controls. As with the VIDEO element controls, there is nothing too fancy.

As with video, you can control the audio playing back using JavaScript and some CSS. Let's start with using JavaScript before we make everything look pretty with CSS. The first step is to create the base web page. The following HTML should be getting familiar to you.

```
<!DOCTYPE HTML>
<html>
<head>
<title>Audio in HTML5</title>
</head>
<body>
</body>
</html>
```

Now, let's add the AUDIO element between the BODY elements.

```
<audio>
  <source src="sample.mp3">
</audio>
```

You will see from the HTML code that the AUDIO element does not have any attributes. The `autoplay` and `controls` attributes have been removed. If you preview this code in your web browser you will see nothing on the page. Using JavaScript, you will add controls onto the page.

Below the AUDIO element, add the following JavaScript.

```
<script>
  var audio = document.getElementsByTagName ('audio')[0];
</script>
```

The role of this script is to create a new variable called "audio" that will interact with your AUDIO element. The following HTML ANCHOR element includes an `onClick` event that plays the audio file.

```
<a href="#" onClick="if (audio.paused) audio.play();
else audio.pause()">Play/Pause</a>
```

At this point, you can preview your web page in Google's Chrome or Apple's Safari. Pressing the Play/Pause link will play the MP3 audio file.

The page, at this point, can now be dressed up using CSS. Add the following CSS.

```
<style type="text/css">
a {
    font-family: "Franklin Gothic Medium", "Arial
Narrow", Arial, sans-serif;
    font-size: large;
    text-decoration: none;
    color: #C0C0C0;
}
h1 {
    font-family: "Franklin Gothic Medium", "Arial
Narrow", Arial, sans-serif;
    font-size: 24pt;
    color: #C0C0C0;
}
body {
    background-color: #000000;
    }
</style>
```

At this point, you are using the AUDIO element, controlled by JavaScript and styled using Cascading Style Sheets. Your entire code should look as follows.

```
<!DOCTYPE HTML>
<html>
<head>
<title>Audio in HTML5</title>
<style type="text/css">
a {
    font-family: "Franklin Gothic Medium", "Arial
Narrow", Arial, sans-serif;
```

```
        font-size: large;
        text-decoration: none;
        color: #C0C0C0;
    }
    h1 {
        font-family: "Franklin Gothic Medium", "Arial
Narrow", Arial, sans-serif;
        font-size: 24pt;
        color: #C0C0C0;
    }
    body {
        background-color: #000000;
    }
    </style>
    </head>
    <body>
    <h1 align="center">Custom JavaScript Controls for an
Audio file</h1><p align="center">
    <audio>
      <source src="sample.mp3">
    </audio>
    <script>
      var audio = document.getElementsByTagName ('audio')[0];
    </script>
    <a href="#" onClick="if (audio.paused) audio.play();
else audio.pause()">Play/Pause</a>
    </body>
    </html>
```

Again, as with VIDEO element control and styling, you can expect more third-party tools to emerge that allow you to more effectively control AUDIO in your web page. One place to look right now is the new iTunes LP Kit, TuneKit. Apple's iTunes now supports customizable themes for LPs in their store. The styles and themes are created using HTML. Complete details on how to use TuneKit can be downloaded at *http://images. apple.com/itunes/lp-and-extras/docs/TuneKit_Programming_ Guide.pdf.*

Encoding Video and Audio for Delivery over the Web

Previous to HTML5 you would have to use a combination of OBJECT and EMBED elements to add video to your web page. Video requires support of a plug-in, such as Adobe's Flash. HTML5 attempts to sidestep support for Windows Media Player, Flash, or RealPlayer plug-ins by adding video CODECs directly to the browser. A CODEC (compression/decompression) is the technology that allows video files to be converted into smaller, streamed files. Currently, two CODECs are gaining support for HTML5. They are the H.264 video standard and the open-source Ogg package for Theora video and Vorbis audio.

Simply put, the H.264 support, also known as MPEG4, is the video and audio format supported on your iPhone, but it is widely used by many companies. The problem is that MPEG4 has patents that protect the technology. You have to pay someone to use the technology, sometimes.

In contrast to H.264 is the open-source Theora video and Vorbis audio. These formats are free from patents. The audio and video quality difference between H.264 and Theora/Vorbis is very minimal. Technically, H.264 is cleaner at higher resolutions, but you would have to be a video maniac to see the difference. Ultimately, consumers of video/audio content will determine which CODEC becomes the format of choice.

To add these video and audio files to your web site you must convert content you have to either MPEG4 or Vorbis/Theora.

The first step is to create the original digital content. There are a number of ways in which you can create video on your computer. If you are running Windows XP, Vista, or 7 then you need to try Windows Live Movie Maker. The tool is very easy to use and will allow you to create video from still images and video shot on your digital flip camera or digital camera. If you are running a Mac then you can use iMovie to create your movies. Boasting more options and features than Movie Maker, iMovie can be used to create professional-looking solutions very easily.

When you are done creating your movies you will need to convert your files so they can run on your web page. For video, you need to convert your media in to Ogg Theora format or H.264 (MP4).

Creating Video in Ogg Theora Format

Creating Ogg Theora video is more complicated to do than creating H.264/MP4 video files. Fortunately, there is a great tool that works in FireFox you can use to convert your video.

The first step you will need to take is to go to *www.firefogg.org*. On the home page you will see a link that allows you to install the Firefogg tool into FireFox (Figure 4.10). When you have the tool installed, Firefogg will present a message telling you that everything is installed and ready to go.

To create an Ogg Theora video you will need to select "Make Ogg Video" from the Firefogg home page. The first step you are presented with asks you to browse for a video file on your computer (Figure 4.11).

Figure 4.10 Firefogg is a FireFox tool that allows you to create Ogg Theora video files.

Figure 4.11 The Firefogg conversion tool.

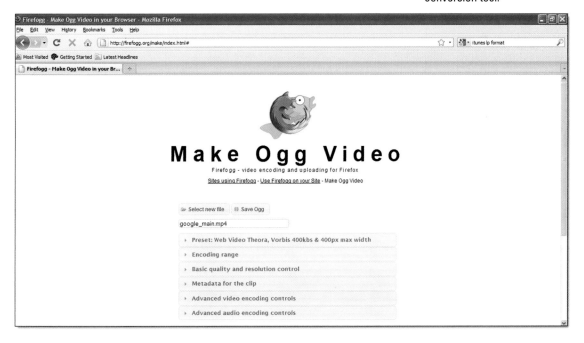

You can, at this point, choose the "Save Ogg" button to create the video file. However, you may want to choose to modify the video using the six different customization types. The first set of properties you can modify are the default video settings (Figure 4.12). You can choose low, medium, and high video encoding settings.

The second option you have is to choose if you want to start converting your video at a specific number of seconds into the movie and before the movie ends (Figure 4.13).

The basic quality options allow you to set high-level video and audio quality settings (Figure 4.14). You will notice that the audio setting is listed as Vorbis. This is because Theora video does not have a default soundtrack. The soundtrack is created using Vorbis audio and then packaged together into the final Ogg file. Using the video and audio options gives you additional control over your content.

The final step is to select "Save Ogg." You will be asked for a place to store the video on your computer. The amount of time it takes to convert the video will depend on how long the video is. The end result is a fully fledged Ogg Theora video file that you can use for video playback in FireFox.

Figure 4.12 Preset file settings.

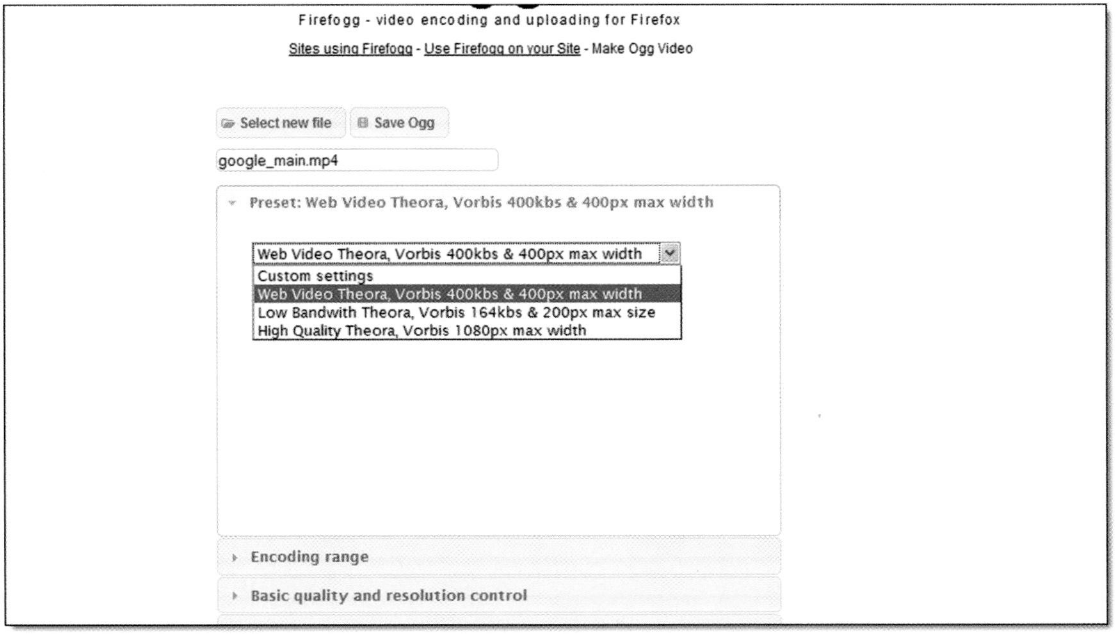

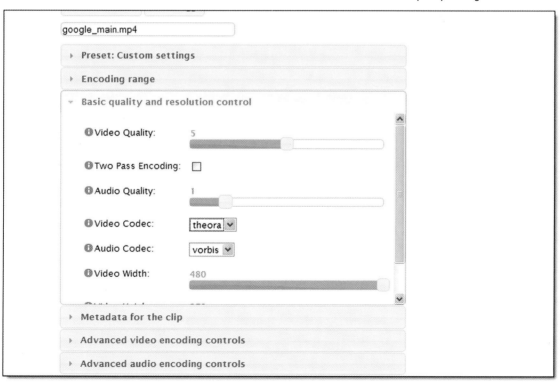

Firefogg - video encoding and uploading for Firefox

Sites using Firefogg - Use Firefogg on your Site - Make Ogg Video

📂 Select new file   💾 Save Ogg

google_main.mp4

▸ Preset: Web Video Theora, Vorbis 400kbs & 400px max width

▾ Encoding range

ⓘ Start Second:

ⓘ End Second:

▸ Basic quality and resolution control

Figure 4.13 You can set the conversion of the video to start and finish at specific seconds.

Figure 4.14 Video and audio quality settings.

google_main.mp4

▸ Preset: Custom settings

▸ Encoding range

▾ Basic quality and resolution control

ⓘ Video Quality: 5

ⓘ Two Pass Encoding: ☐

ⓘ Audio Quality: 1

ⓘ Video Codec: theora ▾

ⓘ Audio Codec: vorbis ▾

ⓘ Video Width: 480

▸ Metadata for the clip

▸ Advanced video encoding controls

▸ Advanced audio encoding controls

Creating Video in H.264 Format

Creating H.264-formatted video is relatively easy. There are dozens of products on the market that will take almost any video format and convert it to MPEG4. Examples include CuCuSoft, MP4 Convertor, and more. For Mac users, it is even easier. Your copy of iMovie already supports MPEG4 format.

The rule of thumb when it comes to creating MPEG4 is simple: Can you play the video back on your iPod or iPhone? If you can, then it's in MPEG4 format, and you can stick it in your web page. What, you don't have an iPod that plays video? Where have you been? Come join the party.

Creating Audio That Plays Back through Your Web Browser

Creating audio that will play back through a web browser is easier to accomplish than video. Again, with WebKit-based browsers, if you can hear the audio in an iPod then you have a good chance of playing the content through Chrome or Safari. For FireFox you will need to play back the video in Ogg Vorbis format.

You can use iTunes on your PC or Mac to create MP3 or AAC audio. iTunes has a neat audio convertor you can use that will take WMV or WAV audio and convert it to MP3 or AAC. Right-click on the converted file and select "Open File in Finder" for the Mac or "Open File in Explorer" for Windows. Ta-da! You have an audio file you can use.

Creating Ogg Vorbis audio takes a little more effort. The tool I have found to be the most effective is an open-source tool called Audacity (Figure 4.15).

Audacity is a complete audio editing tool. The best news is that it is free. The better news is that you run Audacity on Windows (98, ME, XP, Vista, and 7), Mac OS X, and Linux. The tool is an open-source project that should be included with any rich media designer's tool chest. Go to *www.audacity.org* to download the file you need.

To create an Ogg Vorbis audio file you will need to open an audio file in Audacity and then select File → Export as Ogg Vorbis. That's it. Save the file to your hard drive and you are good to go.

In addition to creating Ogg Vorbis audio you can export audio in almost any format from Audacity. It is a great tool to have installed on your computer.

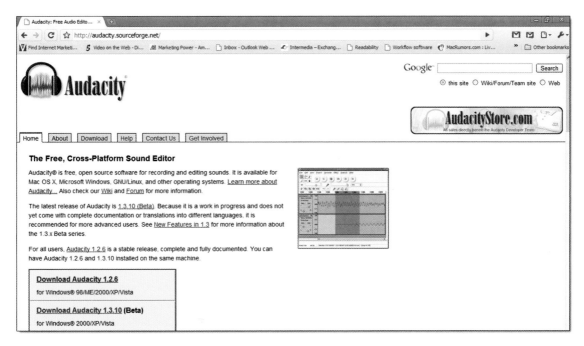

Figure 4.15 Audacity is an audio editing tool that saves files in Ogg Vorbis audio format.

Ensuring That Your Video and Audio Play Back

Currently, FireFox and WebKit do not support the same video playback standards. FireFox supports Theora and WebKit (used in Google's Chrome and Apple's Safari) uses H.264. Google does support Theora, too, but you are still left with the issue of juggling different standards with different browsers. So how do you handle this?

Well, HTML5 has that covered. The VIDEO element allows you to add nested SOURCE elements, as follows.

```
<video autoplay controls>
<source src="sample.mp4">
<source src="sample.ogv">
</video>
```

Using this technique guarantees your HTML5-compliant web browser will play back your video.

The same technique can be used with the AUDIO element. The following shows the AUDIO element with two nested SOURCE elements pointing to an MP3 audio source and a Vorbis audio file.

```
<audio autoplay controls>
<source src="sample.mp3">
<source src="sample.ogg">
</audio>
```

The VIDEO and AUDIO elements are extremely important technologies. Do not expect the battle between Ogg Theora/

Vorbis and H.264 to be over quickly. Take comfort in the fact that you can support both technologies in your HTML.

Serving Video from Your Servers

There are two ways to deliver audio and video to your web page: streaming and download.

Streaming is a technique where the audio and video feed is split into small packets of data and delivered in series of sequential pieces. The web browser receives the pieces and plays back the audio or video as a whole. The end result is that the viewer sees a single, seamless piece.

The download technique requires that a video file is fully downloaded to your computer before it can be played backed. The file is not delivered in packets. Technologies such as Adobe's Flash Video, MPEG4, and Microsoft's WMV will allow the media to start playing before the file is completely downloaded, faking out the streaming technique.

There are benefits and detriments to both techniques. For instance, the streaming technique allows you to broadcast live events, such the 2008 Beijing Olympics. The challenge with streaming, however, is that you do need a special server to deliver live media. In contrast, on-demand media can be downloaded from any web site. On-demand media, however, cannot broadcast live events.

Two additional protocols for delivering video over the Internet are emerging. Apple's QuickTime Live Streaming and Microsoft IIS 7 Live Smooth Streaming are very similar technologies that allow web servers (running the default HTTP protocol) to stream live and prerecorded content over HTTP, a protocol that previously only allowed you to deliver on-demand content. Currently, only Apple's Live Streaming will work with AUDIO and VIDEO elements in HTML5; however, it is likely that Microsoft's format will, too, work with HTML5.

What You Have Learned

Video and audio are big news. Sites such as YouTube, Pandora, and Last.FM are drawing millions of customers every week because of their massive video and audio libraries. Seeing how popular rich media is, HTML5 now includes native support with the VIDEO and AUDIO elements.

Video is supported in two different formats: H.264 and Ogg Theora. Support is currently fragmented between these two formats. Audio is being supported through use of MP3/AAC and

Ogg Vorbis. Again, as with video, support for these formats is fragmented.

Tools, such as Firefogg, Audacity, and iTunes, make it easy to create video and audio content that you can add to your web site. Now is the time for you to start creating HTML5 rich media content and experimenting with the new elements.

The number of people accessing the Internet and demanding rich media on their computers is only increasing. It may be some time before a single standard is supported across all browsers. Of course, as always, the browser that is not supporting the VIDEO and AUDIO elements is Microsoft's Internet Explorer. Hopefully this will change.

PROJECT 4: CREATING SVG LOGOS AND CANVAS CHARTS

SVG and CANVAS are two tools you can use to add illustrations to your HTML5 web sites. In this project chapter you are going to add an SVG logo and a CANVAS-drawn bar chart.

Creating an SVG Logo

First, let's look at what you are going to create for your logo. Figure 4.1Proj shows the final page with a logo used as a watermark.

The background image is created as a single SVG file. Download the files for this project at *www.visualizetheweb.com*. The SVG file is called "logo.svg." You can, of course, create the logo by following these steps:

1. Create a new text document and save the file, labeling it "logo.svg."
2. Open "logo.svg" and enter the following XML to define the content as an SVG image.

```
<?xml version="1.0" standalone="yes"?>
<svg version="1.1"
viewBox="0.0 0.0 800.0 600.0"
fill="none"
stroke="none"
stroke-linecap="square"
stroke-miterlimit="10"
xmlns="http://www.w3.org/2000/svg"
xmlns:xlink="http://www.w3.org/1999/xlink">
```

3. The illustration is created through a path definition in SVG, as follows.

```
<path d="M506 36L498 243L650 306L583 469L490 431L488
476L311 469L316 359L229 323L223 465L46 458L54 251L-98
188L-31 25L62 63L64 18L241 25L236 135L323 171L329 29Z"
```

4. Fill and outline color are defined by the `fill` and `stroke` properties as follows.

```
fill-rule="nonzero"
fill="#ff9900"
stroke="#ffffff"
```

HTML5. doi: 10.1016/B978-0-240-81328-8.00004-5

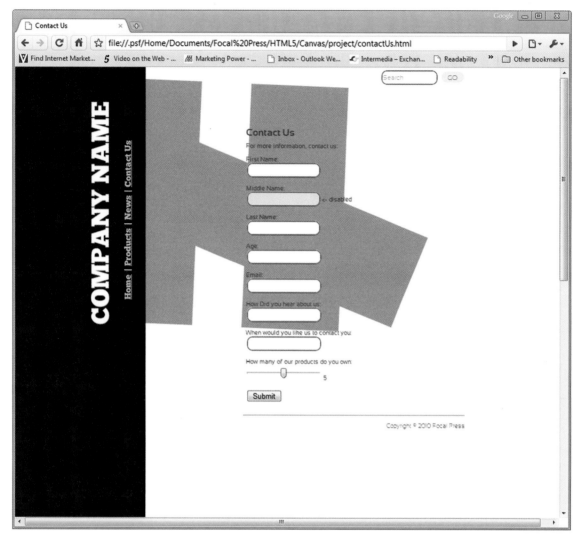

Figure 4.1Proj The orange logo is an SVG illustration.

```
stroke-width="2.0"
stroke-linejoin="round"
stroke-linecap="butt">
</path>
</svg>
```

5. At this point you can save the file. You have your completed SVG logo (Figure 4.2Proj). Drawing SVG illustrations by writing out the image coordinates is complicated. An easier solution is to use a drawing tool. Google's online Google Docs has an SVG illustration tool built into the service.

6. You will need to go to *http://docs.google.com* and create a Google account if you do not already have one.

7. Create a new document (Figure 4.3Proj).

Figure 4.2Proj The SVG logo by itself.

Figure 4.3Proj A blank document created in Google Docs.

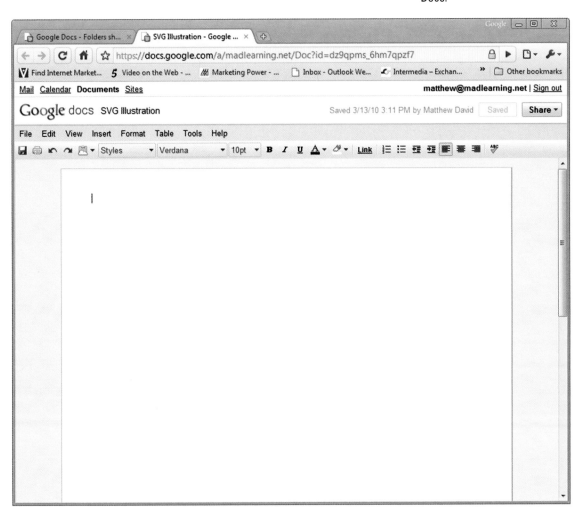

8. Select Insert → Illustration to open the illustration window in Google Docs. The images you now create are all SVG. How cool is that?

9. Go ahead and use the illustration tools. In Figure 4.4Proj you can see SVG text and SVG images have been added.

10. When you have completed your illustration you can choose to export the image from Google Docs by selecting Edit → Download As → SVG. This will export the image as a single SVG document. You now have your own SVG illustration without having to install any software.

11. Add the following IFRAME linking to the SVG document below the BODY element in your HTML pages.

```
<iframe src="logo.svg" name="myframe" width="1000"
height="600" frameborder="0" allowtransparency="true">
</iframe>
```

12. Save your documents and preview the page through a web browser. At this point, you now have an SVG document added to your web site.

Figure 4.4Proj SVG illustrations created in Google Docs.

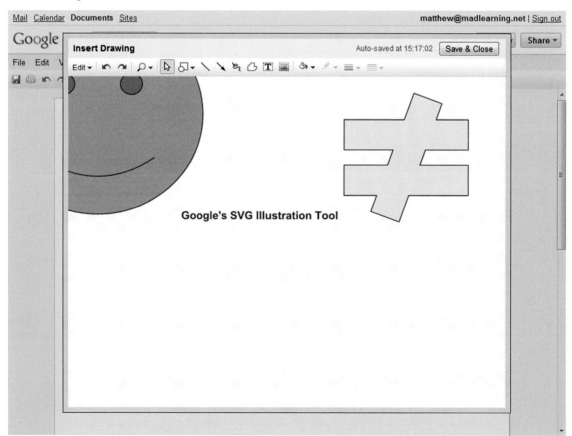

Inserting a CANVAS-Driven Dynamic Chart

The second image-generation tool you can use in HTML5 is CANVAS. The following project will add a dynamically drawn bar chart to your page. The advantages of using dynamic images, such as CANVAS, are that you can programmatically dictate the result. For instance, the chart you will be drawing illustrates growth for the last four quarters and the projected growth for the next quarter.

You can easily update the chart as your data are going to be driven from a JavaScript array. There is no need to get out Photoshop and update a JPEG image of the bar chart. You can update the code in the web page and you are good to go.

Okay, so let's get started. You are going to need to download the files from *www.visualizetheweb.com*.

1. Open the file named "news.html." You are going to add the bar chart. Add the following CANVAS tag to that section to give the chart a place on your page.

   ```
   <article id="article_two" style="position: absolute; left:
   420px; top: 350px; width: 315px; height: 195px; z-index: 2">
   <h1>What we do</h1>
   <p><time datetime="2010-03-15T10:32:17">March 15,
   2010</time></p>
   <H2>2010 Annual Report</H2>
   <video controls><source src='2010 Report.ogv'></video>
   <canvas id="barChart" width="600" height="400">
   </canvas>
   </article>
   ```

2. It is important to notice that the CANVAS element has an ID labeled `barChart`. The `barChart` ID will be used to link the JavaScript definition to the CANVAS element. Begin by adding a new JavaScript element to the page. Place the new JavaScript element inside of the HEAD element.

   ```
   <script type="text/javascript">
   ```

3. The next step is to create a new function that defines the CANVAS element.

   ```
   function graph() {
   var graphCanvas = document.getElementById('barChart');
   ```

4. Ensure that the element is available within the DOM.

   ```
   if (graphCanvas && graphCanvas.getContext) {
   ```

5. Open a two-dimensional context within the canvas.

   ```
   var context = graphCanvas.getContext('2d');
   ```

6. Draw the bar chart.

   ```
   drawBarChart(context, data, 50, 100, (graphCanvas.
   height - 20), 50);}
   ```

7. The following array contains the data you will use to populate the final bar chart.

```
var data = new Array(5);
data[0] = "First Quarter,200";
data[1] = "Second Quarter,120";
data[2] = "Third Quarter,80";
data[3] = "Fourth Quarter,330";
data[4] = "Projected Growth,345";}
```

8. The line of code draws the bar chart with the specified width, height, and starting position.

```
function drawBarChart(context, data, startX, barWidth,
chartHeight, markDataIncrementsIn) {
```

9. The following draws the X and Y axes onto your chart.

```
context.lineWidth = "1.0";
var startY = 380;
drawLine(context, startX, startY, startX, 30);
drawLine(context, startX, startY, 570, startY);
context.lineWidth = "0.0";
var maxValue = 0;
for (var i=0; i<data.length; i++) {
```

10. The following will extract the data from the array.

```
var values = data[i].split(",");
var name = values[0];
var height = parseInt(values[1]);
if (parseInt(height) > parseInt(maxValue)) maxValue = height;
```

11. The date is now written to the chart.

```
context.fillStyle = "gray";
drawRectangle(context, startX + (i * barWidth) + i,
(chartHeight - height), barWidth, height, true);
```

12. The following will add the column markers on the left side of the chart.

```
context.textAlign = "left";
context.fillStyle = "#000";
context.fillText(name, startX + (i * barWidth) + i,
chartHeight + 10, 200);}
```

13. Data markers are added to the Y axis.

```
var numMarkers = Math.ceil(maxValue/
markDataIncrementsIn);
context.textAlign = "right";
context.fillStyle = "#000";
var markerValue = 0;
for (var i=0; i<numMarkers; i++) {
        context.fillText(markerValue, (startX - 5),
(chartHeight - markerValue), 50);
        markerValue += markDataIncrementsIn;
    }}
```

14. The following JavaScript will draw a line on the context start and end points.

```
function drawLine(context0, startx, starty, endx,
endy) {
    context0.beginPath();
    context0.moveTo(startx, starty);
    context0.lineTo(endx, endy);
    context0.closePath();
    context0.stroke();}
```

15. The following draws a rectangle around the charts.

```
function drawRectangle(context0, x, y, w, h, fill) {
    context0.beginPath();
    context0.rect(x, y, w, h);
    context0.closePath();
    context0.stroke();
    if (fill) context0.fill();
                }
        </script>
```

16. An `onLoad` event is needed in the BODY element to load the CANVAS JavaScript into the page.

```
<body onLoad="graph();">
```

17. Save your document and view your CANVAS-driven chart (Figure 4.5Proj). Try changing the data values in the array. You will see that the chart updates automatically.

Figure 4.5Proj The CANVAS element is used to create the bar chart without needing a traditional image format such as JPEG or PNG.

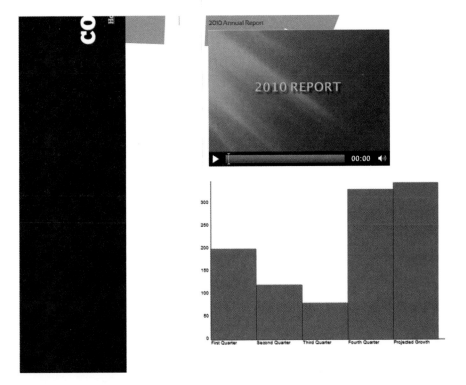

Summary

SVG and CANVAS are technologies that have been a long time coming for HTML. Using scripting languages, such as XML and JavaScript, you can now programmatically create the illustrations you want on your page. You are not limited to the forced restrictions a traditional pixel-based image, such as JPEG, places on you.

In this project you have successfully added an SVG image to your web site. In addition, you have seen how you can create your own SVG illustrations using online cloud services such as Google Docs. You also created a bar chart constructed using the CANVAS object. In the next section of the book you are going to build onto your knowledge of JavaScript and add complex interactivity with Ajax libraries.

HTML5 JAVASCRIPT MODEL

CSS, SVG, and Video are all great improvements to HTML5. The role for HTML5, however, is not to simply add eye-candy, but to enable developers to create applications in web browsers that are equal in performance to desktop applications. To accomplish this, you need a powerful development language that gives developers the ability to create sophisticated solutions. The answer to this is JavaScript, the world's most popular programming language.

Currently, the belief is that web applications simply are not as powerful as desktop applications. The reason for this is not due to JavaScript, but the engines inside of your web browser that process JavaScript. The faster a script can be processed, the more sophisticated your applications can become.

During 2009, web browser companies played a game of leap frog trying to reset speed benchmarks. FireFox, Safari, Google, and Opera played constantly. Toward the end of the year it appeared that the only company that would be left in the dark was Microsoft with the Internet Explorer 8 browser. At the fall 2009 PDC presentation Microsoft showed off an early developer version of IE9 running standard JavaScript tests (such as the SunSpider test at *http://www2.webkit.org/perf/sunspider-0.9/sunspider.html*) that placed its JavaScript engine on par with its competitors (see Figure 5.1).

The goal of this article is to review JavaScript, including how it is used in HTML5, how you can build upon the work of others through Ajax, and how to implement popular Ajax libraries into your work.

HTML5. doi: 10.1016/B978-0-240-81328-8.00010-0

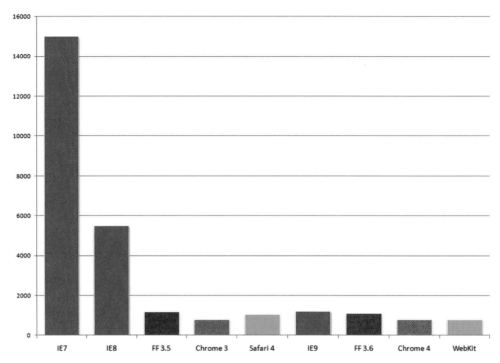

Figure 5.1 IE9 posts dramatic improvements in JavaScript processing speeds over old versions of Internet Explorer.

Understanding JavaScript

The goal of this article is to show how JavaScript can be used with HTML5 by a designer to give exceptional visual control to the layout of your web page. In addition, HTML5 is expanding to support application programming interfaces (APIs) that enable complex system integration inside your web pages. The new APIs, such as Web Workers, Geolocation, and local data storage, are complex and require sophisticated use of JavaScript to make them work.

JavaScript is not a new technology. The roots of JavaScript go back to 1993 when Netscape Communications included a scripting technology called LiveScript in their web browser. Incorporating even a simple programming language that enables interactivity in the web browser became extremely popular.

The current release of JavaScript has dramatically matured the original LiveScript language. Unlike desktop applications that run code optimized for an operating system, JavaScript must be interpreted within a virtual machine translator running inside of the web browser. This process inherently forces JavaScript solutions to run more slowly than desktop applications. To compensate for this, Google uses a technology called

V8 that dramatically improves the processing of JavaScript code. Competitors Mozilla, Apple, and Microsoft also have their own JavaScript engines that compete closely with Google's V8. Their engines—Rhino (FireFox) and SquirrelFish (Safari)—bring web applications extremely close to desktop speed. Sorry, Microsoft does not have a cool name for the JavaScript engine; they just call it JS—not very sexy.

Today's JavaScript allows you to build desktop-like applications that run inside of your web browsers. Google's Wave solution is an excellent example of a massively complex application that is run using JavaScript (Figure 5.2).

JavaScript is the most popular development language in the world, with millions of users. The technology is not too complex to learn; indeed, if you have any experience with C#, Java, or ActionScript, then you will likely learn JavaScript quickly.

JavaScript is so popular that it has its own standard. Ecma International is an industry association founded in 1961 and dedicated to the standardization of information and communication technology (ICT) and consumer electronics (CE). The standardized version of JavaScript is managed by Ecma. The full standard name is ECMA-262, but is often referred to as EcmaScript. ECMA-262 as a standard is well supported by *all* web browsers, including Microsoft's Internet Explorer.

Figure 5.2 Complex JavaScript powers Google's Wave.

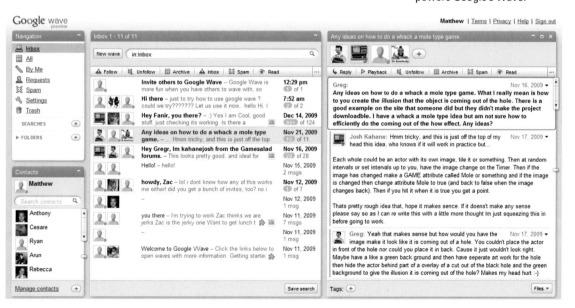

JavaScript as Programming Language

Fortunately, as programming languages go, JavaScript is not too complicated to learn. By the time you get to the end of this section you will understand what is needed to write basic programs.

There are two ways in which you can insert JavaScript into your web page:

- Insert your JavaScript directly into your web page between two SCRIPT elements.
- Add your JavaScript to a text file and link the web page to the text file.

To get started, we will use SCRIPT elements on a page to separate the code. Later, you will create separate files for your JavaScript. Following is a simple JavaScript file.

```
<html>
<body>
<script type="text/javascript">
document.write("Welcome to JavaScript");
</script>
</body>
</html>
```

This is a normal web page with opening and closing HTML elements. Within the BODY element you can see the opening and closing SCRIPT element. You place your JavaScript code within the SCRIPT element.

The SCRIPT element will default to JavaScript as a scripting language. There is, however, more than one scripting language you can use. A popular alternative to JavaScript is Microsoft's VBScript, a version of the VB language in script format. VBScript is natively supported by Microsoft's Internet Explorer. Other web browsers can support VBScript through a plug-in.

This next example JavaScript has one line of code:

```
document.write("Welcome to JavaScript");
```

The `document` is referencing an object. In this case, the document object is the web page itself. The `write` script is a property of the document object that allows you to add code. Figure 5.3 shows what your page will look like when you run this script.

JavaScript can also be placed inside of the HEAD element of a page and executed by an event action. Event actions are driven when something happens. For instance, when a web page loads, you can add an event action called `onLoad` (see Figure 5.4). The following is an example of inserting JavaScript into the HEAD element on the page.

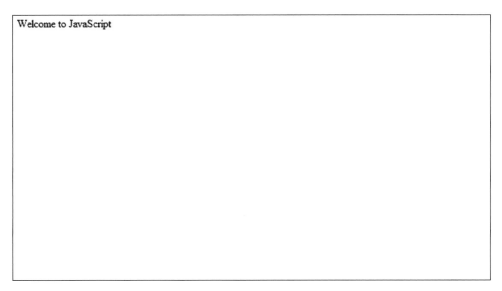

Welcome to JavaScript

Figure 5.3 The text on the web page is created using JavaScript.

Figure 5.4 You can force a JavaScript alert box to pop up when you load a web page.

```
<html>
<head>
<script type="text/javascript">
function popUpAlert()
{
alert("Welcome to JavaScript");
}
</script>
</head>
<body onLoad="popUpAlert ()">
</body>
</html>
```

The JavaScript runs a function. A function is a block of code that executes when it is called by another code. In this case, the other code is an `onLoad` command in the BODY element.

As you might imagine, you can mix up code in the HEAD element and in the main page as shown in the following example.

```
<html>
<head>
<script type="text/javascript">
function popUpAlert()
{
alert("Welcome to JavaScript");
}
</script>
</head>
<body>
<script type="text/javascript">
document.write("<H1>Welcome to JavaScript</H1>");
</script>
<a href="#" onClick="popUpAlert ()">Click me</a>
</body>
```

You will see in the above JavaScript that there is the same function called popUpAlert(). What is different is that the event to call that script has been moved into the main content of the web page. An ANCHOR element is now controlling when the JavaScript function is executed:

```
<a href="#" onClick="popUpAlert ()" >Click me</a>
```

The ANCHOR element cannot be used with the onLoad event, so it is using an onClick event to run the popUpAlert() function. This JavaScript will only run when you click on the link.

Above the ANCHOR element is a JavaScript that dynamically adds content to the page, as follows.

```
<script type="text/javascript">
document.write("<H1>Welcome to JavaScript</H1>");
</script>
```

In addition to adding dynamic text, the JavaScript also inserts HTML H1 elements. Figure 5.5 shows how this all looks in your web page.

A third way to run your scripts is through an external file. Keeping your files in an external file allows you to share the file with other web pages and keep your HTML cleaner.

The external file you will use is really just a text file. Open your favorite text editor such as Notepad, paste the JavaScript function into the file, and save it, naming the file "popup.js." Paste the following JavaScript into your new JS file.

```
function popUpAlert()
{
alert("Welcome to JavaScript");
}
```

You will notice that the JavaScript does not have a leading and closing SCRIPT element. You do not need one when you move your code to an external file. The "js" extension identifies the document as a JavaScript file (see Figure 5.6).

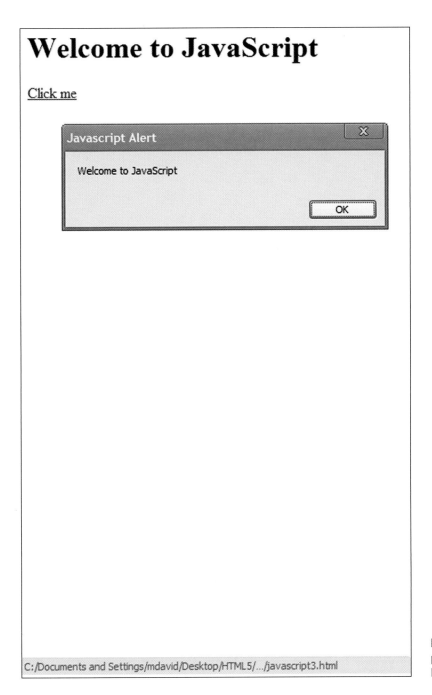

Figure 5.5 JavaScript can be placed within the HEAD and BODY elements.

```
1  <html>
2  <head>
3  <script type="text/javascript" src="popup.js"></script>
4  </head>
5  <body >
6  <script type="text/javascript">
7  document.write("<H1>Welcome to JavaScript</H1>");
8  </script>
9  <a href="#" onclick="popUpAlert ()" >Click me</a>
10 </body>
```

Figure 5.6 You can add your JavaScript to externally linked files.

Now you can link the SCRIPT element in your web file to the JS file:

```
<script type="text/javascript" src="popup.js">
</script>
```

You will see that your JavaScript runs just fine in your web browser.

Working with Variables

JavaScript is a programming language and, as part of this, comes loaded with ways in which you can create data. A simple way to create data is through variables. A variable is a declared object that contains data. For instance, the following is a variable called `color` with the value of red:

```
Var color="red"
```

Now, you can write a JavaScript where you are referencing the variable `color` to substitute the value red.

```
<script type="text/javascript">
document.write("<p>My favorite color is "+color+"
</p>");
</script>
```

The variable named `color` is dynamically added to the content on the page.

Using Math in Your Scripts

Variables can also have mathematical values (see Figure 5.7). For instance, the following two variables can be used to create the value of a third variable.

```
<script type="text/javascript">
var myFirstNumber=4;
var mySecondNumber=3;
var myThirdNumber=myFirstNumber*mySecondNumber;
</script>
```

Figure 5.7 You can mathematically control the values of variables.

My favorite number is 12

You can see that the first two variables are multiplied (the * is the multiplier value) to generate the third variable. The following JavaScript presents the final value in the web page:

```
document.write("<p>My favorite number is
"+myThirdNumber+"</p>");
```

There are seven arithmetic operators you can use in JavaScript:
- +   addition
- -   subtraction
- *   multiplication
- /   division
- %   modulus
- ++   increment
- --   decrement

The following example uses all seven operators to demonstrate how you can use them in your code (see also Figure 5.8).

```
<html>
<head>
<script type="text/javascript">
var varNumber=7;
var varAddition=varNumber+3;
var varSubtraction=varNumber-3;
var varMultiplication=varNumber*3;
var varDivision=varNumber/3;
var varModulus=varNumber%3;
var varIncrement=++varNumber;
var varDecrement=--varNumber;
</script>
</head>
```

Figure 5.8 JavaScript has seven different arithmetic operators you can use to control the value of content dynamically.

```
7+3=10

7-3=4

7*3=21

7/3=2.3333333333333335

7%3=1

Increment 7=8

Decrement 7=7
```

```
<body >
<script type="text/javascript">
document.write("<p>7+3="+varAddition+"</p>");
document.write("<p>7-3="+varSubtraction+"</p>");
document.write("<p>7*3="+varMultiplication+" </p>");
document.write("<p>7/3="+varDivision+"</p>");
document.write("<p>7%3="+varModulus+"</p>");
document.write("<p>Increment 7="+varIncrement+" </p>");
document.write("<p>Decrement 7="+varDecrement+" </p>");
</script>
</body>
```

Assessing Values Using Operators

In addition to mathematical operators, JavaScript also has comparison operators that allow you to take two or more values and compare the differences. There are seven comparison operators:

- == is equal to
- === is exactly equal to
- != is not equal to
- > is greater than
- < is less than
- >= is greater than or equal to
- <= is less than or equal to

Comparison operators become extremely valuable when you start to write functions that have potentially two or more outcomes.

Controlling Outcomes with If/Else and Switch Statements

Common to almost all programming languages is the use of if/else statements. Essentially, the if/else statement looks for a condition and, depending on the value, will execute a statement. Take for instance the following code.

```
<script type="text/javascript">
var myColor="red";
if (myColor=="red")
  {
  document.write("The correct color");
  }
</script>
```

A variable called myColor is created with a string value of red. The script then uses an if statement to look for a value using the comparison operator, ==. If the exact value is met then the text "The correct color" is printed on the page.

If the variable myColor is changed to blue, then the if statement will not run. To help show if an alternative option is available you can use an else statement to show a second option, as follows.

```
<script type="text/javascript">
var myColor="blue";
if (myColor=="red")
    {
document.write("The correct color");
    }
else (myColor=="red")
    {
document.write("This is not the correct color");
    }
</script>
```

The if/else statement can have a third condition set using the else/if statement. For instance, the following allows you to have two correct answers (red and blue), but when the value in the myColor is changed to any other value, then a third result is printed.

```
<script type="text/javascript">
var myColor="green";
if (myColor=="red")
    {
    document.write("The correct color");
    }
else if (myColor=="blue")
    {
    document.write("This is a good color");
    }
else
    {
    document.write("The wrong color was chosen");
    }
</script>
```

If there is a chance for you to have three or more valid choices then you will want to use switch statements to allow you to match your choice from a list of choices. Let's start by creating a variable that we can match different choices to:

```
var myColor="green";
```

The switch statement can now look for the condition of the variable myColor and match it against possible answers. The following switch statement creates three different answers depending whether the variable is green, red, or blue. A final, default value will run if none of the conditions are met.

```
switch (myColor)
{
case "red":
  document.write("You picked red");
  break;
```

```
case "green":
  document.write("You picked green");
  break;
case "blue":
  document.write("You picked blue");
  break;
default:
  document.write("You did not make a valid choice");
}
```

When you run this script the case statement that matches the string value green will print "You picked green" in the web page. Try changing the myColor variable value to red and blue to change the value printed to the page.

JavaScript supports many other tools you can use to control content. For instance, you can create a loop statement that will look through a list to match the correct results. The following uses an array with a for loop to print the results in the web page (see Figure 5.9).

```
<html>
<body>
<script type="text/javascript">
var mycolor;
var mycolors = new Array();
mycolors[0] = "Red";
mycolors[1] = "Green";
mycolors[2] = "Blue";
mycolors[3] = "Yellow";
mycolors[4] = "Orange";
for (mycolor in mycolors)
```

Figure 5.9 A for statement loops through an array to print the results on the screen.

```
Red
Green
Blue
Yellow
Orange
```

```
    {
    document.write(mycolors[mycolor] + "<br/>");
    }
</script>
</body>
</html>
```

Specific Objects You Can Use in JavaScript

JavaScript can be extended further inside of the web browser through the use of objects. JavaScript is an object-oriented programming (OOP) language in the same way that languages such as Java, C++, and C# are OOP. This means you can create and use objects. By default, web browsers support the following objects:

- String—this is text
- Date—allows you to use date and time
- Array—allows you to build a structured collection of data
- Boolean—true or false
- Math—allows you to use mathematical operators
- RegExp—allows you to use regular expressions to define a pattern, such as social security number or phone number

Using these objects enables you to create complex solutions. Do the final solutions meet the same demands of desktop applications? Five years ago I would have said no; today, it is extremely close and tomorrow's solutions will certainly outpace what you can do on the desktop.

Developing JavaScript for HTML5

New APIs in HTML5 can be programmatically interfaced with JavaScript. There are three APIs that stand out:

- Web Workers
- LocalStorage
- Geolocation-aware systems

Using JavaScript, you can interface with these new APIs to create new, Web-centric solutions.

Using Web Workers

JavaScript is a scripting solution that, when runs, will execute the code line by line. Many other development languages, such as C# and Java, can have multiple processes running simultaneously. Web Workers is a technology that frees JavaScript from sequential execution. You can now run multiple scripts at once.

This is easily done in JavaScript. In the following script you will declare a new variable, called `myWebWorker`, as a new Web Workers file:

```
var myWebWorker = new Worker("webWorker.js");
```

The example is loading a second script. In the JavaScript JS file is a second script that triggers another, duplicate Web Workers file to run. The loop forces two programs to run at once. The JavaScript for webWorker.js is as follows.

```
var results = [];
function resultReceiver(event) {
results.push(parseInt(event.data));
if (results.length == 2) {
  postMessage(results[0] + results[1]);
  }
}
  function errorReceiver(event) {
    throw event.data;
}
  onmessage = function(event) {
    var n = parseInt(event.data);
    if (n == 0 || n == 1) {
      postMessage(n);
      return;
    }
    for (var i = 1; i <= 2; i++) {
      var myWebWorker = new Worker("webWorker.js");
      myWebWorker.onmessage = resultReceiver;
      myWebWorker.onerror = errorReceiver;
      myWebWorker.postMessage(n - i);
    }
  }
```

The final for statement triggers the same webWorker.js file to reload. This forces the script to run multiple times.

In your main HTML page you will add the following HTML and JavaScript to load the Web Workers file.

```
<html>
  <title>Test threads fibonacci</title>
  <body>
  <div id="result"></div>
  <script language="javascript">
    var myWebWorker = new Worker("webWorker.js");
      myWebWorker.onmessage = function(event) {
        document.getElementById("result").textContent =
event.data;
        dump("Got: " + event.data + "\n");
      };
      myWebWorker.onerror = function(event) {
```

```
          dump("Web Worker error: " + event.data + "\n");
          throw event.data;
        };
        myWebWorker.postMessage("Success, Web Workers are
working");
    </script>
    </body>
    </html>
```

Enabling multiple JavaScripts to execute simultaneous is essential for complex applications. There is a quick test you can take to see massive numbers of JavaScript programs running. Go to *www.Gmail.com* and log into Google's Web-based email service. The service will run a simple version of the site if you visit Gmail with IE7 or earlier. If you are using FireFox 3.6 or Google's Chrome then you are presented with a jet-fueled alternative loaded with JavaScript. The high-performance alternative requires that the browser can support technologies such as Web Workers to process scripts simultaneously.

Storing Data with LocalStorage

Key to applications is the ability to store data. In the past you have been able to do this through using complex cookies or Ajax commands that leverage the ability to send data back to a database. The ability to store data locally in your web browser is dramatically improved with the implementation of LocalStorage.

LocalStorage is essentially the ability to have an SQL-like database running in your web browser. An example of LocalStorage being used is Google's version of Gmail for the iPhone. Using LocalStorage, you can view and send email with Gmail without having a Web connection. The email is resynchronized with the mail servers when a new network connection is established.

You access LocalStorage in your JavaScript by using the GlobalStorage object. Figure 5.10 demonstrates LocalStorage being used.

The first step for the example in Figure 5.10 is to create an area where you can type some text. You are going to use standard-form controls.

```
    <textarea id="text" class="freetext">
    </textarea> Item name <input id="item_name" type="text"
value="new item"/>
```

An event is going to be added to the INPUT submit button to trigger the JavaScript to run:

```
    <input onClick="writeLocal();" type="button"
value="Save"/>
```

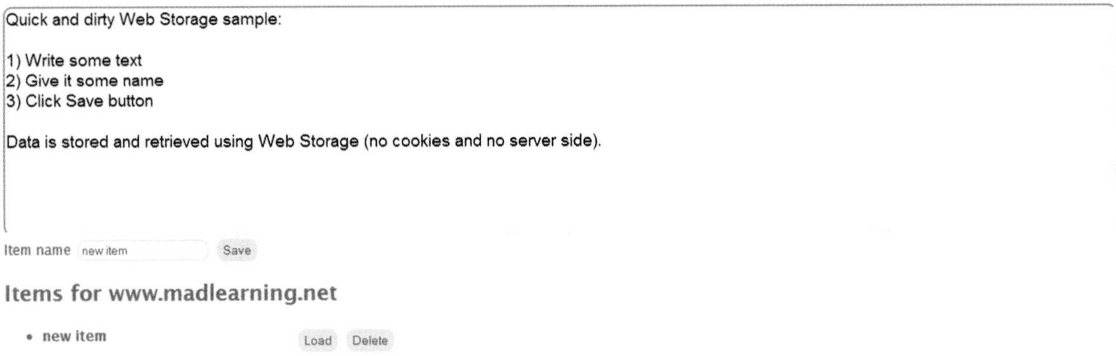

Quick and dirty Web Storage sample:

1) Write some text
2) Give it some name
3) Click Save button

Data is stored and retrieved using Web Storage (no cookies and no server side).

Item name new item   Save

Items for www.madlearning.net

- **new item**   Load   Delete

Figure 5.10 Data can be stored locally in web browsers using the LocalStorage object.

The LocalStorage is going to post the data stored in the browser to the web page. An area with the ID `items` is defined.

```
<div id="items">
</div>
```

The first function run in your JavaScript is to define that the content on the page is going to be associated with the web site your page is being hosted on.

```
function $(id) { return document.getElementById (id); }
var host = location.hostname;
var myLocalStorage = globalStorage[host];
```

The second function allows you to store data using the LocalStorage API.

```
function writeLocal() {
  var data = $('text').value;
  var itemName = $('item_name').value;
  myLocalStorage.setItem(itemName, data);
  updateItemsList();
}
```

As with any SQL database you need to be able to delete entries. The following function allows you to delete items using the `removeItem` property.

```
function deleteLocal(itemName) {
  myLocalStorage.removeItem(itemName);
  updateItemsList();
}
```

The following sample shows you the whole program with some simple CSS styling for presentation.

```
<html><head><title>HTML5 Web Storage / localStorage</
title></head>
  <style>
```

```
.freetext {
    width: 100%;height: 40%;overflow: hidden;
background: #FFE;font-family: sans-serif;font-size: 14pt;-
moz-border-radius: 10px;-webkit-border-radius: 10px;
    }
    li {
      padding: 4px;width: 400px;
    }
    input {
      margin: 2px;border-style: solid;-moz-border-radius:
10px;-webkit-border-radius: 10px;color: #666;padding: 2px;
    }
    body {
      font-family: "Lucida Sans", "Lucida Sans Regular",
"Lucida Grande", "Lucida Sans Unicode", Geneva, Verdana,
sans-serif;color: #FF0000;font-size: medium;
    }
    </style>
    <body><textarea id="text" class="freetext "> </
textarea> Item name <input id="item_name" type="text"
value="new item"/><input onClick= "writeLocal();"
type="button" value="Save"/> <div id="items"></div>
    <script>
    function $(id) { return document.getElementById(id); }
    var host = location.hostname;
    var myLocalStorage = globalStorage[host];
    function writeLocal() {
      var data = $('text').value;
      var itemName = $('item_name').value;
      myLocalStorage.setItem(itemName, data);
      updateItemsList();
    }
    function deleteLocal(itemName) {
      myLocalStorage.removeItem(itemName);
      updateItemsList();
    }
    function readLocal(itemName) {
      $('item_name').value=itemName;
      $('text').value=myLocalStorage.getItem(itemName);
    }
    function updateItemsList() {
      var items = myLocalStorage.length
      // list items
      var s = '<h2>Items for '+host+'</h2>';
      s+= '<ul>';
      for (var i=0;i<items;i++) {
        var itemName = myLocalStorage.key(i);
        s+= '<li>'+
          '<div style="float:right;">'+
          '<input type="button" value="Load" onClick=
"readLocal(\''+itemName+'\');"/'+'> '+
```

```
        '<input type="button" value="Delete" onClick="dele
teLocal(\''+itemName+'\');"/'+'> '+
        '</div>'+
        '<strong>'+itemName+'</strong>'+
        '</li>';
    }
    $('items').innerHTML = s+'</ul>';
    }
    window.onLoad = function() {
    updateItemsList();
    $('text').value=[
        'Quick and dirty Web Storage sample:','',
        '1) Write some text',
        '2) Give it some name',
        '3) Click Save button','',
        'Data is stored and retrieved using Web Storage
(no cookies and no server side).'].join('\n');
    }
    </script></body></html>
```

As you can see, the implementation of LocalStorage allows you to store data without using cookies from a server-side database.

Controlling Geolocation Devices with JavaScript

There is no doubt that the tech world is going mobile. Devices now need to know where they are geographically. In preparation for this, HTML5 includes support for geolocation (see Figure 5.11). The iPhone and Android phones are already geolocation enabled.

The following example uses Google Map's service and the browser's Geolocation API to tell you where you are located. The first step is to load the Map services.

```
<script src="http://maps.google.com/maps?file=api &amp
;v=2&amp;sensor=false&amp;key=ABQIAAAAiUzO1s6QWHuyzxx-
JVN7ABSUL8-Cfeleqd6F6deqY-Cw1iTxhxQkovZkaxsxgKCdn1OCYaq7Ub
z3SQ" type="text/javascript"></script>
```

The Google Map services are publicly accessible. Now you need to start writing JavaScript. The first step is to define a series of variables that you can use in your code.

```
    var map;
    var mapCenter
    var geocoder;
    var fakeLatitude;
    var fakeLongitude;
```

HTML 5 Geolocation

Figure 5.11 Web browsers can now know where they are using the Geolocation API.

With your JavaScript variables defined, you can create the first function that initializes the geolocation services in your web browser.

```
function initialize()
{
    if (navigator.geolocation)
    {
        navigator.geolocation.getCurrentPosition
( function (position) {
        mapServiceProvider(position.coords.
latitude,position.coords.longitude);
        },
    }
    else
    {
        alert("I'm sorry, but geolocation services are not
supported by your browser or you do not have a GPS device
in your computer. I will use a sample location to produce
the map instead.");
        fakeLatitude = 49.273677;
        fakeLongitude = -123.114420;
        mapServiceProvider(fakeLatitude, fakeLongitude);
    }
}
```

The next function instructs the geolocation services to use the
Google Map service.

```
function mapServiceProvider(latitude,longitude)
{
     mapThisGoogle(latitude,longitude);
}
function mapThisGoogle(latitude,longitude)
{
     var mapCenter = new GLatLng(latitude, longitude);
     map = new GMap2(document.getElementById ("map"));
     map.setCenter(mapCenter, 15);
     map.addOverlay(new GMarker(mapCenter));
     geocoder = new GClientGeocoder();
     geocoder.getLocations(latitude+','+longitude,
addAddressToMap);
}
```

The final code completes the mapping.

```
function addAddressToMap(response)
{
     if (!response || response.Status.code != 200) {
          alert("Sorry, we were unable to geocode that
address");
     } else {
          place = response.Placemark[0];
          $('#address').html('Your address: '+place.
address);
     }
}
window.location.querystring = (function(){
     var collection = {};
     var querystring = window.location.search;
     if (!querystring) {
          return{toString: function(){return ""; }};
     }
   querystring = decodeURI(querystring.substring(1));
   var pairs = querystring.split("&");
   for (var i = 0; i < pairs.length; i++) {
          if (!pairs[i]) {
               continue;
          }
          var seperatorPosition = pairs[i].indexOf ("=");
          if (seperatorPosition == -1) {
             collection[pairs[i]] = "";
          }
          else {
               collection[pairs[i].substring(0,
   seperatorPosition)]
                    = pairs[i].substr(seperatorPosition + 1);
          }
     }
```

```
collection.toString = function() {
        return "?" + querystring;
};
return collection;
})();
```

The final result is that you can use geolocation to determine where you are using just your web browser. This is very useful in mobile web browsers where you can link map services to geographically based tools.

Integrating JavaScript with HTML5

It will come as no surprise to find out that JavaScript is tightly integrated with all elements of HTML5. This is clearly seen with the use of the CANVAS element. By itself, the CANVAS element cannot do much. It is the use of JavaScript that allows it to become fully interactive.

The following JavaScript example demonstrates how you can use JavaScript, CANVAS, and a little CSS to create a simple game where you can control a crowd of people. Called "Crowd Control," the goal of this simple game is to chase the people on the screen. What you will find is that each person on the screen will run away from your cursor as you move toward it.

The first step is to create a basic HTML5 page with some simple CSS to control the color of the page. The following will do.

```
<!DOCTYPE HTML> <html> <head> <title>Canvas Example -
Crowd Control</title>
<style type="text/css">
body{
        margin: 0;
        padding: 0;
        overflow: hidden;
        background: yellow;
        color: white;
        text-align: right;
        font-family: Arial, Helvetica, sans-serif;
        font-size: 0.8em;
        }
</style>
</head>
    <body>
    </body>
</html>
```

In-between the BODY elements you will need to add the following CANVAS element. Notice that the CANVAS element has the ID `crowdControl`. You will link to this ID using JavaScript.

```
<canvas id="crowdControl"></canvas>
```

Following this you will start your JavaScript. The first action is to define the contextual structure of the CANVAS element.

```
<script type="text/javascript">
  var context = document.getElementById
('crowdControl').getContext('2d');
  var mousex=0,mousey=0;
```

The `crowdControl` JavaScript will add copies of a PNG file onto the screen. You will want to create a new image object variable that can then point to the PNG file.

```
var imagine=new Image();
  imagine.src="people.png";
```

Now you can start building your functions. The function will declare where on the page the crowd can move.

```
function crowd(){
    this.x=Math.random()*context.canvas.width;
    this.y=Math.random()*context.canvas.height;
    this.vx=0;
    this.vy=0;
    this.move=crowd_move;
    this.draw=crowd_draw;
}
function crowd_move(){
    this.x+=this.vx;
    this.y+=this.vy;
    this.vx*=0.9;
    this.vy*=0.9;
    this.vx+=(Math.random()-0.5) *0.1;
    this.vy+=(Math.random()-0.5) *0.1;
    this.x=(this.x*500+context.canvas.width/2)/501;
    this.y=(this.y*500+context.canvas.height/2)/501;
}
```

Next, let's add the JavaScript that will actually draw the crowd.

```
function crowd_draw(){
    context.save();
    context.beginPath();
    context.translate(this.x,this.y)
    context.rotate(angle(this.vx,this.vy));
    context.drawImage(imagine,-10,-5);
    context.fillStyle = 'white';
    context.fill();
    context.restore();
}
```

The next two functions will allow your mouse to push the people around the screen and allow you to interact with them.

```
var people=new Array();
  function begin(){
     for(var i=0;i<100;i++){
        var temp=new crowd();
        people.push(temp);
     }
  }
function work(){
    var x;
    context.save();
    context.beginPath();
    context.fillStyle = 'yellow';
    context.strokeStyle ='white';
    context.rect(0,0,context.canvas.width,context.
canvas.height);
    context.fill();
    context.stroke();
    context.restore();
      for(x in people){
          var y;
      for(y in people){
        if(y!=x){
            var dx=people[y].x-people[x].x;
            var dy=people[y].y-people[x].y;
            var d=Math.sqrt(dx*dx+dy*dy);
            if(d<40){
                people[x].vx+=20* (-dx/(d*d));
                people[x].vy+=20* (-dy/(d*d));
            }else if(d<100){
                people[x].vx+=0.07* (dx/d);
                people[x].vy+=0.07* (dy/d);
            }
        }
      }
    }
    var dx=mousex-people[x].x;
    var dy=mousey-people[x].y;
    var d=Math.sqrt(dx*dx+dy*dy);
    if(d<100){
        people[x].vx+=1* (-dx/(d));
        people[x].vy+=1* (-dy/(d));
    }
    people[x].move();
    people[x].draw();
  }
}
```

The final functions set the size of the CANVAS element on the screen.

```
function mmouse(event) {
    mousex=event.pageX;
    mousey=event.pageY;
```

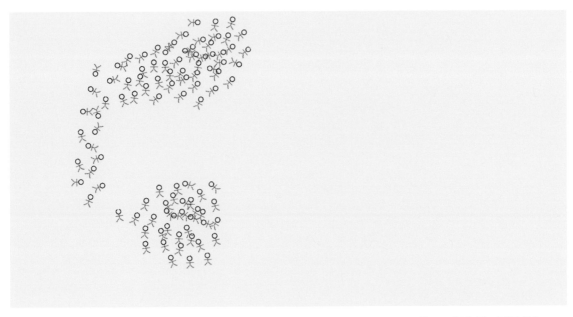

Figure 5.12 The CANVAS element relies heavily on JavaScript to add interactivity.

```
    }
context.canvas.onmousemove = mmouse;
function resize_context(){
    context.canvas.width=window.innerWidth;
    context.canvas.height=window.innerHeight;
}
window.onresize=resize_context;
onLoad=resize_context();
onLoad=begin();
setInterval(work,10);
</script>
```

The final result is shown in Figure 5.12.

JavaScript is central to adding interaction to the CANVAS element. This is where the root power of JavaScript can be found—JavaScript allows you to interact with any HTML5 element on the screen, whether it is HTML, SVG, CSS, or CANVAS. This gives you great control.

Taking JavaScript to the Next Level with Ajax

The good news is that there are a lot of tools that break down the barrier to complex development with JavaScript. You can download JavaScript libraries of code that come prebuilt with functionality such as animation, form validation controls, and data manipulation. These libraries are called Ajax libraries. Originally, called AJAX (Asynchronous JavaScript and XML) the term has now been changed to Ajax (note the lowercase letters) to allow support for a broader range of technologies beyond just XML.

Using Ajax in Your Work

At the core, Ajax is a set of well-written JavaScript programs that you can interact with. Each Ajax library has slightly different ways in which you can use it. The following example demonstrates how you can use the most popular Ajax library, jQuery, in your web site.

There are hundreds of different Ajax libraries, but jQuery is the one that is stepping above the crowd. The library itself is robust and will work with all popular web browsers, including Microsoft's Internet Explorer. The popularity of jQuery is so great that Microsoft is now supporting jQuery as their default Ajax tool in ASP.NET. This means any ASP.NET solution can integrate with the jQuery Ajax library seamlessly.

To get jQuery you need to go to *www.jquery.com*, as shown in Figure 5.13.

Figure 5.13 jQuery can be downloaded at *www.jquery.com*.

You can either download the latest jQuery JavaScript library or simply connect to it over the Internet. The following example will connect jQuery from the Web. Start by creating an empty web page, as follows.

```
<!DOCTYPE html>
<html lang="en">
<head>
1.1 </head>
1.2 <body>
1.3 </body>
1.4 </html>
```

In the BODY section of the page, let's add some content.

```
<section id="container">
<article class="article">
        <h1>A Christmas Carol</h1>
    <p class="thebody">Marley was dead: to begin with.
There is no doubt whatever about that. The register of
his burial was signed by the clergyman, the clerk, the
undertaker, and the chief mourner. Scrooge signed it. And
Scrooge's name was good upon 'Change, for anything he
chose to put his hand to.
  </p>
        <ul class="actions">
        </ul>
    </article>
    <article class="article">
        <h1>David Copperfield</h1>
        <p class="thebody">Whether I shall turn out to
be the hero of my own life, or whether that station
will be held by anybody else, these pages must show. To
begin my life with the beginning of my life, I record
that I was born (as I have been informed and believe) on
a Friday, at twelve o'clock at night. It was remarked
that the clock began to strike, and I began to cry,
simultaneously.
  </p>
        <ul class="actions">
        </ul>
    </article>
</section>
```

When you preview this page you will see that there is no formatting or interaction. What you have is a list of Charles Dickens' books followed by the opening paragraph. This amount of content will get difficult to read if you have lots of entries to skim through. Using a little jQuery you can insert a show/hide action to show and hide the opening paragraph (see Figure 5.14).

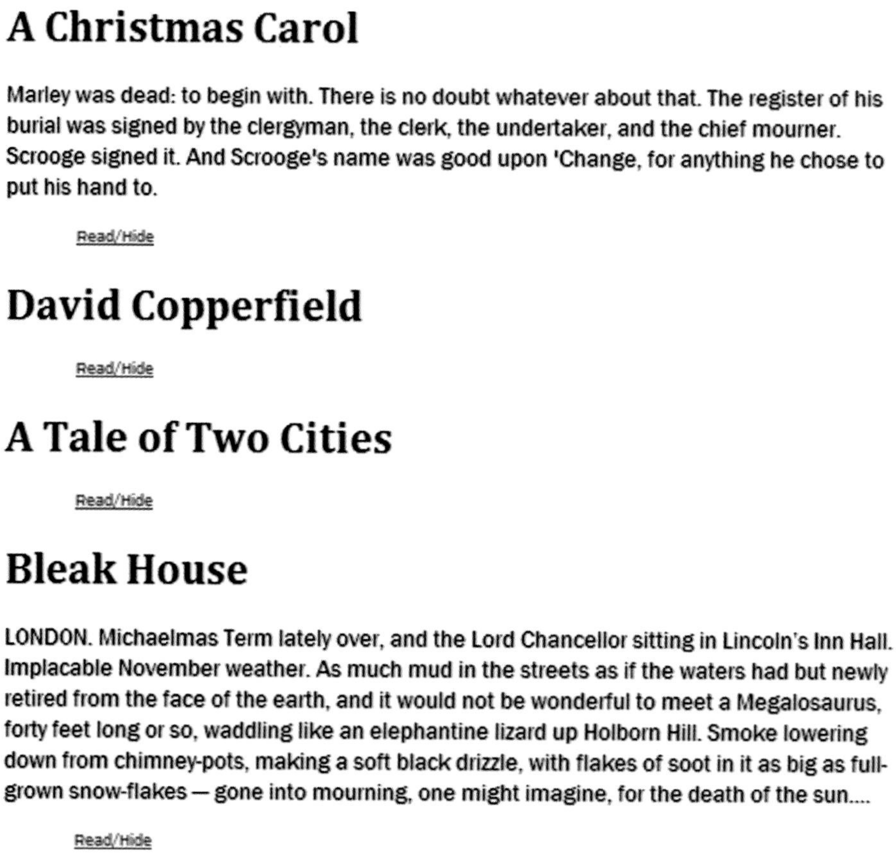

A Christmas Carol

Marley was dead: to begin with. There is no doubt whatever about that. The register of his burial was signed by the clergyman, the clerk, the undertaker, and the chief mourner. Scrooge signed it. And Scrooge's name was good upon 'Change, for anything he chose to put his hand to.

Read/Hide

David Copperfield

Read/Hide

A Tale of Two Cities

Read/Hide

Bleak House

LONDON. Michaelmas Term lately over, and the Lord Chancellor sitting in Lincoln's Inn Hall. Implacable November weather. As much mud in the streets as if the waters had but newly retired from the face of the earth, and it would not be wonderful to meet a Megalosaurus, forty feet long or so, waddling like an elephantine lizard up Holborn Hill. Smoke lowering down from chimney-pots, making a soft black drizzle, with flakes of soot in it as big as full-grown snow-flakes — gone into mourning, one might imagine, for the death of the sun....

Read/Hide

Figure 5.14 jQuery allows you to add effects, such as a show and hide effect, with very few lines of code.

In the HEAD section of the page, insert the following code to call and use the jQuery library.

```
<script src="http://jquery.com/src/jquery-latest.js">
</script>
```

The next JavaScript interacts with the jQuery library to create simple interaction.

```
<script> //<![CDATA[
  // When the page is ready
  $(document).ready(function(){
    $(".article .thebody").hide();
    $("#container .article ul")
      .prepend("<li class='readbody'><a href=''
title='Read/Hide Article'>Read/Hide</a></li>");
      $(".actions li.readbody a").click(function (event){
        $(this).parents("ul").prev(".thebody").toggle();
              // Stop the link click from doing its
normal thing
        event.preventDefault();
      });
```

```
   });
//]]></script>
```

Finally, insert a little CSS to make the page look pleasing, as follows.

```
<style type="text/css">
section {
    width: 500px;
}
ul {
    list-style-type: none;
    right: 0px;
    font-family: "Franklin Gothic Medium", "Arial
Narrow", Arial, sans-serif;
    font-size: xx-small;
    text-decoration: none;
}
h1 {
    font-family: Cambria, Cochin, Georgia, Times,
"Times New Roman", serif;
    font-size: x-large;
    font-weight: bolder;
}
    p {
    font-family: "Franklin Gothic Medium", "Arial
Narrow", Arial, sans-serif;
    font-size: small;
}
</style>
```

Now you can test your page. You will see that you can select the show/hide text to make the opening paragraph appear or disappear. This makes skimming through the content much easier.

The jQuery library comes with hundreds of extensions you can use to expand the effects you can add to your web pages. Check out *http://plugins.jquery.com/*, where you can find the jQuery extensions.

Popular Ajax Libraries

There are quite literally hundreds of Ajax libraries. While jQuery is the most popular, there are many that fill specific niche needs. Below is a list of some really good libraries you can use in your web applications.

Adobe's Spry Framework

Adobe has an Ajax library called Spry. The Spry framework makes this list simply because it is tied directly into Dreamweaver (see Figure 5.15). Dreamweaver is a great web site

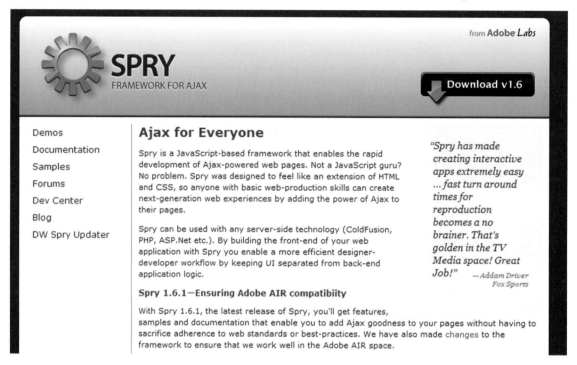

Figure 5.15 Adobe's Spry framework is a mature Ajax library that is built directly into Adobe's Dreamweaver web site management tool.

development tool and now comes with tight integration with the Spry framework. Adding Ajax, interaction controls such as form validation, animation, and data control are very easy for nondevelopers.

You can download the library at *www.labs.adobe.com/technologies/spry/*.

YUI: Yahoo Interface Library

Yahoo is well known for their web services. They're less well known for their work on web standards and functionality. The YUI library is Yahoo's set of Ajax tools you can use in your web site. You can find out more information on the YUI tools at the Yahoo Developer Network at *http://developer.yahoo.com/* (see Figure 5.16).

Controlling Forms with wForms

At some point you will want to control how users complete forms in your web site. Form control covers elements such as how users enter data into the forms, how form fields are controlled

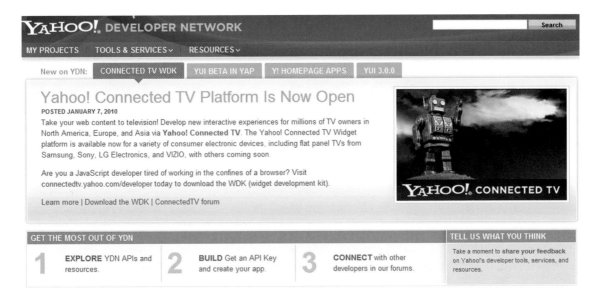

Figure 5.16 Yahoo's Developer Network.

by other elements on the page, and how to hide/show form elements depending on how your users enter data. These functions are all handled easily by wForms (*http://www.formassembly.com/wForms/*). The library is small and well documented.

Animation Control with $fx()

Need a way to add animation in your web page? The $fx() library (*http://fx.inetcat.com/*) allows you to easily add animation in your site.

Visualizing Data with JSCharts

Data visualization is a big thing. The days of just presenting data in rows and columns is dead. We need to have ways in which the data we are looking at mean something. The Ajax library JSCharts (*http://www.jscharts*) will give you ways in which you can transform HTML tables into line charts, bar charts, and pie charts. They look fantastic (see Figure 5.17).

At the end of the day, Ajax libraries are a great way to extend what you are doing with your web page. Coupling CSS, SVG, HTML, and all of the HTML5 family of tools together, you can create compelling web applications.

Figure 5.17 Ajax libraries allow you to convert HTML tables into charts.

What You Have Learned

Throughout this chapter you have learned how JavaScript, the programming language within HTML, is evolving to allow you to develop large, complex applications. Sites such as Google's Gmail are excellent examples of Web-based applications that run with the same level of efficiency as desktop equivalents. The next step for you to take is to download an Ajax library, such as jQuery, and begin to create applications on the Web.

PROJECT 5: WORKING WITH JAVASCRIPT

The speed and power of JavaScript are growing exponentially. All modern web browsers, including Google's Chrome, Mozilla's FireFox, Apple's Safari, and Microsoft's Internet Explorer, can render JavaScript at close to machine code levels. In addition, work by standards groups, such as W3C and WASP, ensures that JavaScript will run consistently from one web browser to another.

Ajax libraries are great examples of demonstrating JavaScript running effectively between browsers. In this final project you are going to extend a popular Ajax library, jQuery, to create a simple lightbox effect to a product photo library.

Working with jQuery

There are many Ajax libraries you can use to rapidly extend what you can do on your web site. You can download the files for this project at *www.visualizetheweb.com*. You will see that there are two Ajax libraries included in the package: jQuery and Spry. Both libraries are open source. The first, jQuery, is arguably the most popular Ajax library. You can check out *www.jquery.com* for detailed information on how to use the library. The second library, Spry, is developed as an open-source project managed by Adobe (Figure 5.1Proj). Adobe's web management tool, Dreamweaver, now ships with native support for Spry.

Allowing the core jQuery script to be extended has allowed for hundreds of jQuery extensions to be written and made available. A jQuery extension is written in JavaScript, which makes it difficult to protect. For this reason, you will find that most jQuery extensions are managed as open-source projects.

HTML5. 10.1016/B978-0-240-81328-8.00005-7

Figure 5.1Proj Adobe's home page for the Spry Ajax framework.

Developing a Lightbox Image Management Tool

A lightbox effect enhances what you can do with image libraries on the screen. Traditionally, if you have images in a web page, you either provide the complete image or a link to a larger version of the image. The lightbox effect adds a thumbnail image to a page (Figure 5.2Proj).

When you select the thumbnail the main page darkens and a larger version of the image is loaded (Figure 5.3Proj). Navigation buttons allow you to tab from one image to another image in your library. The key is that you never leave the page you are on.

The entire lightbox effect is created through a combination of images, jQuery, custom JavaScript, CSS, and HTML.

Creating the Images

The first step in this project is to create the images you need for the thumbnails and full-size images (Figure 5.4Proj). You can use your favorite editing tool, such as PhotoShop, Gimp, or Expression Design. Take your original file and create a thumbnail version of the image at 72 pixels by 72 pixels.

Figure 5.2Proj The page contains a lightbox effect. Each thumbnail can be selected.

Figure 5.3Proj The lightbox effect is used to zoom in on each image.

Figure 5.4Proj You will need to create a thumbnail and full-size version of each image you want to see in the lightbox photo library.

Create a subfolder in your web site and call it Photos. Place your thumbnail and full-size images into the new folder.

A second folder, called Images, contains all the files that you will use for navigation buttons to move from image to image.

Working with JavaScript

The most complex part to creating the lightbox functionality is the JavaScript library you need to create.

Create a new folder called JS in the same folder containing all of the files in the site. Download from *www.jquery.com* the latest version of the jQuery JavaScript library and add it to the JS folder. A version is included with the downloaded files for this project.

Create a new JavaScript file and label it "lightbox.js." Open the "lightbox.js" file in your favorite text editor. You will need to add the following JavaScript. You will see the use of a $ sign. This is an alias that connects to the jQuery object.

```
(function($) {
$.fn.lightBox = function(settings) {
```

1. The first set of properties control how you want the lightbox to appear on the screen. The `overlayBgColor` attribute sets the background color when you select an image, and the `overlay-Opacity` attribute defines how transparent the background is.

```
settings = jQuery.extend({
overlayBgColor: 'black'
overlayOpacity:0.8
```

2. The following configuration points to the images used for the navigation.

```
fixedNavigation:false
imageLoading:'images/lightbox-ico-loading.gif',
imageBtnPrev:'images/lightbox-btn-prev.gif'
imageBtnNext:'images/lightbox-btn-next.gif'
imageBtnClose:'images/lightbox-btn-close.gif',
imageBlank:'images/lightbox-blank.gif',
```

3. The `containerBorderSize` attribute sets the padding around the container that opens with the full-size image.

```
containerBorderSize:10,
```

4. The following setting specifies in milliseconds how fast the window will open and close.

```
containerResizeSpeed:400,
```

5. The following controls the text that appears in the lightbox. You can customize all of these settings to your own preferences.

```
txtImage:'Image',
txtOf:'of',
```

6. The following properties allow you to use the keyboard to navigate through the lightbox. The "c" key will close the lightbox, and the "p" and "n" keys will move to the previous and next image in the set, respectively.

```
keyToClose:'c',
keyToPrev:'p',
keyToNext:'n',
```

7. The following will set up the dynamic array that will correctly load the data for each image.

```
imageArray:[],
activeImage:0
},settings);
```

8. The next function allows you to start extending the default jQuery objects.

```
var jQueryMatchedObj = this;
function _initialize() {
```

9. This script uses the jQuery object to determine if the user has
   selected a thumbnail on the screen.

```
_start(this,jQueryMatchedObj);
return false;
}
```

10. The following function will dynamically create the lightbox as it
    appears on the screen. You will see at the end of this script the
    dynamically generated HTML. You can modify this HTML to
    include your own content—for instance, you can add a dynamic
    title.

```
function _start(objClicked,jQueryMatchedObj) {
$('embed, object, select').css({ 'visibility' :
'hidden' });
_set_interface();
settings.imageArray.length = 0;
settings.activeImage = 0;
if (jQueryMatchedObj.length == 1) {
settings.imageArray.push(new Array(objClicked.
getAttribute('href'),objClicked.getAttribute('title')));
} else {
for (var i = 0; i <jQueryMatchedObj.length; i++) {
settings.imageArray.push(new
Array(jQueryMatchedObj[i].getAttribute('href'),jQueryMatc
hedObj[i].getAttribute('title')));
}
}
while (settings.imageArray[settings.activeImage][0] !=
objClicked.getAttribute('href')) {
settings.activeImage++;
}
_set_image_to_view();
}
function _set_interface() {
$('body').append('<div id="jquery-overlay"></div>
<div id="jquery-lightbox"><div id="lightbox-container-
image-box"><div id="lightbox-container-image"><img
id="lightbox-image"><div style="" id="lightbox-nav">
<a href="#" id="lightbox-nav-btnPrev"></a><a href="#"
id="lightbox-nav-btnNext"></a></div><div id="lightbox-
loading"><a href="#" id="lightbox-loading-link"><img
src="' + settings.imageLoading + '"></a></div></div>
</div><div id="lightbox-container-image-data-box"><div
id="lightbox-container-image-data"><div id="lightbox-
image-details"><span id="lightbox-image-details-
caption"></span><span id="lightbox-image-details-
currentNumber"></span></div><div id="lightbox-secNav">
<a href="#" id="lightbox-secNav-btnClose"><img src="' +
settings.imageBtnClose + '"></a></div></div></div>
</div>');
```

11. The following script will determine the page size and set the CSS settings along with adding the correct navigation buttons.

```
var arrPageSizes = ___getPageSize();
$('#jquery-overlay').css({
backgroundColor:settings.overlayBgColor,
opacity:settings.overlayOpacity,
width:arrPageSizes[0],
height:arrPageSizes[1]
}).fadeIn();
var arrPageScroll = ___getPageScroll();
$('#jquery-lightbox').css({
top:arrPageScroll[1] + (arrPageSizes[3]/10),
left:arrPageScroll[0]
}).show();
$('#jquery-overlay,#jquery-lightbox').click(function() {
_finish();
});
$('#lightbox-loading-link,#lightbox-secNav-btnClose').
click(function() {
_finish();
return false;
});
$(window).resize(function() {
var arrPageSizes = ___getPageSize();
$('#jquery-overlay').css({
width:arrPageSizes[0],
height:arrPageSizes[1]
});
var arrPageScroll = ___getPageScroll();
$('#jquery-lightbox').css({
top:arrPageScroll[1] + (arrPageSizes[3]/10),
left:arrPageScroll[0]});});};}
```

12. Set the parameters for the animation as you load an image.

```
function _resize_container_image_box(intImageWidth,
intImageHeight) {
var intCurrentWidth = $('#lightbox-container-image-
box').width();
var intCurrentHeight = $('#lightbox-container-image-
box').height();
var intWidth = (intImageWidth + (settings.
containerBorderSize * 2));
var intHeight = (intImageHeight + (settings.
containerBorderSize * 2));
var intDiffW = intCurrentWidth - intWidth;
var intDiffH = intCurrentHeight - intHeight;
$('#lightbox-container-image-box').animate({
width: intWidth, height: intHeight },settings.
containerResizeSpeed,function() { _show_image(); });
```

```
if ((intDiffW == 0) && (intDiffH == 0)) {
if ($.browser.msie) {
___pause(250);
} else {
___pause(100);}}
$('#lightbox-container-image-data-box').css({ width:
intImageWidth });
$('#lightbox-nav-btnPrev,#lightbox-nav-btnNext').
css({ height: intImageHeight + (settings.
containerBorderSize * 2) });};
```

13. The following function prepares the images for preloading.

```
function _set_image_to_view() {
$('#lightbox-loading').show();
if (settings.fixedNavigation) {
$('#lightbox-image,#lightbox-container-image-data-box,
#lightbox-image-details-currentNumber').hide();
} else {
$('#lightbox-image,#lightbox-nav,#lightbox-nav-
btnPrev,#lightbox-nav-btnNext,#lightbox-container-image-
data-box,#lightbox-image-details-currentNumber').hide();}
var objImagePreloader = new Image();
objImagePreloader.onLoad = function() {
$('#lightbox-image').attr('src',settings.
imageArray[settings.activeImage][0]);
_resize_container_image_box(objImagePreloader.width,
objImagePreloader.height);
objImagePreloader.onLoad=function(){};};
objImagePreloader.src = settings.imageArray[settings.
activeImage][0];};
```

14. You can now run a function that will load the image, followed
by a second function that will present the associated thumbnail with the image.

```
function _show_image() {
$('#lightbox-loading').hide();
$('#lightbox-image').fadeIn(function() {
_show_image_data();
_set_navigation();});
_preload_neighbor_images();};
function _show_image_data() {
$('#lightbox-container-image-data-box').
slideDown('fast');
$('#lightbox-image-details-caption').hide();
if (settings.imageArray[settings.activeImage][1]) {
$('#lightbox-image-details-caption').html(settings.
imageArray[settings.activeImage][1]).show();}
if (settings.imageArray.length> 1) {
$('#lightbox-image-details-currentNumber').
html(settings.txtImage + ' ' + (settings.activeImage + 1)
+ ' ' + settings.txtOf + ' ' + settings.imageArray.
length).show();}}
```

15. The final sets of scripts control the navigation buttons and keyboard controls. Start by adding the following function.

```
function _set_navigation() {
$('#lightbox-nav').show();
$('#lightbox-nav-btnPrev,#lightbox-nav-btnNext').
css({ 'background' : 'transparent url(' + settings.
imageBlank + ') no-repeat' });
```

16. The following JavaScript controls how the previous button works.

```
if (settings.activeImage != 0) {
if (settings.fixedNavigation) {
$('#lightbox-nav-btnPrev').css({'background' : 'url('
+ settings.imageBtnPrev + ') left 15% no-repeat'})
.unbind()
.bind('click',function() {
settings.activeImage = settings.activeImage - 1;
_set_image_to_view();
return false;});
} else {
$('#lightbox-nav-btnPrev').unbind().hover(function() {
$(this).css({'background' : 'url(' + settings.
imageBtnPrev + ') left 15% no-repeat' });
},function() {
$(this).css({'background' : 'transparent
url('+settings.imageBlank + ') no-repeat' });
}).show().bind('click',function() {
settings.activeImage = settings.activeImage - 1;
_set_image_to_view();
return false;});}}
```

17. Now add the controls for the next button.

```
if (settings.activeImage != (settings.imageArray.
length-1)) {
if (settings.fixedNavigation) {
$('#lightbox-nav-btnNext').css({ 'background' :
'url('+settings.imageBtnNext + ') right 15% no-repeat' })
.unbind()
.bind('click',function() {
settings.activeImage = settings.activeImage + 1;
_set_image_to_view();
return false;
});
} else {
$('#lightbox-nav-btnNext').unbind().hover(function() {
$(this).css({ 'background' : 'url(' + settings.
imageBtnNext + ') right 15% no-repeat' });
},function() {
$(this).css({ 'background' : 'transparent url(' +
settings.imageBlank + ') no-repeat' });
```

```
}).show().bind('click',function() {
settings.activeImage = settings.activeImage + 1;
_set_image_to_view();
return false;});}}
```

18. The following function checks that the images have loaded
correctly.

```
function _preload_neighbor_images() {
if ((settings.imageArray.length -1)> settings.
activeImage) {
objNext = new Image();
objNext.src = settings.imageArray[settings.activeImage
+ 1][0];}
if (settings.activeImage> 0) {
objPrev = new Image();
objPrev.src = settings.imageArray[settings.activeImage
-1][0];}}
function _finish() {
$('#jquery-lightbox').remove();
$('#jquery-overlay').fadeOut(function() { $('#jquery-
overlay').remove(); });
$('embed, object, select').css({ 'visibility' :
'visible' });}
```

19. The following will allow you to use the keyboard to navigate
through the image library.

```
_enable_keyboard_navigation();}
function _enable_keyboard_navigation() {
$(document).keydown(function(objEvent) {
_keyboard_action(objEvent);});}
function _disable_keyboard_navigation() {
$(document).unbind();}
```

20. The following functions confirm that the key is selected correctly.

```
function _keyboard_action(objEvent) {
if (objEvent == null) {
keycode = event.keyCode;
escapeKey = 27;
} else {
keycode = objEvent.keyCode;
escapeKey = objEvent.DOM_VK_ESCAPE;}
key = String.fromCharCode(keycode).toLowerCase();
if ((key == settings.keyToClose) || (key == 'x') ||
(keycode == escapeKey)) {
_finish();}
if ((key == settings.keyToPrev) || (keycode == 37)) {
if (settings.activeImage != 0) {
settings.activeImage = settings.activeImage - 1;
_set_image_to_view();
_disable_keyboard_navigation();}}
if ((key == settings.keyToNext) || (keycode == 39)) {
```

```
if (settings.activeImage != (settings.imageArray.length - 1)) {
settings.activeImage = settings.activeImage + 1;
_set_image_to_view();
_disable_keyboard_navigation();}}}
```

21. Save your file.

At this time you have completed the JavaScript for your lightbox application.

Stitching It All Together in HTML

At this point you have the groundwork completed for your project. The final step is to stitch it all together with HTML.

1. Let's start by opening "products.html." In the HEAD element of the HTML add the following links to the CSS and JavaScript libraries you have created.

```
<link rel="stylesheet" type="text/css" href="../style-
projects-jquery.css"/>
    <script type="text/javascript" src="js/jquery.js">
</script>
    <script type="text/javascript" src="js/lightbox.js">
</script>
    <link rel="stylesheet" type="text/css" href="css/
jquery.lightbox-0.5.css" media="screen"/>
```

2. Next, add a localized function for your lightbox application.

```
<script type="text/javascript">
$(function() {
$('#gallery a').lightBox();
    });
</script>
```

3. The final code that needs to be added to the HEAD element is an extended CSS style.

```
<style type="text/css">
/* jQuery lightBox plugin - Gallery style */
#gallery {
background-color: #444;
padding: 10px;
width: 420px;
}
#gallery ul { list-style: none; }
#gallery ul li { display: inline; }
#gallery ul img {
border: 5px solid #3e3e3e;
border-width: 5px 5px 20px;
}
#gallery ul a:hover img {
border: 5px solid #fff;
```

```
border-width: 5px 5px 20px;
color: #fff;
}
#gallery ul a:hover { color: #fff; }
</style>
```

4. The final step is to insert into the main BODY element a new, updated ARTICLE element that contains a DIV tag with the ID `gallery` linking it to the JavaScript lightbox application.

```
<article id="article_one" style="position: absolute;
left: 420px; top: 100px; width: 315px; height: 195px;
z-index: 2"> <h1><m>Horticultural Products</m></h1><br/>
<div id="gallery">
<ul>
<li> <a href="photos/image2.jpg" title="Red leaf
trees was a popular seller this last quarter. $('#gallery
a').lightBox();"> <img src="photos/thumb_image2.jpg"
width="72" height="72" alt=""/> </a> </li>
    <li> <a href="photos/image3.jpg" title="Green will
be our next area of horticultural expansion $('#gallery
a').lightBox();"> <img src="photos/thumb_image3.jpg"
width="72" height="72" alt=""/> </a> </li>
    <li> <a href="photos/image4.jpg" title=" $('#gallery
a').lightBox();"> <img src="photos/thumb_image4.jpg"
width="72" height="72" alt=""/> </a> </li>
    <li> <a href="photos/image5.jpg" title=" $('#gallery
a').lightBox();"> <img src="photos/thumb_image5.jpg"
width="72" height="72" alt=""/> </a> </li>
</ul>
</div>
</article>
```

At this time you can save the project. Preview the "products. html" page in your favorite modern browser to view the interactive lightbox solution.

Controlling Forms with jQuery

You can do a lot with jQuery. This section discusses how you can use jQuery to control how people fill out forms. Even with enhanced functionality in HTML5 Forms, forms can still miss certain key features. Validating data is a key element. The goal of this section is to add form validation to the contact us page in the web site.

The best place to start is with the default form (Figure 5.5Proj). Open up "contactus.html." Following is the code.

```
<form method="POST" action="http://fp1.formmail.com/
cgi-bin/fm192">
    <input type="hidden" name="_pid" value="119137">
```

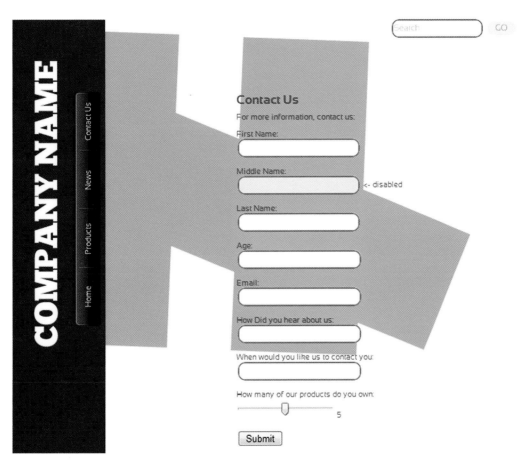

Figure 5.5Proj This is a standard form in HTML5.

```
    <input type="hidden" name="_fid" value="FNNZXGED">
    <input type="hidden" name="recipient"
value="matthewadavid@gmail.com">
    <label>First Name:</label><br/>
    <input name="FirstName" type="text" maxlength="25"
required><br/><br/>
    <label>Middle Name:</label><br/>
    <input name="MiddleName" type="text" disabled>
<- disabled<br/><br/>
    <label>Last Name:</label><br/>
    <input name="LastName" type="text" maxlength="25"
required>
<br/><br/>
    <label>Age:</label><br/>
    <input name="age" type="number" min="18"
max="100"><br/>
    <br/>
    <label>Email:</label><br/>
    <input name="email" type="email" required><br/><br/>
```

```
<label>How Did you hear about us:</label><br/>
<input name="HowDidYouHear" type="uri" list="mylist">
<br/><br/>
<datalist id="mylist">
<option label="google" value="http://google.com">
<option label="yahoo" value="http://yahoo.com">
<option label="Bing" value="http://bing.com">
</datalist>
<label>When would you like us to contact you:</label>
<br/> <input name="ContactDate" type="date"><br/><br/>
<label>How many of our products do you own:</label>
<br/>
<input id="slider" name="sliderValue" type="range"
min="0" max="10" value="5">
</input>
<output name="NumberOfProducts" value="5" onforminput=
"value=sliderValue.value">5</output><br/><br/>
<button type=submit>Submit</button>
</form>
```

Now, let's add some Ajax that will check to see if the content entered into the form is correct. Start by adding a reference link to the latest release of jQuery, as shown here.

```
<script src="http://ajax.googleapis.com/ajax/libs/
jquery/1.4/jquery.min.js" type="text/javascript"></script>
```

A key element to jQuery is its extensibility. To demonstrate this you are going to build your own set of rules that will extend the functionality of the form so that it requires that all fields must be entered before the form can be submitted. To accomplish this you will extend the default jQuery library with your own plug-in library.

Start by creating a new JavaScript text file in the JS library. Name the new JavaScript file "jquery.formvalidation.js." You will notice that it is standard to add the prefix "jquery" for all plug-ins.

You are going to start by adding a base object that you can call from anywhere in your code. This is called a *singleton*. The following is the base validation. The code creates everything with anonymous IDs. This allows you to easily reuse the code. Here you are creating a variable named `rules` that tests for email, URL address, and required content.

```
var Validation = function() {
    var rules = {
```

The following definition is your email rule. Notice that the pattern uses a regular expression to format the rule.

```
email : {
    check: function(value) {
      if(value)
        return testPattern(value,".+@.+\..+");
      return true;
    },
```

```
            msg : "Enter a valid e-mail address."
      },
```

The following definition is for a valid URL rule. As with the email rule, a regular expression is set up to create a pattern that is used by the validation rule. The validation rule then checks the content entered into the form field to confirm it is valid.

```
url : {
        check : function(value) {
          if(value)
            return testPattern(value,"https?://
(.+\.)+.{2,4}(/.*)?");
          return true;
        },
        msg : "Enter a valid URL."
      },
```

The final validation rule is simply looking to see if any content has been entered into the field.

```
required : {
        check: function(value) {
          if(value)
            return true;
          else
            return false;
        },
        msg : "This field is required."
      }
    }
```

A test pattern extends the script you are creating to mimic the jQuery format by adding a $. This makes is easier to integrate the plug-in with other jQuery plug-ins.

```
var testPattern = function(value, pattern) {
  var regExp = new RegExp("^"+pattern+"$","");
  return regExp.test(value);
}
return {
  addRule : function(name, rule) {
    rules[name] = rule;
  },
  getRule : function(name) {
    return rules[name];
  }
 }
}
```

To control HTML Forms in the DOM, where Ajax is run, you need to communicate with the form. The following form factory code achieves this.

```
var Form = function(form) {
  var fields = [];
```

```
               form.find("input[validation],
textarea[validation]").each(function() {
             fields.push(new Field(this));
          });
          this.fields = fields;
       }
       Form.prototype = {
         validate : function() {
           for(field in this.fields) {
             this.fields[field].validate();
           }
         },
         isValid : function() {
           for(field in this.fields) {
             if(!this.fields[field].valid) {
                this.fields[field].field.focus();
             return false;
             }
           }
           return true;
           }
         }
       var Field = function(field) {
             this.field = $(field);
             this.valid = false;
             this.attach("change");
        }
```

The JavaScript looks to see if you have entered content into the form as you are typing in the form fields. The following prototype object looks to see the activity in the field. The `keyup` command instructs the script to run as you complete releasing a key on your keyboard.

```
       Field.prototype = {
         attach : function(event) {
           var obj = this;
           if(event == "change") {
              obj.field.bind("change",function() {
                return obj.validate();
              });
           }
           if(event == "keyup") {
              obj.field.bind("keyup",function(e) {
                return obj.validate();
              });
           }
         },
```

The following function adds the error message onto the screen. In this instance, you will see that the error message is added as an unordered list (UL) element. Of course, you can change this. This

is the beauty of working with jQuery. You can change the error to
a label or tie additional CSS to the error.

```
validate : function() {
  var obj = this,
    field = obj.field,
    errorClass = "errorlist",
    errorlist = $(document.createElement("ul")).
addClass(errorClass),
    types = field.attr("validation").split(" "),
    container = field.parent(),
    errors = [];
  field.next(".errorlist").remove();
  for (var type in types) {
    var rule = $.Validation.getRule(types[type]);
    if(!rule.check(field.val())) {
       container.addClass("error");
       errors.push(rule.msg);
    }
  }
  if(errors.length) {
     obj.field.unbind("keyup")
     obj.attach("keyup");
     field.after(errorlist.empty());
     for(error in errors) {
  errorlist.append("<li>"+ errors[error] +"</li>");
     }
     obj.valid = false;
  }
  else {
     errorlist.remove();
     container.removeClass("error");
     obj.valid = true;
  } }}
```

The final step in the JavaScript library extends the base form validation rules in the core jQuery library with your new extensions.

```
$.extend($.fn, {
  validation : function() {
    var validator = new Form($(this));
    $.data($(this)[0], 'validator', validator);
    $(this).bind("submit", function(e) {
      validator.validate();
      if(!validator.isValid()) {
         e.preventDefault();
      }
    });
  },
  validate : function() {
  var validator = $.data($(this)[0], 'validator');
```

```
                validator.validate();
                return validator.isValid();
    }
  });
    $.Validation = new Validation();
  })(jQuery);
```

At this point you can save your JavaScript file. Now you need to add the functionality to your form. Open "contactus.html" in a text editor. Add a reference to your new "jquery.formvalidation.js" library, as follows:

```
<script src="js/jquery.formValidation.js"></script>
```

The code you created in your "jquery.formvalidation.js" JavaScript file is generic. You need to now associate it directly with a form field.

At this point you now can add your validation rules to your form elements in your web page, and it could not be easier. You have created three validation rules: required, email, and URL. All you have to do to apply them to a form is to insert a new attribute, called `validation`, and specify which rule you would like to apply. Following is an example of the required rule.

```
<label>Last Name:</label>
      <br/>
<input name="LastName" type="text" maxlength="25"
validation="required" required>
```

The whole form looks like the following.

```
<form action="submit" id="html5Form" method="post">
<fieldset>
<legend>Contact Us</legend>
<label>First Name:</label>
<br/>
<input name="FirstName" type="text" maxlength="25"
validation="required" required>
<br/><br/>
<label>Middle Name:</label>
<br/>
<input name="MiddleName" type="text" disabled>
<- disabled <br/>
<br/>
<label>Last Name:</label>
<br/>
<input name="LastName" type="text" maxlength="25"
validation=
"required" required>
<br/><br/>
<label>Age:</label>
<br/>
```

```
    <input name="age" validation="required" type="number"
min="18" max="100">
    <br/><br/>
    <label>Email:</label>
    <br/>
    <input name="email" type="email" validation="email"
required id="emailTo">
    <br/><br/>
    <label>How Did you hear about us:</label>
    <br/>
    <input name="HowDidYouHear" validation="url" type="uri"
list="mylist"><br/>
    <br/><datalist id="mylist">
    <option label="google" value="http://google.com">
    <option label="yahoo" value="http://yahoo.com">
    <option label="Bing" value="http://bing.com">
    </datalist>
    <label>When would you like us to contact you:</label>
    <br/>
    <input name="ContactDate" validation="required"
type="date">
    <br/><br/>
    <label>How many of our products do you own:</label>
    <br/>
    <input id="slider" name="sliderValue" type="range"
min="0" max="10" value="5">
    </input>
    <output name="NumberOfProducts" value="5"
onforminput="value=sliderValue.value">5</output>
    <br/><br/>
    <div class="submit-area">
    <input value="Validate on Submit" type="submit"/>
    </div>
    </form>
```

Below the Submit button input element, add the following
JavaScript code, linking the form by name to the HTML form name.

```
<script>
var thisForm = $("#html5Form");
thisForm.validation();
</script>
```

At this point you can test your form in your web browser. If
you do not complete the form correctly, the validation messages
will appear (Figure 5.6Proj).

A final step you can do is to add CSS to style the error messages. The following CSS will change the error messages to red
with no bullet points.

```
fieldset ul, fieldset ul {
    margin: 0px 0 0px 0px;
```

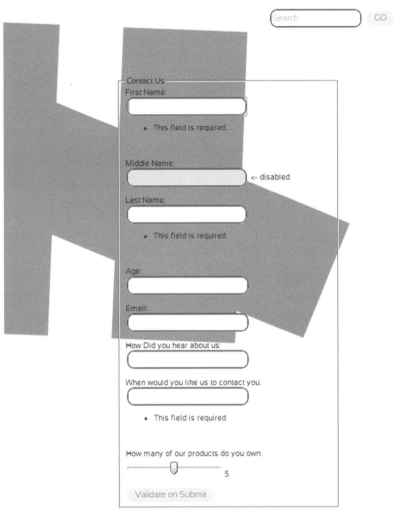

Figure 5.6Proj Validation messages appear when a field is not completed correctly according to the jQuery plug-in extension you created.

```
}
fieldset li, fieldset li {
    list-style-type: none;
    margin-bottom: 0px;
    line-height: 12px;
    font-size: 16px;
}
fieldset li {
    font-size: 12px;
    color: red;
    margin-bottom: 0px;
}
```

Save the CSS to "style.css" and preview the page. You now have clear, recognizable error messages. What is more, you can now use this library with any web form you create.

Inserting a Tabbed Interface to Build on Top of Your Existing jQuery Projects

Blocking Ajax/JavaScript solutions into reusable libraries allows you to build complex web pages very quickly. The next library you will add to the web site will introduce a tabbed window that allows you to navigate through different screens of content without having to leave the current page (Figure 5.7Proj).

To demonstrate how you can quickly begin building complex web pages, the tabbed interface is going to be added to the contact us page. Let's refresh what is going on in this page so far:

Figure 5.7Proj Tabs give you a tool to clearly organize content on the page.

- HTML5 Forms elements add richer controls.
- An HTML5 search form is located in the top right corner.
- CSS is used to format the page.
- CSS is used to create the navigation.
- A reusable custom jQuery plug-in is used to add validation to the form.
- The final step is to add a reusable jQuery plug-in to add tabs.

There is a lot going on in this page. Let's keep adding. The latest web browsers have no problems rendering pages like this.

The first thing to do is to create a custom jQuery JavaScript plug-in. In keeping with the default jQuery plug-in standard, create a new JavaScript file in your JS folder and name it "jquery.tabbed.js." Open "jquery.tabbed.js" and you can begin to add the JavaScript.

The tab plug-in inherits and extends a lot of functionality built into jQuery. Below you will see the $ sign used by jQuery to extend the functionality you need on the page. In this instance, you are telling jQuery to apply the tabbed feature when it sees the DIV element that contains the "tabs" class.

```
$(function () {
var tabContainers = $('div.tabs> div');
tabContainers.hide().filter(':first').show();
$('div.tabs ul.tabNavigation a').click(function () {
tabContainers.hide();
tabContainers.filter(this.hash).show();
$('div.tabs ul.tabNavigation a').removeClass('selected');
$(this).addClass('selected');
return false;
}).filter(':first').click();
});
```

Save your JS file. That's it. Nice and neat.

Open up your "contactus.html" page. Find the SECTION element at line 51. It should look like this:

```
<section id="section_articleOneIdentifier" class=
"sectionOne">
```

There are three parts to the tab interface: first is the main container that allows JavaScript to see that you are using a tab; second is the tabs you will select; and third is the content that appears in the container under the tabs. The third DIV element defines the container area for the tabs. Notice that the class is called "tabs" as called out by the JavaScript library created above.

```
<div class="tabs">
</div>
```

The tabs across the top start life as LI elements. A pseudo link on each LI element is used to show a container.

```
<ul class="tabNavigation">
```

```
  <li><a href="#first">First</a></li>
  <li><a href="#second">Second</a></li>
  <li><a href="#third">Third</a></li>
</ul>
```

Each of the following DIV elements contains an ID that is the same as the pseudo link in the LI elements above. Selecting each LI element will show and hide the following containers.

```
<div id="first">
  <h2>First</h2>
  <p>content goes here<p>
</div>
<div id="second">
  <h2>Second</h2>
  <p>content goes here<p>
</div>
<div id="third">
  <h2>Third</h2>
  <p>content goes here<p>
</div>
```

In theory, you could stop your design here and be done. But, let's face it, the design does not look like tabs. All you have is a list of links that shows and hides sections of the page. The next step is to add CSS to give your design the look it deserves.

Create a new CSS file named "tabbed.css" and save it to the CSS folder. Open the CSS file in your favorite text editor. The most complex element is changing the LI elements into tabs. So, let's start there. The first CSS class is to remove the default styling you have with the UL element.

```
UL.tabNavigation {
    list-style: none;
    margin: 0;
    padding: 0;
}
```

Now you can begin to design how you want the LI elements to be shown. First, let's modify the display to inline.

```
UL.tabNavigation LI {
    display: inline;
}
```

Now that you have your lists running horizontally, you can control the visual layout. You will see in the following CSS that rounded corners are being used to create a tabbed effect.

```
UL.tabNavigation LI A {
    padding: 3px 5px;
    background-color: #ccc;
    color: #000;
    text-decoration: none;
```

```
    border-top-right-radius: 10px;
    border-top-left-radius: 10px;
    -moz-border-top-right-radius: 10px;
    -moz-border-top-left-radius: 10px;
    -webkit-border-top-right-radius: 10px;
    -webkit-border-top-left-radius: 10px;
}
```

With this all being CSS you can add a hover style to the abs to visually show users which tab they are about to select.

```
UL.tabNavigation LI A.selected, UL.tabNavigation LI
A:hover {
    background-color: #333;
    color: #fff;
    padding-top: 7px;
}
UL.tabNavigation LI A:focus {
    outline: 0;
}
```

You now have the styles for the tabs created. The next step is to modify the container for the content on the screen. This takes just one style.

```
div.tabs> div {
    padding: 5px;
    background-color:#FFF;
    margin-top: 3px;
    border: 5px solid #333;
    border-bottom-right-radius: 10px;
    border-bottom-left-radius: 10px;
    -moz-border-bottom-right-radius: 10px;
    -moz-border-bottom-left-radius: 10px;
    -webkit-border-bottom-right-radius: 10px;
    -webkit-border-bottom-left-radius: 10px;
}
```

Save your files. Test the page—you can tab through the content.

At this point you can copy the Contact Us form you created earlier and paste it into one of the tabs. The JavaScript, HTML, and CSS will all behave very nicely.

Using Additional Ajax Libraries: Working with Adobe's Spry Framework

Up to this point we have talked a lot about jQuery and how you can use it and extend it with your own JavaScript. True, jQuery is very powerful, but it is not the only Ajax library you can use. In fact, there are loads of great libraries you can use. If you are a user of Adobe's Dreamweaver then you can take advantage of their Spry Ajax framework.

Spry is an open-source library that can be easily extended in much the same way as jQuery. There is, however, some great functionality built into the core framework that you can apply directly to your web sites.

Spry can be downloaded from *http://labs.adobe.com/technologies/ spry/home.html*. The files contain a core script and several additional scripts that extend the functionality of the core. Expand the downloaded ZIP file and extract the files to your web site into a new root folder called SpryAssets.

You are going to add to the "contactus.html" page. This time, you are going to add content as follows to the first tab, "Who We Are," to allow users to see who is located at the company (Figure 5.8Proj).

1. The control you are going to create allows you to select the person's name and see additional information such as his or her title, email, and phone number. Data change and come from many sources. In this instance, the data are coming from another web page. You can use both XML and HTML as data sources within the Spry framework. In this example you are going to use a web page for the source data.

2. Begin by creating a new HTML web page in the root of the site and name it "whoweare.html." The web page contains a TABLE element. The TABLE has the ID `whoweare`. The ID will be used

Figure 5.8Proj The Spry framework is using a TABLE element in a second web page to show data.

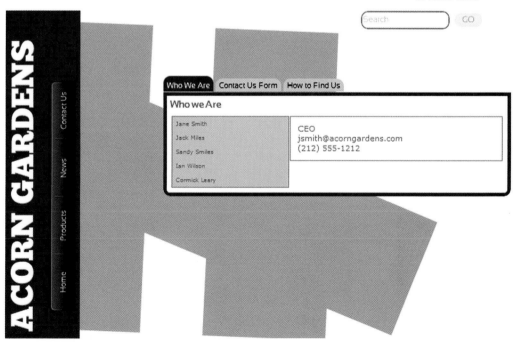

by the JavaScript to know it has the correct data source. Add the following HTML TABLE element.

```
<table width="100%" border="1" id="whoweare">
<tr>
  <td>Name</td>
  <td>Title</td>
  <td>Email</td>
  <td>Phone</td>
</tr>
```

3. The first row of the table created identifies the values of each column of data. Adding the data source to the "contactus.html" file is very easy. The rest of the following rows are entries in the table. Following are the core data.

```
<tr>
  <td>Jane Smith</td>
  <td>CEO</td>
  <td><a href="mailto:jsmith@acorngardens.com">jsmith@
acorngardens.com</a></td>
  <td>(212) 555-1212</td>
</tr>
<tr>
  <td>Jack Miles</td>
  <td>COO</td>
  <td><a href="mailto:jmiles@acorngardens.com">jmiles@
acorngardens.com</a></td>
  <td>(212) 555-1213</td>
</tr>
<tr>
  <td>Sandy Smiles</td>
  <td>VP-Sales</td>
  <td><a href="mailto:ssmiles@acorngardens.com">
ssmiles@acorngardens.com</a></td>
  <td>(212) 555-1214</td>
</tr>
<tr>
  <td>Ian Wilson</td>
  <td>CIO</td>
  <td><a href="mailto:iwilson@acorngardens.
com">iwilson@acorngardens.com</a></td>
  <td>(212) 555-1215</td>
</tr>
<tr>
  <td>Cormick Leary</td>
  <td>CFO</td>
  <td><a href="mailto:cleary@acorngardens.com">cleary@
acorngardens.com</a></td>
  <td>(212) 555-1216</td>
</tr>
</table>
```

4. Open "contactus.html" and add a link to the two following Spry JavaScript files in the SpryAssets folder.

```
<script src="SpryAssets/SpryData.js" type="text/
javascript"></script>
   <script src="SpryAssets/SpryHTMLDataSet.js" type="text/
javascript"></script>
```

5. You only need one line of additional JavaScript to link to the table with the ID of `whoweare` in the web page "whoweare.html." The following script is added to the HEAD element of the page.

```
<script type="text/javascript">
var ds1 = new Spry.Data.HTMLDataSet("whoweare.html",
"whoweare");
   </script>
```

6. If you leave the script as is, then the email links will come in as plain text. You can, however, change this by adding the following to convert the column called "Email" into HTML.

```
ds1.setColumnType("Email", "html");
```

7. As this point everything is very functional. Cascading Styles Sheets to the rescue! From the SpryAssets folders you can find a file called "sprymasterdetail.css."

```
.MasterDetail
   {
       font: 100% Verdana, Geneva, sans-serif;
       margin: 2px;
   }
```

8. This is the selector for the MasterContainer element, which manages all the MasterColumn classes. By default the master column occupies about 35% from the width of the entire structure.

```
.MasterDetail .MasterContainer
   {
       background-color: #EAEAEA;
       border: 1px solid gray;
       width: 35%;
       float: left;
       overflow: hidden;
   }
```

9. This is the selector for a MasterColumn element that holds the actual data for a master column.

```
.MasterDetail .MasterColumn
   {
       font-size: 75%;
       background-color: #CCCCCC;
```

```
                padding: 5px;
                cursor:pointer;
            }
```

10. This is the selector for a highlighted MasterColumn element.

```
    .MasterDetail .MasterColumnHover
        {
            background-color: #EAEAEA;
        }
```

11. This is the selector for a selected MasterColumn element.

```
    .MasterDetail .MasterColumnSelected
        {
            background-color:#848484;
            color: white;
        }
```

12. This is the selector for the DetailContainer element, which houses all the DetailColumn classes. By default the detail column occupies about 60% from the width of the entire structure.

```
    .MasterDetail .DetailContainer
        {
            border: 1px solid gray;
            padding: 10px;
            width: 60%;
            float: right;
            overflow: auto;
        }
```

13. This is the selector for a DetailColumn element that holds the actual data for a detail column. In addition, there are selector styles to format ANCHOR elements.

```
    .MasterDetail .DetailColumn
        {
            margin-bottom: 1px;
        }
    .DetailColumn a:hover{color:#F00}
    .DetailColumn a{color:gray}
```

14. Save your files and review the site.

You should now be able to save the file and preview the content. Data can be added to the HTML TABLE being used for the data source. The next time the "contactus.html" page is reloaded then the new data will be added.

Working with Additional Ajax Libraries: Using Yahoo's YUI Framework

Think that Adobe and jQuery are the only two big players in the Ajax market? Yahoo also shifts some major weight with the implementation of their YUI framework. The core YUI framework is structured the same as Spry and jQuery. What you have is a series of anonymous scripts that you can tie into your own pages. Again, as with other frameworks, you can extend the functionality of the YUI framework with your own extensions.

In the following example, you are only going to add a small feature to the current Contact Us form. The feature is a comments box—nothing too special. Using the YUI framework you will change the comments box from plain HTML into a rich text box editor. Let's get started.

1. Start by opening up the "contactus.html" page. In the HEAD element add the following link to the YUI frameworks. You can, of course, copy these frameworks to your web site.

```
<script type="text/javascript" src="http://yui.
yahooapis.com/2.8.0r4/build/yahoo-dom-event/yahoo-dom-
event.js"></script>
<script type="text/javascript" src="http://yui.
yahooapis.com/2.8.0r4/build/animation/animation-min.js">
</script>
<script type="text/javascript" src="http://yui.
yahooapis.com/2.8.0r4/build/connection/connection-min.js">
</script>
<script type="text/javascript" src="http://yui.
yahooapis.com/2.8.0r4/build/element/element-min.js">
</script>
<script type="text/javascript" src="http://yui.yahooapis.
com/2.8.0r4/build/container/container-min.js"></script>
<script type="text/javascript" src="http://yui.
yahooapis.com/2.8.0r4/build/menu/menu-min.js"></script>
<script type="text/javascript" src="http://yui.
yahooapis.com/2.8.0r4/build/button/button-min.js"></script>
<script type="text/javascript" src="http://yui.
yahooapis.com/2.8.0r4/build/editor/editor-min.js"></script>
```

2. Now you need to extend the scripts with your own plug-in. Create a new JavaScript file, name it "yui.editor.js," and save it into your JS folder. Open your favorite text editor. The first function sets up the default configuration for the rich text area. Add the following.

```
(function() {
var myConfig = {
height: '300px',
width: '600px',
```

```
animate: true,
dompath: true,
focusAtStart: true
};
```

3. The following links the rich editor control to your HTML text area form field.

```
YAHOO.log('Editor created..', 'info', 'example');
myEditor = new YAHOO.widget.Editor('editor', myConfig);
YAHOO.util.Event.onAvailable('iconMenu', function() {
YAHOO.log('onAvailable: (#iconMenu)', 'info',
'example');
YAHOO.util.Event.on('iconMenu', 'click', function(ev) {
var tar = YAHOO.util.Event.getTarget(ev);
if (tar.tagName.toLowerCase() == 'img') {
var img = tar.getAttribute('src', 2);
YAHOO.log('Found an icon, fire inserticonClick Event',
'info', 'example');
var _button = this.toolbar.
getButtonByValue('inserticon');
_button._menu.hide();
this.toolbar.fireEvent('inserticonClick', { type:
'inserticonClick', icon: img });
}
YAHOO.util.Event.stopEvent(ev);
}, myEditor, true);
});
myEditor.on('toolbarLoaded', function() {
YAHOO.log('Editor Toolbar Loaded..', 'info', 'example');
```

4. The following variable allows overlays to be added to the application.

```
var imgConfig = {
type: 'push', label: 'Insert Icon', value:
'inserticon',
menu: function() {
var menu = new YAHOO.widget.Overlay('inserticon', {
width: '165px', height: '210px', visible: false });
var str = '';
for (var a = 0; a < 9; a++) {
for (var i = 1; i < 9; i++) {
str += '<a href="#"><img src="assets/suit' + i + '.gif"
border="0"></a>';
}
}
menu.setBody('<div id="iconMenu">' + str + '</div>');
menu.beforeShowEvent.subscribe(function() {
menu.cfg.setProperty('context', [myEditor.toolbar.
getButtonByValue('inserticon').get('element'), 'tl', 'bl']);
});
menu.render(document.body);
```

```
    menu.element.style.visibility = 'hidden';
    return menu;
    }()
    };
    YAHOO.log('Create the (inserticon) Button', 'info',
'example');
    myEditor.toolbar.addButtonToGroup(imgConfig,
'insertitem');
    myEditor.toolbar.on('inserticonClick', function(ev) {
    YAHOO.log('inserticonClick Event Fired: ' + YAHOO.lang.
dump(ev), 'info', 'example');
    var icon = '';
    this._focusWindow();
    if (ev.icon) {
    icon = ev.icon;
    }
    this.execCommand('inserthtml', '<img src="' + icon + '"
border="0">');
    return false;
    }, myEditor, true);
    });
    myEditor.render();
    })();
```

5. Save your JavaScript file.
6. Now you need to add some HTML to your "contactus.html" file. All you have to do is add the following text area to your form. The ID links the form to the JavaScript.

```
    <textarea id="editor" name="editor" rows="20"
cols="75">
    </textarea>
```

7. The final step is to make the form look nice. Fortunately, the YUI framework comes with a set of prepackaged CSS files you can link to over the Web. Add the following to the web page.

```
    <link rel="stylesheet" type="text/css" href="http://
yui.yahooapis.com/2.8.0r4/build/menu/assets/skins/sam/
menu.css"/>
    <link rel="stylesheet" type="text/css" href="http://
yui.yahooapis.com/2.8.0r4/build/button/assets/skins/sam/
button.css"/>
    <link rel="stylesheet" type="text/css" href="http://
yui.yahooapis.com/2.8.0r4/build/fonts/fonts-min.css"/>
    <link rel="stylesheet" type="text/css" href="http://
yui.yahooapis.com/2.8.0r4/build/container/assets/skins/
sam/container.css"/>
    <link rel="stylesheet" type="text/css" href="http://
yui.yahooapis.com/2.8.0r4/build/editor/assets/skins/sam/
editor.css"/>
```

8. Of course, as with any CSS implementation, you can extend the designs. The following are an extension to the core YUI CSS files. Add this style to the HEAD element of the page.

```
<style>
    .yui-skin-sam .yui-toolbar-container .yui-toolbar-
inserticon span.yui-toolbar-icon {
        background-position: 1px 0px;
        left: 5px;
    }
    .yui-skin-sam .yui-toolbar-container .yui-button-
insertdate-selected span.yui-toolbar-icon {
        background-position: 1px 0px;
        left: 5px;
    }
    #inserticon {
        border: 1px solid #808080;
        padding: 5px;
        background-color: #F2F2F2;
    }
    #inserticon a {
        display: block;
        float: left;
        border: 1px solid #F2F2F2;
    }
    #inserticon a:hover {
        border: 1px solid #808080;
    }
</style>
<style>
.yui-toolbar-group-insertitem {
  *width: auto;
}
</style>
```

9. Save your work.

You now have a fully functional, rich text editor in your web page. No more boring comments box.

Linking to Content Hosted on Different Web Sites

As we come to the end of the book, I want to take some time to remind you that HTML5 is built on top of the Web you are already used to working with. To this end, there are some techniques you can use to add content from other web sites into your own.

Open up "contactus.html" and locate the section for the third tab. Add the following HTML into the third content.

```
<div id="third">
  <h2>How to Find Us</h2>
```

```
    <iframe width="400" height="300" frameborder="0"
scrolling="no" marginheight="0" marginwidth="0"
    src="http://dev.virtualearth.net/embeddedMap/
v1/silverlight/road?zoomLevel=16&center=44.263_-
88.2885&pushpins=44.263_-88.2885"/>
    </div>
```

The iFrame above adds a link directly to a bing map in SilverLight. Wait! I hear you scream, this is an HTML5 book, why add SilverLight? The reason is simple: Web technologies are complex. New solutions are always coming forward that you need to be able to integrate with. Fortunately, SilverLight is a technology that is easily integrated into your HTML.

Save your file. Your final web site is magnificent. This is what you have done:

- Built your web site with 100% HTML5 elements.
- Have images constructed from PNG files, CANVAS, and SVG.
- CSS3 techniques are used on every page to tilt the angle of text and add rich animation.
- Built complex Ajax libraries using jQuery, Spry, and YUI open-source frameworks.
- Integrated SilverLight mapping technology.

You have done well, grasshopper. Next-generation browsers, such as Chrome, IE9, Safari, and FireFox, can now all view sites using the technologies you have covered in this book. HTML5 is not a future technology. It is available for you to use now.

Summary

The lightbox project exemplifies how you can take modern JavaScript libraries and extend them to build your own solutions. It is the strength of HTML5 technologies that enables you to effectively build out these types of solutions.

jQuery is at the core of many of the web technologies used today. The reason why so much of this chapter is dedicated to this one specific Ajax library is because you can save yourself a lot of time by learning jQuery and using the library techniques in building your own extensions and plug-ins.

Processing JavaScript takes powers. The "contactus.html" page by itself has close to 10,000 lines of JavaScript. You can even argue that the page is very basic in its functionality. It is important that web browsers have JavaScript engines powerful enough to render these complex pages. Fortunately, all of the browser companies—Google, Apple, Mozilla, Opera, and Microsoft—are building JavaScript engines that will render increasingly more complex and massive JavaScript libraries. The time for building applications online is now here.

INDEX

Note: Page numbers in *italics* refer to mentions within the Project chapters, and as such refer primarily to examples in the text.